THE IMPOSSIBLE REVOLUTION

Making Sense of the Syrian Tragedy

Yassin al-Haj Saleh

Foreword by Robin Yassin-Kassab

Haymarket Books
Chicago, Illinois

First published in the United Kingdom in 2017 by
C. Hurst & Co. (Publishers) Ltd., London

This edition published in 2017 by
Haymarket Books
P.O. Box 180165
Chicago, IL 60618
773-583-7884
www.haymarketbooks.org
info@haymarketbooks.org

ISBN: 978-1-60846-850-8

Trade distribution:
In the US, Consortium Book Sales and Distribution, www.cbsd.com
In Canada, Publishers Group Canada, www.pgcbooks.ca
In the UK, Turnaround Publisher Services, www.turnaround-uk.com
All other countries, Ingram Publisher Services International,
IPS_Intlsales@ingramcontent.com

This book was published with the generous support of Lannan Foundation and Wallace Action Fund.

Printed in Canada by union labor.

Library of Congress Cataloging-in-Publication data is available.

10 9 8 7 6 5 4 3 2 1

To Samira, the auspicious symbol of Syria,
And to Syria, the symbol of a progressively Syrianized world.

CONTENTS

ACKNOWLEDGEMENTS

For a long time, I resisted the temptation of publishing a 'book' about the Syrian revolution. Writing from within a great upheaval, I was worried about my own naivety. It is possible that I carried the seeds of this apprehension from Hegel, some of whose work I had read during my years in prison. This German philosopher said that we live the present with a naive consciousness. This naivety stands in opposition to absolute knowledge, a Hegelian concept that entered Marxist thought under the rubric of 'science' and scientific socialism. The Syrian revolution released me from such Hegelianisms. For me, naivety has come to mean the *shahada* (testimony) of a witness, my own *shahada* about what I was part of, and my sense of things when the seemingly impossible erupted into vivid existence in my country. The impossible was a revolution.

And in the course of six years, that impossible was crushed out of existence. So maybe it is time in this seventh year to tell the story, or to retell it, to try to represent our struggle.

This *shahada* would have been impossible to put together as a book if it were not for the initiative and the valuable help of Danny Postel and Nader Hashemi from the Center for Middle East Studies at the University of Denver in the US. Without previous personal acquaintance, Danny and Nader introduced me and my work to wider circles of readers when I was still walking my first steps outside Syria in early 2014.

ACKNOWLEDGEMENTS

I cannot thank Kelly Grotke and Stephen Hastings King enough. Along with Nader and Danny, they are the embodiment of solidarity and partnership. Even more, humanity. Steve and Kelly helped diligently with this book, as if it were their own. It is.

Everything would have been far more difficult in Turkey if it were not for Senay Ozden's invaluable help in so many ways. Her comments on many points made in this book were always insightful and illuminating.

And of course I bear responsibility for any mistakes in information or analysis. The *shahid* (the one who gives a *shahada*) does not expect any tolerance about this.

Istanbul, February 2017

FOREWORD

Robin Yassin-Kassab

'The world is sick and its sickness is aggravating our sicknesses, both inherited and acquired.'[1]

Yassin al-Haj Saleh is a burningly relevant political thinker. Unlike most of his counterparts, he speaks not only from theory but from a lived experience of repression, revolution, counterrevolution, and war. Objective but never neutral, he is engaged and in tune with the rapid shifts and turns of his tormented society, urgently seeking answers to the most wide-ranging and inclusive of questions, and unearthing more, previously un-thought of, questions as he goes.

His context is Syria, where 12 million are homeless, and perhaps half a million dead. Syria which, in the seventh year of the upheaval, has become a truly global issue. The war Assad unleashed to marginalise and destroy a democratic opposition has given rise to a series of increasingly complicated conflicts, often bearing ethnic or sectarian tones. Fanned by overlapping, sometimes competing foreign interventions, these conflicts have infected the region and the world in turn. Regional and international imperialisms are feasting on Syria. Battle lines and forced demographic changes are fueling a hunger to redraw the maps. The spectre of Syrian refugees and/or terrorists, meanwhile, is shaping America's domestic politics and helping undo the European Union. As hopes for freedom and prosperity are crushed, new strains are injected into old authoritarianisms, and twenty-first century forms of nativism are taking root, west and east.

Yassin speaks from the heart of this turmoil. Yet, you hold in your hand the first book-length English translation of his work.

It's been a long time coming.

'They simply do not see us,' he laments. If we don't see Syrian revolutionaries, if we don't hear their voices when they talk of their experience, their motivations and hopes, then all we are left with are (inevitably orientalist) assumptions, constraining ideologies, and pre-existent grand narratives. These big stories, or totalising explanations, include a supposedly inevitable and ancient sectarian conflict underpinning events, and a jihadist-secularist binary, as well as the idea, running counter to all evidence, that Syria is a re-run of Iraq, a Western-led regime-change plot. No need to attend to detail, runs the implication, nor to Syrian oppositional voices, for we already know what needs to be known.

Purveyors of such myths—ideologues and regime-embedded journalists, 'experts' who don't speak more than a few words of Arabic—often seem to rely on each other to confirm and develop their theories. They brief politicians, they dominate opinion pages, learned journals and TV panels. And, to a large extent, we the public rely on them too. We see through their skewed lens, through a certain mythic framework which 'covers' the Syrian revolution only in the sense of hiding it from view. As a result we are unable either to offer solidarity to this most profound and thoroughgoing of contemporary social upheavals, or to learn any lessons from it.

Yassin al-Haj Saleh was born in 1961 in a village near Raqqa. His concern for social justice arose from his immediate environs: the poor rural hinterland of a troubled post-colonial state.

Karam Nachar, an academic and sometime collaborator of Yassin's, illustrates Syria's urban/rural and class divides by comparing the situation of his relatives in bourgeois Aleppo, who attended cinemas back in the 1920s, with—a mere 200 kilometres away—the Raqqa that Yassin grew up in forty years later, where there were still no cinemas, nor even paved roads.

While studying medicine in Aleppo, Yassin joined the Syrian Communist Party (Political Bureau), a group formed in 1972 after the mainstream Communist Party had been co-opted by the Assad regime. The 'Political Bureau' advocated democracy as well as social justice, and agitated against the regime's 1976 intervention in Lebanon on the side of right-wing Falangists.

Yassin was arrested in 1980, and languished as a political prisoner for the next sixteen years. He spent the last year in Tadmor prison, near the ruins of Palmyra. Tadmor is a name, or a crime scene, which resonates terribly in the Syrian imagination. Poet Faraj Bayraqdar, a fellow prisoner, called Tadmor 'the kingdom of death and madness'.

But languish is not quite the word. Despite the torture and unliveable conditions, Yassin read and thought as much as he could, liberating himself from the 'internal prisons' of political and ideological regimentation. *With Salvation, Oh Youth: Sixteen Years in Syrian Prisons* is his memoir of the period, an addition to Syria's rich 'prison literature' genre (though Yassin, considering all of Assad's Syria a prison, preferred to slip the label and categorise the text more generally as 'a matter of concern').

Released in 1996, he completed his long-interrupted medical studies in Aleppo, then moved to Damascus. In 2000 he met his wife, Samira al-Khalil, also a former political prisoner.

In the summer of that year, Hafez al-Assad died and his son Bashaar inherited the presidency. A brief and illusory 'Damascus Spring' unfolded shortly thereafter. The president seemed to encourage constructive criticism, and dissenters took him at his word, speaking against corruption, organising discussion forums, and soon signing petitions and issuing declarations calling for democratic reforms and human and civil rights. A fragile civil society began to develop.

By autumn 2001, spring had turned back to winter. The key figures of the democratic movement were imprisoned. Yet most Syrians remained unaware of the drama, because the intellectual dissenters, forbidden to directly appeal to the people, were unable to either galvanise them or express their concerns. 'The masses', in any case, often confounded the expectations of older oppositionists. They could no longer be mobilised by outworn slogans. The Syrian demographic was increasingly young, and increasingly tightly-squeezed economically.

Yassin's criticism of the opposition he belonged to was coruscating:

> The opposition must change itself first in order to be an example of change to society ... Neither communism nor Arab nationalism can solve the problem. The democratic opposition needs new ideas about Syrian patriotism and the current economic and social transformation taking place in Syria ... It must be independent from the outside. The only way to exit this crisis of failure is to focus on ... developing knowledge of Syrian society, which the opposition in all its different branches lacks completely.[2]

In most cases, the eruption of the 2011 protests took the various strands of the opposition, whether co-opted, repressed or exiled, by complete surprise. Gathering huge crowds from all of Syria's regions, sects and ethnicities, the protest movement was famously 'leaderless'. No single figure, ideology or political platform dominated, yet a grassroots organisational structure was quick to emerge, often staffed by young people with little or no prior political experience. Yassin and Samira took part in this early ferment. They worked with key activists including human rights lawyer Razan Zeitouneh, a founding member of both the Local Coordination Committees—which connected each neighbourhood's revolutionaries to the rest of the country—and the Violations Documentation Centre—which recorded and publicised the escalating repression.

Yassin lived in hiding for the first two years of the revolution. In April 2013 he moved to Douma, a suburb of Damascus liberated from the regime but besieged, bombarded, and increasingly prevailed over by a Salafist militia called Jaysh al-Islam. He planned to head straight on north to Raqqa, but circumstances forced him to wait until July. By this time, Samira had arrived in Douma, where she helped establish women's centres and small income-generating projects. She stayed on to continue this work, planning to join Yassin later in Turkey.

Yassin's journey to Raqqa (documented in the film *Our Terrible Country*) took him out of range of one tyranny and into the domain of another. Daesh (ISIS, or so-called "Islamic State") had imposed its own brand of totalitarianism on the city and had detained Yassin's friends and fellow activists, including his brothers.

Then, on 9 December 2013, Samira was abducted in Douma, along with Razan Zeitouneh, Wael Hamada, and Nazem Hamadi. The four activists have not been heard of since. Yassin considers Jaysh al-Islam accountable for their fate.

> Her abductors represent an Islamist recreation of the cruelty against which the revolution originally erupted. The case of Samira and her colleagues represents the case of Syria, trapped between the regime, the embodiment of brutality, and the Islamists, the embodiment of inhumanity. For the two, the prisons were the first thing they cared about in whatever area they control.[3]

We would expect most men to buckle under the pressure of such personal and national tragedy. But Syrians very often find they have no such option. Living in Istanbul, Yassin has helped set up the cultural and discussion centre Hamisch. He writes for al-Jumhuriya, the online journal he helped establish in 2012, addressing the current crisis and imagining the shape of a better future.[4] And he constantly engages with his tormented and scattered society, whose creativity and resilience he shares.

We should read Yassin al-Haj Saleh to learn more about Syria, but also because the implications of his work, like the effects of the war, stretch far beyond Syria.

Large swathes of the Western left have failed to adequately analyse and respond to the Syrian revolution, to the extent that they've ended up rehashing the security discourse of the right, and sometimes even its war-on-terror rhetoric. When Yassin laments this, he also throws down a challenge:

> My impression about this curious situation is that they simply do not see us; it is not about us at all. Syria is only an additional occasion for their old anti-imperialist tirades, never the living subject of the debate ... We, rank-and-file Syrians, refugees, women, students, intellectuals, human rights activists, political prisoners ... do not exist ... But honestly I've failed to discern who is right and who is left in the West from a leftist Syrian point of view ... Before helping Syrians or showing solidarity with Syrians, the mainstream Western left needs to help themselves.[5]

Yassin resists authoritarianism in all its manifestations, and confronts lazy thinking and prejudice wherever he finds them. He lashes orientalists and Islamophobes, for instance, as much as he does Islamists. Anyone looking for the reassurance of simplistic binaries will be disappointed, for he sides with neither Saudi Arabia nor Iran, neither Russia nor America, neither (to use his terms) 'necktie fascists' nor 'long-bearded fascists'.[6]

His writing is ethically concerned. Very usefully, he recognises that cultural and political analysis can't be disentangled. Cultural production, from educational projects and newspapers to radio stations and online poetry, has been central to the revolutionary process, and the key achievements of the revolution—self-organisation, the formation of democratic councils, the opening of debate—are part of cultural life as much as of politics, because they concern people's lived values in community practice.

The writing is multilayered, finding a welcome balance between localism and reductive geo-strategic discourse, when it delineates the links—the cross-infection of political illnesses as well as emancipatory possibilities—between an internationalised Syria and a Syrianised world.

Yassin al-Haj Saleh's is an important voice for our uncomfortable historical moment, in which distinctions between left and right are dissolving and reforming, when notions of sovereignty and identity are in flux, when the freedom of all is in question.

INTRODUCTION

The chapters of this book were written over the course of about four years in four cities: Damascus, Douma, Raqqa, and Istanbul. Except for Damascus, where I had lived in hiding for two years following the start of the Syrian revolution, only one chapter was written in each city. I have been living in Istanbul for more than two years now, but I prefer not use the term 'exile' to describe my life in Turkey, since the word has elitist connotations in Syria and conjures up images of certain intellectuals or politicians living in Europe. It also does not seem an appropriate term for other reasons: not only am I just one individual among many in a continuing exodus involving more than 4 million Syrians (even according to the questionable statistics of international bodies), but I live here while the whereabouts of my wife, Samira al-Khalil, remain unknown. She was abducted by a local Salafist organization in Douma near Damascus in December 2013, along with three of our friends, Razan Zaitouneh, Wael Hamada, and Nazem Hamadi. In addition, my brother Firas was abducted by Daesh (ISIS, or so-called "Islamic State") in July 2013 and remains missing, as do other friends and acquaintances: Ismail al-Hamidh, Paolo Dall'Oglio, Ibrahim al-Ghazi, Abdullah al-Khalil, and Mohammad Nour Matar. These circumstances are not something from which one can be exiled; rather, they remain very present and personal.

I am also not an 'exiled' person because throughout the past six years, and up until the moment of writing, Syrians, including myself, have not been allowed a single day of reprieve. Not one day has passed without Syrians being killed by airstrikes or under torture. We are not distant from these events, and we have not had time to catch our breath and look around, to check on ourselves and on our neighbours, to think about where we are and ponder the path that has taken us to where we are today; most important, we have not been able to mourn and bid farewell to our loved ones who have crossed over to the other side, and to re-examine our new condition and start wrestling with it.

The following introductory pages address my personal journey between Damascus and Istanbul over the course of fifty-six months, in order to clarify the circumstances in which the book's ten chapters were written and to make a connection between personal and public experiences. One striking thing about the Syrian tragedy is that it has ruthlessly obliterated the space between what is personal or private, and what is public. Almost every Syrian individual has become a public person, and the public sphere contains endless tales, different and similar, narrated by numerous people who have had first-hand exposure to the ordeal—people whose voices have long been silenced. Today, and since the beginning of the revolution, possession of discourse has been an essential aspect of Syrians' attempts to own politics in their country, and to own the country itself.

This book was written by someone involved in the conflict, though I have tried to provide enough general information to benefit an impartial, open-minded reader.

* * *

I moved to Damascus in late 2000, so had been living there for a little over ten years at the time the Syrian revolution broke out in March 2011. Before that, I was in Aleppo, labouring to finish my higher education after a seventeen-year hiatus, sixteen years of which I spent in prison for belonging to a communist party that opposed the Hafez al-Assad regime. After moving to Damascus, I dedicated myself to writing and translation. This was just after Bashar, Hafez's son, became president and sole possessor of Syria by means of hereditary succession. My move to Damascus put me in a good position to observe the development of conditions in Syria during the years of Assad Jr.'s rule, both before the revolution and for two and a half years after it broke out. Throughout that time, Samira, herself a former political detainee who spent the years 1987–1991 in prison, was my perfect support and ideal partner, both in our private life and in our public cause, and even in my writing. She read what I wrote, sometimes before publication and sometimes after, and found it not too bad. Her enthusiasm for many of my articles is what marks them warmly in my memory. Our relationship began in September of 2000, and in two years we were married.

On the night of 30 March 2011, I gathered a few of my books and belongings and left the house to live in seclusion for an indefinite period of time. Back then I was not wanted by authorities. I wished to live in hiding so that I could freely say and write what I wanted. Bashar al-Assad had just finished his first speech after the revolution erupted in mid-March, and an Arab satellite channel asked me to comment on it. When I did, I found myself beating around the bush. At that moment, I decided to live in hiding.

My name was known but not famous, and hardly anyone would have recognized my face. Samira was not known in the public sphere. The task I set for myself was to try to explain what was going on in the country as clearly as possible, without self-censorship.

During the first four months, my new residence was not in a house, though it was located in a good spot in the centre of the city. Samira was able to come by every now and then, but couldn't stay with me. Each time, she had to engage in complex manoeuvres so as to leave no trace that might lead to my hideout.

At that time, I wrote a weekly column for *Al-Hayat* newspaper, and also gave interviews and wrote for other publications from time to time. I averaged two articles a week. The selection of ten articles for this book was taken from nearly 380 published articles and interviews, written between the eruption of the Syrian revolution in March 2011 and November 2015, 235 of which were written before I left the country in October 2013. With so much material to consider, the resulting selection could only be somewhat arbitrary, sacrificing a lot of what might have provided a more detailed testimony about Syria and the revolution, and about me personally.

The first essay that appears here, 'Revolution of the Common People', was published in June 2011, about three months after the revolution began. As the reader may notice, the article is dominated by a sense of confidence and hope. It tries to demonstrate the democratic, liberatory nature of the intifada, or the 'uprising,' as I used to refer to it at that time. The article highlights the revolution's creation of new identities, for many people as well as for many big cities and towns that were resurfacing from under the Assadist eclipse, which had obscured the majority of Syrians. I also discuss two social components of the revolution: a 'traditional' component that is close to conservatism and comes out of impoverished towns and neighbourhoods; and a 'modern' component comprising the educated middle class. These two components are united by the centrality of work in their social, political, and moral perspectives. The Syrian revolution is one of a working society, of people who make a living from their work as opposed to those who live on the profits of their position or power-associated privilege. The essay also objects to the exclusion of Islamists from the conceptualization of a new, democratic Syria, since not once have Islamists been excluded in Syria (or its neighbouring countries) without the exclusion of all independent opposition currents as well: leftist, secular, and liberal ones; exclusions that left the country (and the Arab region) a political wasteland. While it is true that including Islamists in a pluralistic political system is not an easy task, the alternative has been tried-and-tested, and is unsatisfactory.

After four months of living in hiding, I moved to what was almost a house. There, Samira was able to live with me, which she did most of the time. It was also close to the city centre, and I could work there all day, unlike my former residence, where I had no privacy until the evening. Shortly after I moved to this place in July 2011, the regime's troops seized Hama and Deir ez-Zour with tanks. The two cities had witnessed major protests with hundreds of thousands of participants, akin to the Egyptian model of Tahrir Square. There was a failed attempt to reproduce that same model in Damascus in early April 2011, and I personally witnessed vehicles loaded with intelligence officials and *shabiha* (regime thugs) from Damascene neighbourhoods and peripheral areas opening fire on the demonstrators. After midnight on 18 April 2011 in Homs, about 200 protestors were killed at the Clock Square. Protestors had apparently believed they could erect their tents and impose a fait accompli. The bodies of the victims were carried by bulldozers to an unknown destination, and fire brigades washed the blood off the streets.

Alongside the intelligence services, the *shabiha* were the champions of repression during the early stages of the revolution. The word *shabiha* then became known outside Syria and around the world, though it used to be familiar in Syria only on a small scale; the terrifying phenomenon itself was not very well-known, however, and hardly any literature touched upon it. Writings about the *shabiha* phenomenon began to increase from the beginning of the revolution, proportionate to the rise of *shabiha* themselves. I wrote the essay 'The *Shabiha* and Their State' in September 2011. It explores the social and political roots of the phenomenon and works to expose the ways it is connected to the Assad regime's structure. In the context of the regime's widespread practice of *tashbih* (i.e., the thuggish practices of *shabiha*), specific political, intellectual, and economic *tashbih* that have characterized Baathist rule since its inception are addressed, since these directly relate to the regime's weak legitimacy and narrow social base.

That same September I wrote another essay, reflecting a new concern about the possibility that the Syrian revolution could enter into what I called 'the state of nature,' 'The Danger of a "State of Nature"'. Armed resistance was on the rise in unmistakable proportion to the repression of peaceful protests. I was worried that we were heading towards a state of open warfare dominated by a logic of necessity—the necessity of fighting desperately against the offender, leaving little room for the positive aspirations of the revolution. Things like democracy and justice, knowledge and art, would become luxuries when people were being murdered, tortured, and humiliated in great numbers. It became obvious to me that such a situation was an imminent danger, in which the 'rational self' would be subdued in favour of the 'angry self': a logic of desperation, with a consequent marginalization of those who identify with the rational self, including intellectuals and activists.

Like most Syrian activists and intellectuals who were advocates of the revolution, I thought that the fall of the regime was both possible and relatively close at hand throughout 2011. Ben Ali's regime was toppled in Tunisia within less than a month, and in Egypt, Mubarak's regime fell in less than three weeks. In Yemen, Ali Abdullah Saleh was dethroned within months, and Libya's Gaddafi was ousted and killed also within months, although NATO intervention played a decisive role. Only the Bahraini revolution had been crushed, by Saudi forces and with American approval. It never occurred to us that the Syrian revolution, with all its vitality and broad social support, would not be allowed to succeed either. That year, whenever I was asked whether I would continue to live in hiding, I jokingly made an analogy to the condition of pregnancy: by the end of the year, the Syrian revolution will be nine months and ten days along, and will deliver a living, breathing child. I didn't think about changing my living situation before that time.

The forty weeks of pregnancy passed, however, and delivery did not take place.

A few days after New Year's in 2012, I sensed that I was being watched, as did one of the friends with whom I had a meeting close to my residence. That night, I did not go back to my place. In fact, I never returned. Another friend of mine arranged to retrieve a few belongings: two computers along with some personal items. For about a month afterward, I lived in a real house, also in the city centre, and Samira was with me most of the time. The overall situation in the country was becoming more and more unmanageable. It was also becoming increasingly clear that the unimaginable situation we had discussed privately—that the regime would be willing to destroy the country for the sake of staying in power—was its only political agenda, and that it was already being implemented.

Around that time, I tried to broaden my work so that it was not limited to political coverage of current events; I tried instead to examine the social, historical, and cultural origins of the Syrian conflict.

It seemed important to trace the roots of the terrifying, fascist violence that the Assad junta had unleashed on the people. How could it be possible for those who run the country to treat those who are presumably their own people with such brutality and villainy, and with so much hatred? The essay 'The Roots of Syrian Fascism' tries to address these questions. A form of Arab nationalism adopted by the ruling Baathist party, which I refer to as Absolute Arabism, facilitated this process through the militarization of public life and the construction of barriers that separated Syrians from the rest of the world, which was seen as evil and dangerous. Absolute Arabism was also a facilitating factor for repressing internal diversity among Syrians, which helped strip them of any right to civic or political life: to conduct meetings, hold speeches, and protest in the public sphere. Attempts at local political activism and efforts to mingle with the outside world were both sure recipes for accusations of treason and consequent detainment, torture, and perhaps death.

Sectarianism is the second root of fascism, and it played a key role in facilitating identification with the regime, which helped provide it with a low-cost and easy-to-mobilize source of oppressive power, as well as a reservoir for the application of a violence mixed with hatred and humiliation.

Finally, there was the emergence of a neo-bourgeoisie during the years of Bashar al-Assad's rule, a class that owes everything to the regime and has a lot to lose were the revolution to emerge victorious. The ideology of this class is 'Development and Modernization,' and it simultaneously denies the necessity for political reform while giving a 'modern' appearance to the regime's elite. Arab nationalism was not well-suited to these tasks, but even so, the ascendant neo-bourgeoisie was unwilling to dispense with some of its main implications, especially those which painted the world as a dangerous place and which concealed the internal diversity of Syrian society. The ideology of 'Development and Modernization' is a culturalist one that attributes socio-political reality to 'mentalities' and calls for 'modernity'—moves that allow it to project a completely inverted image of reality. According to this distorted approach, Bashar al-Assad, if not a victim of the backward Syrian majority, is at very least constantly compelled to confront it. Within this ideological perspective, the general public is viewed with contempt and disdain, in a manner no different from a colonizing power's view of the colonized; this justifies the use of violence against the 'backward' masses and cheapens the value of their lives, so much so that killing them is a matter of no great concern. In chapter 5, I also emphasize the role of certain intellectuals in justifying the tyranny of the state and in eroding the intellectual, symbolic, and political defences that helped protect people's lives.

During the late winter and then spring of 2012, I was living at my fourth residence, in al-Muhajireen, which is a bit further from the centre of Damascus. Samira, cautious as ever, took care of providing for the home, along with a friend of mine. I moved between my new residence and a few other friends' houses that were closer to the city centre. I always moved on foot, which provided exercise and was also a way of dodging the regime's stationary and roving checkpoints. Naturally, I took back ways and avoided main roads as much as I could.

In the face of the regime's fascist violence, armed resistance was on the rise. An initiative by the Arab League had failed, and Kofi Annan, who was the UN-Arab League Joint Special Envoy for the Syrian Crisis, looked incapable of achieving anything. The regime was never interested in a political settlement or a ceasefire: it wanted to monopolize power completely. Things were heading toward open warfare with an unknown end. 'Arms and the Revolution' was written in March 2012 as a contribution to the discussion over the militarization of the revolution; it was an attempt to understand the path which led to it, and to look at its possible outcomes. Syrian society was breaking the Assad state's monopoly over arms in order to take ownership of the political, a goal that had proven unreachable through peaceful and political means. But it lacked a centralized body that could coordinate confrontation with the regime. Covert efforts to organize had a limited impact, due to a prolonged disconnect between the majority of the population and the well-educated sectors, who were more experienced in such things; in addition, local organizers lacked the 'backbone' of war, i.e., funds. I generally resist the urge to make predictions, but one appeared in this article: 'If the regime continues to escalate its militarized confrontation with the revolution—and there is not the slightest indication that it will not do so—then we will see an escalating tendency toward armament and military confrontation on the part of the revolution. And perhaps we will also see the FSA, originally a loose umbrella for armed resistance, replaced by jihadist groups. The latter do not have a national cause but rather a religious one, and they use nihilistic violence, or "terrorism."'

Although rebellious Syrians continued with their peaceful protests in the early spring of 2012, they were left with no good options. In fact, there were ongoing calls for civil disobedience and a general strike, and one actually took place in the very heart of Damascus in May 2012, following the al-Houla massacre that had claimed the lives of more than a hundred victims at the hands of the regime's *shabiha*. The fear factor, however, was always more powerful in the capital. When the strike took place, Bashar called some of the city's merchants and industrialists, and threatened to destroy the commercial district over their heads.

Most Western powers only half-heartedly condemned the regime, since they were motivated by their preferences for order, stability, and protection of the 'state', which always worked to the advantage of Bashar and his ilk, and in fact implied that the murderous regime apparatus would be maintained. The Russian/Chinese veto on the UN Security Council saved those powers from embarrassment and the regime from condemnation. It also suggested that Assad had been given a free pass to deal with 'his' people as he saw fit. This was the context in which the components of a nihilistic mixture began to crystallize, which I analyze in 'The Rise of Militant Nihilism'. Its elements are unrestricted violence, increasingly strict religiosity, and an intensified withdrawal of trust from the world. In May 2012, when I wrote the essay, I was not the only one uncertain about the existence of the so-called 'al-Nusra Front', an organization that had announced itself in January of that year. I was also one among many who had absolutely no trust in the Assad state, which had released Salafist prisoners nearly three months after the revolution began, all while our friends and colleagues were being prosecuted or brutally tortured in jail. From what we know about the regime, it would hardly be a surprise to learn that it had organized its own jihadist group. The story behind the Salafist 'Jund al-Sham' organization, which allegedly assassinated former Lebanese Prime Minister Rafiq al-Hariri, was still in recent memory. Another Salafist organization, 'Fatah al-Islam,' led by Shaker al-Absi, was a Frankenstein's monster created by Assad's intelligence service, which had held al-Absi captive. The noteworthy achievement of al-Absi and his organization was involvement in a war with the

Lebanese army in 2007 that caused the destruction of Nahr al-Bared, a Palestinian refugee camp in northern Lebanon. Yet it seemed to me that even if the Assadist regime had not invented its own Salafist jihadist organization, circumstances were becoming more and more accommodating for the emergence of such a thing. Large numbers of Syrians were becoming ever more enraged and feeling consigned to a dark and unknown fate. It appeared that the odds were getting better and better for the emergence of nihilistic groups as the revolution stumbled and Syrians' chances for achieving worldly justice broke down.

One late night in April, a friend showed up unexpectedly. It was the friend who had helped me and Samira find our house. She informed us that the houses in the neighbourhood were being searched, and warned us that it was highly likely that it would be our turn the following day. Leaving at night was dangerous; back then (and throughout my life in Syria), I used to work through the night and wake up late. That night I did not sleep at all. I woke Samira up early, and by 7 am we were on our way out of the house and the neighbourhood. We carried only our computers, since there was nothing else of value in the house anyway. Two days later, I found my fifth residence, close to the city centre. This time, I would spend nearly a year living in the same place.

Our new house was comfortable indeed: it was owned by a Damascene friend, without whom my second year of living in hiding would not have gone so smoothly. Samira stayed in this house with me most of the time.

All the houses where I lived were rent-free, friends' ways of showing support for what they saw as my and Samira's useful contributions to the revolution. Up until the day I left the country, many Syrians showed a spirit of solidarity, partnership, and generosity—in contrast to how they were accustomed to being treated and in a manner far removed from the values of selfishness, isolation, and avoidance of involvement in public affairs on which they had been raised under the Assad state.

In June 2012, fifteen months into the revolution, weekly peaceful demonstrations reached their highest peak in more than 700 revolutionary hotbeds around the country. A month later, they had disappeared almost completely. By that time, the regime had started using air power and Scud missiles against cities and towns. On 18 July 2012, a mysterious event took place: a few of the regime's security officials were assassinated, the very ones who comprised the 'Crisis Management Cell'. The common narrative back then was that the armed resistance had somehow been able to assassinate them, but no one could give a convincing account of what had happened. In my opinion, that mysterious incident was a turning point in the Syrian struggle. It ushered in a victory of the Iranian faction within the upper echelons of the Assadist state, and it is very likely that Bashar and the Iranians disposed of the victims. Shortly after that, in August 2012, the regime began to drop bombs on bread lines. This coincided with Kofi Annan's resignation, at which time he described Bashar al-Assad as 'a man...willing to employ any means to retain power.'

The Iranian presence became tangible and the national framework of the Syrian conflict was rapidly collapsing. Before that time of mid-2012, it was said that Hezbollah helped with training and recruiting for guerrilla warfare, but I personally believe that it was already participating in the war many months before that fact was explicitly announced in April 2013. There was also confirmation that Sunni jihadists had entered the scene in the summer of 2012. I watched footage aired on Al-Jazeera in June of 2012 showing that al-Qaeda's 'Mujahideen Shura Council' had seized Bab al-Hawa, a border crossing from Turkey to Syria. This was a bad omen. It became clear that the conflict was no longer contained within Syrian borders, but had spilled over to regional and international borders, with its sectarian dimension gaining momentum and intensity.

Chapter 7—'Assad or No One'—is an attempt to describe the nihilistic structure of the regime and the basic agenda guiding its policy, which is indicated by this slogan. It also tracks the resemblance between Assadist nihilism and religious nihilism, and between religious *shabiha* (jihadists) and the *shabiha* of Assad.

During the second half of 2012, the regime was in a steady state of decline despite its use of air power and long-range missiles, and despite the introduction of chemical weapons into the scene (most likely, Obama wouldn't have talked about his infamous 'red line' if he didn't already possess reports on the regime's mobilization of its chemical weapons). By 2012, the regime had lost its grip on the Eastern Ghouta, along with neighbourhoods in East Damascus.

Early in 2013, I began planning to move to the north of the country. The regime had also lost its grip over the countryside in Aleppo and Idlib, which added to my feeling of suffocation in Damascus, where my presence was not beneficial to any general cause and where dangers were multiplying with the increasing number of checkpoints and inspections of homes in the city's neighbourhoods. Samira was my partner in decision-making, and she also wanted to change our situation. The two of us were well aware of the great risks and the temporary separation, but, by that point, we had grown accustomed to danger and temporary separation as parts of the life we shared.

After consulting friends, I made up my mind to head first for Douma in Eastern Ghouta, and then travel north. Once there, I would arrange for Samira either to get to Raqqa, where my sister and two brothers lived, or to head toward Beirut and then to the north of Syria via Turkey. Raqqa, where I originally come from, had been out of the regime's control since March 2013, and was the first liberated provincial centre. It was a natural destination for me, when I was finally able to secure my transport to Douma on 3 April 2013. In an arrangement made by friends, I was aided by two young men from the rebels whom I had never met before. One of them was later detained the following autumn. He was killed under torture. The other was detained before him, and was probably allowed to escape in exchange for turning in his friend along with another rebel in the fall of 2013.

When I arrived in Douma (12 kilometres east from the centre of Damascus), the regime had regained control over al-Utaybah, which functioned as the entrance to Ghouta in the north. I have no definitive account about how this happened, but while I was in Douma I was able to gather information that local rebels in Ghouta and Daraa in the south were pressured by Saudi Arabia and urged by the US to steer clear of entering Damascus and toppling the regime by force. In my opinion, such an outcome was possible: the process of liberation had been substantial and fighters were sincere and enthusiastic. At the time, the armed resistance was particularly popular. However, there was a Salafist military group among them that called itself 'Sariyyat al-Islam' (Company of Islam) led by Zahran Alloush, a former prisoner in Sednaya Prison who was released in June 2011. Zahran's father, Abdullah Alloush, was a prominent Wahhabi cleric who had lived in Saudi Arabia for many years. 'Sariyyat al-Islam' was a small group that had made a negligible contribution to the liberation of Douma and Eastern Ghouta in the autumn of 2012. The liberators were local, popular fighters without a specified ideological orientation. When I arrived in the city in April 2013, the 'Sariyyat' had grown and turned into 'Liwa al-Islam' (Brigade of Islam) and had become the strongest (but not the only) military organization in the city. Could it be that the expansion of such a dependent Salafist organization was the bill to be paid in order to prevent a military toppling of the regime? This is what I tend to believe, as did other local activists in Douma, including Muhammad Flitani, who was assassinated in May 2014, most likely by 'Jaysh al-Islam' (Army of Islam), previously known as 'Liwa al-Islam.' At any rate, during my stay in the city between April and July 2013, the general atmosphere was one of frustration and confusion among the region's rebels and fighters, who also felt let down. The only party that seemed to continue to grow and prosper was Sariyyat/Liwa/Jaysh al-Islam.

I stayed with the Civil Defence Unit (that came later to be known as the White Helmets) in Douma for about a month, observing, learning, and helping out as much as I could. Then I moved to a neighbouring town in Eastern Ghouta named al-Mliha, and stayed there for another month. On 18 May 2013, it was possible to smuggle Samira to join me there. She arrived, sporting short hair and riding a motorbike behind two rebels. Samira had recently become wanted by the authorities in Damascus; she also wanted to try a new lifestyle. Before Samira's arrival and three weeks after my own, Razan Zaitouneh, the well-known lawyer, writer, and activist also came to Eastern Ghouta. She wasted no time and immediately started work as soon as she got there: she rented a residence, and used it as an office for the Violations Documentation Centre (VDC) of which she was one of the main founders, at the beginning of the revolution.

We spent the whole month of May in al-Mliha, then returned to Douma and lived together: Razan, Samira, and myself.

While there, I finished working on six portraits of fighters in the Free Syrian Army (FSA). They were later published in al-Jumhuriya

(The Republic), the online platform I co-founded along with younger activists and writers in March 2012. I also published a small report on a restricted chemical weapons attack committed by the regime against Jobar, a neighbourhood in Damascus. The report was based on interviews with one of those injured during the attack as well as doctors working in the region. I also wrote a letter to European intellectuals, urging them to pressure their governments to aid Syrians in their struggle for justice. The letter was published in a few European newspapers.

From what I observed at this time while working in the field, it appeared to me that there was a conflict among four Syrias: 'Assad's Syria', the Syrian Arab Republic, a rebellious Syria, and a Salafist Syria. I detailed my observations in the essay 'An Image, Two Flags, and a Banner', in which I combined social analysis with an interpretation of symbols (Kurdish Syria, under the current one-party system with its expansionist national tendency, was not around yet). The essay raises the prospect of a new inclusive Syria, one that unites rebellious Syria and the non-Assadist components of the current 'Syrian Arab Republic' against both Assad's Syria and Salafist Syria. The article was published as I left Douma on 10 July 2013. I had been looking for a way out since I arrived: it took me about 100 days to find one.

I embraced Samira that night, and said goodbye to Razan. It was not possible for Samira to accompany me on such a dangerous, arduous journey, but we had a plan to meet later. At the time, our plan seemed feasible: Samira would be smuggled back to Damascus, and from there the next steps would be much easier.

I spent nineteen days on the road, travelling in the summer heat and across the Syrian desert with its burning sun.

At one point, on my way to Raqqa, I was able to contact my friend, Dr. Ismail al-Hamidh, to ask him about my brother

Ahmed, a member of the local council in the city of Tell Abyad. He had been captured by Daesh the day I left Douma. Ahmed was still captive, but then I learned that they had also kidnapped my brother Firas, who was active in organizing protests against them following Ahmed's detainment. Firas, who left a wife and a toddler, is still captive and his whereabouts have remained unknown since 20 July 2013.

I was compelled to live in hiding again as soon as I arrived in Raqqa. Along with my two brothers, Paolo Dall'Oglio, the Syrian rebel and Italian Jesuit priest, was captured while trying to meet the leaders of Daesh on the day of my arrival. It was extremely hard for me to be unable to walk around the city where I spent years of my adolescence, where most of my brothers lived, and where my parents had lived until their deaths, while some religiously-obsessed, enraged Tunisians, Saudis, Egyptians, and Europeans roamed freely, unable to engage in anything other than murder. While in Raqqa, I wrote the essay 'The Destiny of the Syrian Revolution', which is probably the most pessimistic of all the book's chapters.

I had been in Raqqa for three weeks when the chemical massacre occurred in Eastern Ghouta, where Samira was still staying. She was safe. For a moment, it seemed like the regime's evil deed would be punished, since it had crossed the 'red line', as defined by the Obama administration. Many Syrians, including myself, had no reason to regret that the junta might be punished for at least one of its crimes, after it had used air power, long-range missiles, and chemical weapons against its own people, and after it had killed thousands of them under torture, committed sectarian massacres, and even invited other murderers to join the killing spree. Yet American officials raced in to say that punishment, if it happened, would be appropriate and limited. It was an absurd situation: those who had appointed themselves the guardians of international law were reassuring a murderer that they might be compelled to punish him for violating their law, but without affecting his ability to kill his people and with no reference to his other crimes, which had already claimed the lives of nearly 100,000 Syrians. In this situation, the crime was apparently not the murder of 1,466 people in Ghouta during a chemical massacre: the problem was the weapon used in the crime. Since that time, it became clear that punishing a murderous regime was something too progressive for the US Establishment. A few days later, the Obama administration sealed a deal with the Russians, one worthy of Roosevelt's description of the Japanese attack on Pearl Harbor: treacherous and dastardly; an act that will live in infamy. America, the 'friend of the Syrian people', joined with the enemy of the Syrian people, Russia, leaving the Syrian people at the mercy of a mass murderer, Bashar al-Assad. They told him: 'You are forbidden from killing Syrians with the weapons we prohibited, but it is none of our business if you continue to kill them with other weapons that we did not prohibit!' In my opinion, the deal revealed the extent of the criminality at the heart of the current international order. Not only was the deal a free pass for Bashar al-Assad to go on killing Syrians by other means, but it was also a warrant of immunity against any form of punishment. It was an earth-shattering blow for Syrians who were looking forward to a new progressive Syria. It was also an invaluable boon to Daesh and the Al-Nusra Front, as well as to the Assads. Impunity is the mother of terrorism: more impunity means more terrorists ranging free.

After this, and in a way that I took to be intimately connected with the disgraceful chemical deal, Western media outlets voluntarily launched a free publicity campaign for Daesh—a dangerous, bizarre, magical, and ultra-sexy lifestyle. We saw a sort of 'enchantment of the world' that stimulated the fantasies of many young men and women in the West who joined this fascist organization, which was enjoying ten times more coverage than the crimes of the Assad state, even though Assad's victims outnumber those of Daesh tenfold.

After receiving reassurance that it could deal with Syrians as it saw fit, and with encouragement from the Russians and Iranians, the regime expanded its use of barrel bombs. These, by the way, are immeasurably more destructive than chemical weapons when used against homes, neighbourhoods, and towns, and they claim just as many lives. Late in the summer of 2015, I co-wrote a satirical letter to Staffan de Mistura (the United Nations and Arab League Envoy to Syria), asking him to work on issuing a resolution from the UN Security Council to return chemical weapons to Assad and permit him to use them again, in exchange for a ban on barrel bombs. We suggested that the UN form an International Barrel Bomb Agency (IBBA) with headquarters in Tehran, the capital of the state that has made the greatest outside contribution toward murdering Syrians. Despite translation into English, French, Spanish, and Turkish, the letter received little attention.

Meanwhile, back in 2013, Samira and Razan covered the events in Eastern Ghouta, each in her own way, from the chemical massacre to barrel bombings to the conditions of daily life. Samira directed the 'Women Now' centre, which supported local women in producing what they needed to provide for their families. She used to write short posts on her Facebook page about the living conditions in the region. Razan was the woman behind the most important report on the chemical massacre, as well as many other stories of former detainees and reports on detention centres, to name a few. She also directed the staff network of the Violations Documentation Centre in most areas across the country.

Samira was also a valuable source of information for me in Eastern Ghouta. Even after my arrival in Raqqa, I was still planning to explore the areas in the north to learn about and familiarize myself with the region. Yet it became more and more obvious that the situation was unwelcoming except for fighters and those with sufficient ties to protection. Having spent two and a half months in Raqqa, Samira (still in Ghouta) and my other brothers, living in different countries, were becoming increasingly anxious about my safety and continued to urge me to leave. They were afraid that I would fall captive to Daesh. I left for Turkey on 11 October 2013, nearly two years and seven months after the revolution began. Turkey was the first country that I had ever 'visited', after Lebanon (before I was banned from visiting Lebanon in 2004), and the first country I had ever lived in outside of Syria.

Three weeks later, my friend and physician Ismail al-Hamidh was kidnapped by Daesh. At that point, I would have been compelled to leave Raqqa had I still been living there. Today, Ismail is still captive: there has been no information whatsoever about him. His wife and five children stayed in Raqqa for some months, before having to leave first for Turkey and then France some months later.

When she learned that I had left the country, Samira was relieved. But I was becoming more anxious. Ghouta was completely besieged at the time of my departure. It had been besieged before as well, but moving to Damascus used to be possible through checkpoints that were under the regime's control. My main concern was to provide Samira with resources to live on until we found her a way out. Most important was covering our communication expenses, which used a satellite internet device that required a costly gasoline-operated generator. When I first arrived in Ghouta in April 2013, the price of gasoline was about $1 per litre. A hundred days later, it had soared to more than $10 a litre. The generator was defective, and it also used at least a litre of gasoline per hour. Samira and Razan were online daily for about 3–5 hours on average. Our last conversation revolved around finding a way to cover Samira's living costs until we could find her a way out of Ghouta. I was supposed to send money to someone in Damascus, who would contact someone else in Douma in order to deliver the money to Samira, for a fee. The strict control over people's basic needs in the besieged areas was a source of income for businessmen, who were no longer exclusively pro-Assad.

Toward the end of that horrible year, the worst thing occurred. Samira was abducted along with Razan Zaitouneh, Wael Hamada, and Nazem Hamadi on the night of 9 December 2013. Up until my departure from Ghouta in July 2013, it never occurred to us that there could be a more dangerous threat to their lives than the regime's bombs. Wael and Nazem had joined Razan and Samira in September, two months after my departure. Samira never thought that there were potential risks threatening her life or freedom: she never expressed any fears in that regard. Razan, on the other hand, had received a death threat from 'Jaysh al-Islam' if she did not leave Douma. Unfortunately, none of us, our friends in Ghouta included, took the matter seriously then.

That was a fateful error.

For some time, I was unable to absorb what had happened. I thought the matter would be resolved quickly, and the four would be released. But our opponent was the de facto authority in the area. All available evidence pointed to 'Jaysh al-Islam,' a Salafist power the regime had cultivated—until it took control of the region—in exchange for the rebels being prevented from entering Damascus. This authority did not conduct an investigation into a crime that had occurred in its 'capital', nor did it help anyone who wished to do so.

A few days after the crime occurred, I stated that I held 'Jaysh al-Islam' politically accountable, and suggested its legal responsibility too.

The kidnapping of Samira, Razan, Wael, and Nazem was the biggest blow to the revolution by a party other than the regime or Daesh. Today, more than three years after the incident, we still have no information about these two women and two men, and as such the kidnapping is a crime against the four detainees, but also against their loved ones, and against the betrayed revolution.

What bestows a particularly tragic status on this abduction is that it was an outcome of our own struggle, and that we ourselves had made this horrible incident possible. Throughout the past two years, this incident has occupied my mind more than the long years of my imprisonment. Telling their story, constructing its meaning and politics, is the commitment that I made to myself for as long as they are absent, and for as long as I am alive and breathing.

In the spring of 2014 in Istanbul, I spoke at a meeting held by a Turkish leftist organization about sectarianism in Syria. What I said during that meeting provided the basis for the book's closing chapter, which is also the longest. It was published in the spring of 2015. The essay explains that sectarianism does not inevitably stem from inherited cultural differences, since those have always existed in every society, but is rather the outcome of social and political privileges. Sectarianism is essentially a tool for governing and a strategy for control. The piece aims at providing conceptual tools to think about sectarianism and its political economy in Syria. It also shows that the world of sects and denominations is not separate from the world of classes. Generally speaking, it offers an alternative view to the culturalist tendency common in the West, which attributes sectarianism to inherent differences among religions.

Approaching the matter in this way is beneficial for constructing a critical approach to both culturalism and cultural determinism as well as theories of 'civilization' that have prospered around the globe since the end of the Cold War. The 'clash of civilizations' is sectarian war on a global level. It does not exist because there are primordially different civilizations, but because the concept of civilization is being used to protect the financial and political privileges of the 'civilized,' and to exclude the 'uncivilized' or those who descend from 'inferior civilizations' from any real sense of equality or partnership in the shaping of world politics.

In general, this book does not tell the story of the Syrian revolution: it is rather an attempt to trace and chronicle some of its paths; its overall narrative was produced through direct involvement with the course of the Syrian struggle and its developments. In the essays that appear here, and in my writing more broadly, I have tried to build an ethical case against the Assadist state. Today, building an ethical case against Salafists occupies an increasingly significant place in my work, along with the case against the current international order, which seems to have lost its moral compass and proven an effective element in the destruction of Syria and in the claiming of countless lives.

It seems to me that the complicated entanglements between the local struggle against tyranny and religious, sectarian, and ethnic conflicts, along with all the complex and intertwined international interventions, constitute as a whole what could be called 'The Syrian Question.' History is full of Questions, most notably the 'Eastern Question', the 'Jewish Question' and the 'Palestinian Question.' Such questions are complex, multifaceted, and enduring: they are coupled with wars and hatred, blood, decay, and despair. Such questions condense and intensify the state of the world at the time they arise. Somehow, I imagine that these 'Questions' reflect the machinations of the powerful in history and their handiwork, which transforms human history into a convoluted, ugly novel with no way out, a novel whose characters are criminals, thieves, murderers, and professional liars. History has another face, and that is the face of revolutions and rebellions of the vulnerable. They cut the Gordian knots of Questions, and open up clearer and more youthful prospects, richer in hopes for themselves and for the world. The Syrian Question is the response of the powerful (locally, regionally, and internationally) to the Syrian Revolution, and the revolutions of the region as a whole. The powerful tie many Gordian knots, which the vulnerable spend a lifetime trying to undo. Posing Questions is a strategy through which all the vulnerable people in the world are disciplined.

Many players have been involved in creating the 'complex' Syrian Question: 'Holy Russia,' inheritor of the Tsarist Empire Marx dubbed the 'prison of the peoples,' is involved; also the USA, holder of the keys to the 'Middle East,' a modern prison of the peoples; the Saudi theocracy, which is a global source of decay and 'Questions' even more than it is a source of oil; the Iranian theocracy, which is another source of hatred, 'Questions', and oil; Turkey, the primary heir to the Eastern Question along with two lesser heirs, Jordan and Lebanon; secular European republics and kingdoms that prioritize Christian and other 'minority' refugees; Israel, the state that lives in a permanent 'state of exception' and strikes whenever it so wishes, enjoys absolute impunity, and is always consulted by both Americans and Russians on the Syrian Question; and finally, the two poles of the underground world—the terrorist jihadist groups (which are basically independent intelligence agencies run by fanatics) and the international intelligence agencies (which are essentially a torturing and murdering apparatus). All of these elements are now operating in a country that suffered enormously from the Western solution to the Jewish Question, the creation of the Palestinian Question, and was also a fragment of the Western solution to the Eastern Question.

Broadly considered, the Syrian Question indicates that we are currently facing an international crisis within a world that is being run by the powerful to a greater extent than at any other time dating back at least a century, a world that is becoming more depressing and complex by the minute, a world that is losing direction and at the same time concealing possibilities for emancipation and democracy.

The crisis is no longer a Syrian one. It is a crisis of the world.

Facing an international crisis and the danger of an international civil war requires new principles and new institutions, starting with the principle of global responsibility: of our own responsibility for the world, of the world's responsibility for us, and of the whole world's responsibility for the whole world. No one is too distant to be a neighbour, no one is too alien not to belong to 'us', no one is too monstrous to be involved in politics. No one is Daesh, Daesh does not exist. What exists is a progressively Syrianized world.

It is especially important to have effective international institutions other than the United Nations. The UN Security Council is particularly problematic: it imposes the rule of an oligarchy over the international majority. It is not necessary to stand around waiting for a world war in order to topple these ineffectual institutions that are so bereft of justice.

The principle of universal responsibility, and new international institutions, are the prerequisites for saving democracy which retreats everywhere as soon as it stops progressing anywhere, as we see today on a daily basis. The antithesis of global progress toward democracy is a throwback to international aristocracies, to the spread of a model of gated communities and gated states that raise up their walls in the face of menaces from the vulnerable and the barbarized, much in the way that Western powers, the rich and the powerful, are doing today in the face of Syrians and other refugees.

1

REVOLUTION OF THE COMMON PEOPLE

DAMASCUS, JUNE 2011

For hundreds of thousands of Syrians, the Syrian popular uprising has been an extraordinary experience, ethically and politically: an experience of self-renewal and social change, an uprising to change ourselves and a revolution to change reality.

I

The young and the elderly, women and men, are changing their lives and renewing themselves through their participation in the protest movement, bravely facing arrest, torture, or death. After confronting danger face to face, they have emerged stronger and more courageous, more dignified and more open. Such an experience is not available to those who refrain from participating in the protests, nor has a similar experience on such a large scale been possible for about two generations of Syrians. Through their engagement in a costly, collective venture, these renewed Syrians have developed a hitherto unmatched spirit of selflessness and lively solidarity. Out of desperation (in the literal sense of the word—which in Arabic, as *istimata*, denotes putting your life into your struggle, risking death to achieve your purpose) for a more common purpose, Syrians who are participating in the uprising have been freed of both fear and selfishness. The always edgy and dangerous and often catastrophic and tragic nature of these experiences guarantees that they will remain in the national memory for generations to come.

It is appropriate to speak in terms of a revolution because many Syrians are radically changing themselves while struggling to change their country and emancipate their fellow Syrians. For that reason in particular, it will be very difficult to defeat the uprising.

Over the past forty years, the regime has imposed a narrow and impoverished existence on Syrians, lives devoid of new experiences, rejuvenation, and passion. We have lived 'material' lives in every sense of the word, deprived of any moral, ethical, spiritual, and aesthetic dimensions; purely worldly lives to the point of abject cynicism, in the context of which religion might have seemed the sole spiritual confection to be found in an arid desert.

Today, the uprising provides bountiful new experiences for a large number of Syrians. The voluntary and emancipatory nature of this extraordinary experience renders it a democratic uprising. It is unprecedented under the Assadist regime.

2

Thanks to the communications revolution (and modern cell phone technology in particular), the distance between field activity and media coverage has shrunk considerably, allowing for more democratic forms of organization and leadership to emerge within the movement. Widely supported by modern means of communication (specifically cell phones, Facebook, Twitter, and YouTube videos) and the instantaneous delivery of news and images to TV channels, new technologies have filled the gaps that resulted from news correspondents being prevented from working in Syria.

Each activist, young ones in particular, is making a new reality in multiple ways. By taking to the streets in defiance of a tyrannical power that has come to represent the past, and working to change it, and then again through documentation, he or she creates a new reality and ensures that it becomes known and tangible by broadcasting it across public media outlets. Such actions provide (relative) protection for the movement, allowing it to address public opinion in the country and in the world, gaining the sympathy of broad segments of Syrians, Arabs, and people further afield. If it were not for this vital 'central nervous system' (i.e., the young men and women who cover their own activities on-site) the uprising would be isolated, and much easier for the regime to destroy.

Moreover, the activities of those armed with a cell phone camera create an objective memory of the uprising, and build an enormous audio-visual archive. This archive is made up of the efforts of thousands of Syrians, and is being watched by millions of Syrians everywhere, which provides additional immunity from oblivion. Verbal testimony is fragile compared to photography; the latter is also more likely to persist in collective memory. Both cell phones and Facebook have played roles in differentiating and individualizing independent contributors. New media have also played an expanded role in democratizing participation in the production of information, and in the creation of a different public space, a 'virtual' arena that is impenetrable by authorities. New technologies are playing a communicative role in the creation of new and resilient communities working against the regime, in addition to their role in building a memory of the uprising by keeping an immense record of all its minutiae, day by day and area by area.

Besides the visual archive, there is also a large and growing number of stories written and posted online by direct participants. These narratives will find their way into the public sphere one day.

In addition to assembling a memory that is resistant to confiscation and erasure, the process of photo-documentation of the uprising has allowed for a decisive victory in the media battle. The regime possesses nothing that even remotely resembles the credibility, dynamism, and broad-based coverage of the uprising's documents, which were compiled at nearly no financial cost. The human cost, however, has been very high.

This new reality forged by activists has also reinforced the moral superiority of the intifada. Those who sacrifice their freedom and risk their lives to cover their uprising stand in stark contrast with the 'Party of the Couch', to borrow a term used by Egyptian activists during their revolution (i.e. those who follow the revolution on TV). Still less can those who sacrifice their freedom and risk their lives be compared with the regime's ideologists and journalists, its apologists and *shabiha* (thugs), its tools of oppression or its murderers, junior and senior.

The courage, sacrifice, and collective spirit that characterize the uprising are certain to eventually constitute a national experience, one that will make a contribution to the reconstruction of the country.

This is to say that a regime capable of engaging in a war against the rebellion of the governed is entirely incapable of fighting a war against their memories. The regime may be able to overcome the intifada by force, but such a victory will only mark the first round in a longer struggle, one in which Syrians will already have recourse to a sophisticated memory of exceptional experiences, a source of support for them in any future rounds of their liberation struggle.

REVOLUTION OF THE COMMON PEOPLE

3

Today, there are two powers in Syria: the regime and the popular uprising.

The regime possesses arms, money, and intimidation. The regime kills, but is devoid of meaning or substance. The uprising, on the other hand, has had to meet the challenge of overcoming fear and is consequently infused with the spirit of freedom.

The uprising is the embodiment of selflessness, which amounts to sacrificing life, whereas the regime is the embodiment of selfishness, which amounts to the destruction of the country for the survival of an intellectually, politically, and ethically degenerate junta. The uprising is an ethical and political rebellion, and the most positively transformative event in the history of modern Syria since independence. But the regime has turned on Syrians, because it can only thrive over a meek, divided, and unconscious body politic.

The uprising allows for personal identities, while the regime invalidates all names save for the one it has imposed on everything in the country: 'Assad'. Streets, squares, the largest lake, hospitals, the largest library, are all named after Assad; even the country itself is known as 'Assad's Syria'. The uprising revives the original names of places: in Daraa Governorate: Jasim, Nawa, Bosra, Da'el, Inkhil; in Damascus: Kanaker, Douma, Harasta, al-Midan, Barza, Rukned-Din, Moadamiyeh, al-Tal, al-Kiswah, Qatana, Jdeidat Artouz; in Homs: Bab al-Sebaa, Bab Dreeb, al-Waer, al-Rastan, Talbiseh, al-Qusayr; in Hama: al-Hader, al-Souq, al-Assi Square, al-Salamiyah; in Idlib: Maarrat al-Nu'man, Jisr al-Shughour, Kafranbel, Binnish, Khirbat al-Jawz, Mount Zawiya; in Aleppo: the University, Sayfed-Dawla, Salah ed-Din, as-Sakhour, Ainal-Arab, Tall Rifaat, Manbij, al-Bab; in al-Hasakah: al-Qamishli, Ras al-Ayn, Amuda, Derbassiyeh; in

Latakia: al-Saliba, ar-Raml al-Falastini, al-Skantori, Jableh; in Tartus: Banias, Al-Bayda, Raqqa, and Tabaqa; in Deir ez-Zour: al-Mayadeen, al-Bukamal, and al-Ghourieh.

The uprising also gives names to Friday protests: The Good Friday (as a sign of respect to the Christian communities), Friday of Anger, Azadi (Freedom, in Kurdish) Friday, Saleh al-Ali Friday (named after an Alawi leader of resistance against the French in early 1920s), and Irhal (leave) Friday, among many others. The uprising is freeing the country's name from its shackles. It is 'Syria,' not 'Assad's Syria', nor is it the 'State of the Baath.'

Through its revival of names, the uprising has been creating personalities, i.e. active centres for initiatives and free will. By contrast, the regime was established upon the idea of turning Syria and all Syrians into the subjects of a single free agent: 'The Assad Self.'

The uprising reveals the stifled richness of Syria: the social, cultural, and political richness of Syria and its damaged population, those whom the hand of tyranny has long alienated or excluded. The uprising has given them a stage for speaking in public upon which they can cheer, object, satirize, chant or sing: they can occupy the public sphere and liberate it from totalitarian control.

Through the revival of individualizing names, the uprising also makes it possible for Syrians to regain control of their lives and their environments by telling their stories and repairing their language, opening it up to some of their most vivid emotions.

4

The 'modernization and development' policies attributed to Syrian President Bashar al-Assad were superficial makeovers at the material level of tools and devices (modern cars, malls and restaurants, lavish hotels and bank branches, 'Ivy League' schools, etc.). They were devoid of any humane, ethical, or political essence. Values such as political rights, public freedoms, social solidarity, and cultural progress all remained unheard of. In fact, social and national solidarity declined significantly among Syrians, and the humanitarian and emancipatory dimensions of culture deteriorated beneath the cliquish, intolerant ideologies perpetuated by ideologues of 'modernity'.

The real identity of the regime consists of the combination of an obsolete, inhumane political apparatus with a glamorous material façade. This makes for more than just an authoritarian political system: it is a social, political, and ideological system based on racial discrimination with respect to the population, as well as holding a monopoly on power, wealth, and patriotism. This supercharged monopoly is one of the reasons for the popular protests, which perhaps explains why the protests began in Syria's hinterland and 'peripheral' towns. The ongoing economic liberalization in Syria spurred a model of development that favoured cities at the expense of rural areas, city centres at the expense of outlying neighbourhoods, and wealthy modern suburbs at the expense of the crowded traditional suburbs where those excluded by the neoliberal authoritarian development model found a last refuge. These areas have all been marginalized, and unemployment levels have soared due to the requirements asked of prospective employees within the new labour market (proficiency in foreign languages and familiarity with new technologies, to name but a few). At the same time, there has been a decline in the social role of the state, with government representatives transformed into a rich elite, ruling the locals with scorn and disdain as if they themselves were foreign dignitaries. The president's cousin, Atef Najib, arrested and tortured children in Daraa before the outbreak of the uprising and then suggested to their parents that they just forget their children, telling the fathers that he and his men will impregnate their wives if they failed to do so. This is an example of a powerful, brutish, affluent, and savage man who enjoys absolute immunity.

Syrians have seethed under these developments, which have also provoked new levels of contempt and psychological detachment. And although these developments are not entirely new, during recent years they have brought about degrees of social and cultural segregation equivalent to apartheid.

Intellectuals have contributed to the institutionalization of these social conditions by propagating an authoritarian form of secularism, one obsessed with monitoring the role of religion in public life while entirely ignoring the roles played by the political system and power elites. This aristocratic and dishonest form of secularism has justified the regime's heavy-handed mechanism of political governance: it has reduced the intellectual and moral fortifications that protect the lives of the general public; and it has joined with a racist international cultural and political climate (as Benedict Anderson has explained, racism is an ideology of class, not an ideology of identity). This secularism contributed to legitimating the transfer of power, concentrating it in the hands of those that rule in Syria today. Atef Najib did not emerge from the doctrines of the likes of Adonis, George Tarabichi, or Aziz al-Azmeh (three well known Syrian secularist intellectuals), but this dogma strongly reduced the intellectual, moral, and symbolic barriers that would have prevented him from emerging, along with other, similar monsters.

To sum up, one can say that the Syrian revolution erupted against a form of modernization that was merely economic liberalization catering to the rich; against a modernist ideology without any emancipatory implications; and against a cosmetic modernity marked by devices and possessions, from banks to private universities to cars. It is a revolution against an elitist regime that has turned 'development and modernization' into a doctrine that conceals power relations and privileged, illegal wealth; it is a revolution against the wealthy regimists who stole fortunes during the days of 'socialist' Baathism and then became masters of the economy in liberal times; and it is a revolution against the elite's ideologues who have turned 'modernism' into an object of worship along with its practical interpretation in the form of the Assadist 'development and modernization' policy.

5

The fact that 'traditional' social environments are hotspots of the Syrian revolution raises a political and conceptual question concerning the possible links between democracy and that type of social base.

In 'Assad's Syria', the aforementioned communities have suffered under political persecution, cultural alienation, and economic exploitation. These factors place them in a proletarian position: they have little to lose and a lot to win from a revolution. Besides, these communities restore their cultural esteem through their courageous and widespread participation in the uprising. They work to emancipate themselves politically by challenging an authoritarian, modernist and ultra-reactionary regime. Their political presence in the revolution will perhaps contribute to a relative adjustment of socio-economic forces to their advantage.

In fact, the presumed 'traditionalism' of these communities is the by-product of their segregation from public life, in addition to declines in developmental activity, income, and education, alongside a spontaneous local inclination toward greater independence. There is nothing traditional about this so-called 'traditionalism': it is incomprehensible outside of very particular political and economic circumstances that, in their outcomes, resemble the effects of colonialism.

These social environments were in a process of dissolution until the 1970s. However, the prolonged deterioration of economic conditions, the collapse of the public education system, and an imposed political quarantine all played a role in their isolation and were active engines for 'traditionalizing' them.

Contrary to claims that there is a widespread 'modernizing' political culture in Syria, the most vibrant local environments are in fact those most resilient to tyranny, which possess the greatest potential to nurture and support democracy. Moreover, increased local autonomy and decentralization are desirable from a developmental, administrative, and political perspective in both these areas and the country as a whole. The regime's extreme centralization was an obstacle to development, a source of social and cultural impoverishment, and an instrument of dictatorship.

6

How, then, are we to comprehend this article's opening statements about the uprising as an experience of self-transformation—which tens and hundreds of thousands of Syrians have engaged upon—in relation to the section just above, which positioned 'traditional' social environments as seemingly the natural habitat of the Syrian uprising? Are 'traditional' environments compatible with self-transformation? Doesn't the word 'tradition' mean precisely that an ideal model for the self is given in advance, and that the ultimate goal is for individuals to approximate this model?

Actually there is nothing traditional about these communities. Their supposed traditionalism is a projection from outside, produced by the modernist ideology that isolated them and was always suspicious about their political loyalties.

The Syrian uprising combines local and civic networks rebelling against various forms of deprivation, with modern, educated, and cultured women and men who are motivated by aspirations of freedom, individuality, and autonomy—values associated with an educated middle class emancipated from local frameworks. The commonalities that unite these two groups include their connections to work and an exclusive reliance on it to make a living, their perceptions of justice, and their world views. Together, these two components constitute the 'common people' of Syrian society, as against the 'elites' who define themselves through power, wealth, or alleged cultural distinction.

The freedom desired by the youth of the educated middle- and lower middle class—both believers and non-believers—requires the rebuilding of political and ethical systems around work and the value of work. Here, work contrasts socially, politically, and ethically with power and privilege, which is the basis for an opposite kind of social alliance, one that did not raise an eyebrow over the killing and brutal torturing of fellow Syrians.

But why freedom and not justice, as one might expect from the centrality of work in the formation of the Syrian uprising's social coalition as well as from the centrality of justice in Islamic values? This affinity is probably a response to the ways power was exercised in the current, privileged social system, which caused the collapse of the material and moral value of work, the collapse of the society of work itself and the deterioration of its political weight. The priority accorded freedom in the Syrian uprising indicates that the elimination of tyranny is a condition of justice, though the question of justice does not end there. Elevating the status of freedom and using it as the basis for justice could be a step towards restructuring the supreme values in our culture.

What we take away from it all is this: the differences in tastes and lifestyles between the uprising's two allied components are less significant than their common separation from the new feudal lords, from those who own and govern but do not work.

7

Is it possible that political developments in a post-Assad Syria might result in a 'tyranny of the majority'? Will we see an Islamic tyranny, hostile to religious minorities (mainly Christians), or a sectarian Sunni Islamist tyranny (against Alawites, Ismailis, Druze, and Shiites)?

In reality, this hypothesis has no precedent in the modern history of Syria. During the pre-Baath era, social and political conditions were beginning to favour the reduction of material and political differences among cultural groups, rather than the reverse. Baathist rule itself, with Assad père et fils, would not have been possible had it not been for this development. Before they were being excluded by the one-party state, active political parties represented diverse religious and ethnic constituencies in the public sphere. Nationalist and communist parties offered an answer to society's need to overcome its vertical divisions. The Baath Party rallied Christians and Muslims, Sunnis and Alawites, and many others. Moreover, at earlier stages communists rallied Arabs, Kurds, Armenians, and Jews. Once these parties were dissolved, including the Baath Party itself, ordinary people were left with nothing to identify with beyond their civic affiliations. To make matters worse, the dissolution of political parties during the reign of Hafez al-Assad was accompanied by the subjugation of the army, which revoked its general, national character; the subjugation of the universities, which extinguished their independence; and the subordination of the trade unions, which stifled their public role. The establishment of a personal tyranny took the country into a new phase of clannish rule, against which Syrians are revolting today, following the lead of Tunisians, Egyptians, Yemenis, Bahrainis and Libyans.

Anyone with some knowledge of Syrian society realizes that Syrian Sunnis cannot be defined except passively—they are only known by their otherness, since they are not Christians, nor Alawites, nor Druze, nor Ismaili. This is troublesome to Islamists first and foremost, the self-proclaimed representatives of Syrian Sunnis, and to others with sectarian motives, no different from the Islamists in their core beliefs.

The only relevant question in this context is: what explains a warning against a 'tyranny of the majority' being issued by the very same people who stammer when it comes to discussing an already existing, incontestable tyranny? The answer can be found in a modernist doctrine that establishes an essentialist link between the West and modernism, rather than a historical connection. Through this association, this modernist doctrine acquires the West's essentialist, hostile predisposition against Islam, one rooted in Judeo-Christianity rather than in the secular, democratic, and liberal heritage of the West. Throughout history, this predisposition has always sympathized with the marginalized within Islamic society, but not out of concern with justice for the disadvantaged—or else we would have seen its advocates supporting the Palestinians against Israel and evincing less scepticism towards the current revolutions. Rather, it is due to identity and the 'chemistry of identities,' a topic for another time.

We would be in the best position to object to a possible Islamization of our current revolutions and of our post-revolutionary societies, were we to break the link between this objection and the essentialist or fundamentalist predisposition of hostility toward Islam itself. The latter lacks any democratic or emancipatory content, but is rife with retrograde, authoritarian, and racist tendencies. This is a pivotal point because the scepticism of some toward Islamic aspects of the Arab revolutions is deeply rooted in a fundamentalist antagonism toward Islam itself. It would be fatal for a truly secular democrat to be a partner to this tendency, one that has prospered since 9/11, continuing a moderate post-Cold War boom.

8

But is it not likely that political Islamists will have the final say in post-Baath Syria? As we have seen in Tunisia, political Islamists have gained a strong political presence after the revolution for the first time since the country declared independence about sixty years ago. Likewise, in Egypt, they are the likeliest candidates to administer, or at least occupy influential positions in, the country. There is nothing to suggest that they would not be influential in a new Syria.

This is a valid speculation. However, it is not a new issue, nor is it the worst possibility when it comes to personal and clannish dictatorships.

Certainly, it would not be easy to welcome Islamists into our new political system, but their exclusion has been tried and tested and the results of doing so are well documented. In fact, wherever Islamists have been excluded in the Arab world (Egypt, Tunisia, Syria, Libya, Algeria), others have been excluded as well, and these comprehensive exclusions have only benefitted tyrannical rule. There is not a single exception to this pattern, no instance where Islamists were suppressed while leftists, liberals, and seculars were embraced. Moreover, such a policy doesn't merely result in the alienation of any active political or intellectual powers—it also generates Islamic extremists with a penchant for political violence who would be most likely to contest the ruling cliques for power politically and militarily, and who would aggressively oppose any compromise over religion, morality, and culture, seeking to impose their own doctrine as the only acceptable option.

Perhaps the legitimate emergence of Islamists onto the social and political scene in our ever-changing societies would bring intellectual and moral conflicts to the surface that would push the opposition to fuse democracy and secularism in order to ward off the possible tyranny of the Islamists. The previous separation of these two—democracy and secularism—has weakened democracy, corrupted secularism, radicalized Islamism, and served only the interests of ruling cliques.

9

What to expect from the Syrian uprising?

An answer to this question is important, so that exaggerated expectations and consequent disappointment may be avoided—but without abandoning the aspirations that spurred the uprising. It would be unreasonable to expect a stable democracy during the initial years following such political upheaval. Achieving political conditions that render reform feasible is imperative because the main problem in Syria is not hardship, but that the regime has posited itself as perfect and thus incapable of reform.

Daunting challenges await post-Baathist Syria, nothing less than rebuilding state and society, and restoring trust among

Syrians on the basis of citizenship. Trust must be restored because it has been ravaged by the regime—the ruling royal junta that does not work—which spread an atmosphere of ongoing cold war among the people, and which today confronts the uprising through an undeniably hot war. Syria would be fine if it could maintain its unity as a country and society, develop mechanisms of self-reform, and say goodbye to the system of permanent internal war.

Problems of educational reform, judicial reform, and administrative reform will appear immediately, as well as issues related to reconstructing the political system on new foundations. The security apparatus will have to be reshaped entirely from the ground up, because the core of the existing security services is predicated on hostility to and contempt for the people. Similarly, the media will need to be re-built completely, since the current media is predicated on lying, trickery, and worship of the regime, rendering it beyond repair. There is also the rebuilding of the army, given that the long process of Baathification has factionalized it and stripped it of patriotism.

From clearing away the ruins left by the Baathist regime, to rebuilding the country on a basis that is open to reform, there is a tremendous burden weighing on the shoulders of the Syrian youth, who are paying dearly for reclaiming life and politics.

2

THE SYRIAN *SHABIHA* AND THEIR STATE

DAMASCUS, NOVEMBER 2011

I take no pride in seeing how the term *shabiha* (Assadist thugs) entered into the global lexicon by way of Syria, while the term's referent was taking to our country's streets, terrorizing, murdering, and mouthing obscenities (in Arabic, the present tense verb *yushabbih*). This term, hitherto unknown outside Syria and for a long time not even widely known within Syria itself, first appeared in the local Arabic dialect, and, soon enough, it spawned derivatives—*shabbaha*, *yushabbihu* (past and present tense of the verb denoting thuggish actions), *tashbih* (infinitive, *shabiha* actions)—all of which were primarily used in reference to regime loyalists. Young revolutionaries, on the other hand, earned the catchall equivalent *mundasseen* (infiltrators) in response, and they now jokingly use it to identify themselves. The term *shabiha* was then deployed in new contexts, such as the '*shabiha* of the pen,' a phrase first coined by the Syrian-British writer Rana Kabbani, to describe Western writers biased toward the Syrian regime, such as the late Patrick Seale, or Robert Fisk (who remains most deserving of it). There is also the '*shabiha* of the opposition,' as well as the '*shabih* of philosophers,' an epithet bestowed upon Bernard-Henri Lévy in particular, who was rebuffed from the revolution's frontlines early on. Finally, we have the '*shabiha* of the revolution,' applied to those who professed their loyalty to the revolution but who turned out to be crude, boorish, and excessively aggressive toward others.

The etymology of the term *shabiha* is obscure. Is it perhaps derived from *ashbaah* (ghosts), since the *shabiha* are outlaws who work in the dark, both literally and figuratively, flickering in and out, and vanishing just as swiftly? Does it stem from the *shabah*, a once popular and plateless Mercedes Benz that senior *shabiha* seemed to prefer for their operations and to set themselves apart?[1] Or, perhaps it has to do with the idea of *shabh*, the 'extending and expanding of privileges and powers,' as when someone is forced under torture to a position where his feet barely touch the floor while his hands are high up, tied to a horizontal metal bar?[2] In this case, 'privileges' refers to an official authorization for a task, while *tashbih* is the act of torturously 'stretching and extending' this authorization, which is what the *shabiha* do.

I

Though its origins remain obscure, it is likely that the term *shabiha* first surfaced in Syria during the second half of the 1970s, particularly after Syria's intervention in Lebanon in 1976 and the corresponding rise in smuggling from an exceedingly economically open country like Lebanon into its economically isolated Syrian neighbour. The term gained national currency at a time of major national crisis over thirty years ago. However, up until the outbreak of the Syrian revolution in 2011, its application was limited to young Alawite-born males from the Syrian coastal regions, along with their leaders in the Assad family. Later, it spread to other influential families: the Deebs (kin to the Assads) and the Makhloufs (maternal cousins to Hafez al-Assad). They made their living from smuggling (electronics, tobacco, drugs, alcohol, antiquities, etc.) and imposing *khuwwa* (extortion). They were notoriously brutal, cruel, and blindly devoted to their leaders, usually referred to as *mu'allim* (boss) or *khaal* (maternal uncle).[3] In this respect, they were similar to the mafia. Like the mafia, they were well-known both to the central authorities (who deliberately ignored their activities) and to the local authorities (who collaborated with them and granted the leaders immunity from prosecution by virtue of their kinship ties). And if by chance a conflict of interests arose between the *shabiha* and the local authorities, the latter wouldn't dare to defend themselves.[4]

By the 1980s, the *shabiha* were untouchable, operating freely and with impunity in the coastal city of Latakia. Once, they entertained themselves by forcing patrons in one of the city's cafes to lie on the floor beneath their tables—among them was the late and respected Syrian intellectual Elias Murqus (1928–1991). On another occasion, they amused themselves by killing a young man who objected to their insults.[5] They routinely used threats to seize property and possessions for cheap, even for free: their leaders raped attractive young women; and they also offered to resolve disputes in exchange for a hefty commission from the winner—most certainly the richer one.[6]

Their victims came from all backgrounds, and a few of them were Alawites. Stories from the early 1990s tell of a young and beautiful woman, Hala Aqel, who was abducted, raped, and murdered, her corpse dumped outside her parents' house. Around the same time, a university professor, Samir Ghafar, was killed for refusing to pass a female student in his class who turned out to be linked to a senior *shabih*. Since the *shabiha* lived in predominantly Alawite areas, the first to suffer at their hands were their neighbours. Take the *shabih* Abu Rammah of Latakia, for example: first he mocked his neighbours, before he blocked the previously public entrance to an alley passageway, erecting swing sets for his children as well as an awning under which to receive guests of his ilk.[7]

2

One of the primary features of the Syrian *shabiha* phenomenon is the fluidity of the boundaries that separate them from the regime's official agencies. The origin of this uncertainty can be located in the ties of kinship that bind their *mu'allimun* with an autocratic president (also known as the *mu'allim*), as well as in the structural resemblance between the regime itself and the *shabiha*, since both exercise power through the arbitrary use of violence and other practices known locally as *taballi* and *salbata*.[8] *Salbata* is a uniquely Syrian term that condenses several ways power is exercised in 'Assad's Syria' into one word: an amalgamation of *salb* (looting or robbery), *labt* (the act of kicking) and *tasallut* (tyranny). *Taballi* is roughly equivalent to making false or malicious accusations against someone for which that person will pay a hefty price: charging them with cursing the president, for example, or with making sectarian statements, which is taboo.[9]

Starting in the latter half of the 1970s and for a decade afterwards,
the Saraya ad-Difaa (Defence Brigades) were the closest thing Syria had to a militia: they were above the law and lavishly funded by the state. Rifaat al-Assad, the commander of the Defence Brigades until 1985, was a *shabih* in every sense of the word. A coarse, vulgar, dissolute and predatory man, he was known for his

flashes of temper and self-aggrandisement, and once enjoyed a near monopoly over the trade in antiquities beyond the borders of Syria. While his brother Hafez al-Assad was a man of deliberation, Rifaat was a man of instinct and impulse. It has been widely alleged that Rifaat was aware of the the 982 massacre in Hama, as well as the earlier massacre at Tadmur Prison on 27 June 1980. Hafez, however, was ultimately the force behind everything. The daily, arbitrary torture carried out for twenty years against Islamist prisoners in the cells of Tadmur Prison is a most efined example of Hafez's style.

In any case, the fact that the regime placed its own survival before all other considerations was enough to guarantee a suspicious view of the governed, who were seen as a source of danger requiring constant surveillance. This attitude is a cornerstone of the creed adopted by the Syrian *mukhabarat* (security apparatuses) throughout the Assad era. It intersects with the narrative of historical victimhood prevalent in the Alawite community, from which the majority of senior security officials and staff in Assad's Syria originate. It comes as no surprise, then, that unofficial agents with this background should manifest the same attitudes as their official counterparts—indeed, such attitudes are evident in the spiteful and retaliatory treatment of dissidents today (Alawites and non-Alawites alike) and of society as a whole. In times of crisis, moreover, it is only to be expected that state officials will start acting like *shabiha*. Syrians and observers outside Syria have documented videos showing groups of *mukhabarat* carrying out acts of violence similar to punitive expeditions and colonial campaigns, using tactics that have also characterized sectarian militias from Lebanon and Iraq. A film from al-Baidha village is the most famous among these clips, but it is not the only one.[10] There are other videos capturing armed *shabiha* in uniform, forcing an unarmed man to chant: 'There is no god but Bashar'.[11] Another shows them commanding a different man to do the same, until their commander ordered them to 'bury that animal'; this man kept declaring 'There is no god but God,' while they proceeded to bury him alive.[12]

Four characteristics are combined in the basic concept of the *shabiha*. The first is the bonds of blood and sect they share with the ruling family. The second is an inclination to hostility towards society, which makes the *shabiha* a perfect device for executing organized and arbitrary violence against civilians. These anti-social tendencies may well be a variant of the anti-authoritarian attitudes usually found in abundance among marginalized and minority social groups. Although such attitudes usually exhibit proto-democratic elements, in this case these have been distorted by the Assad era into a hostile, conservative worldview that reinforces both dictatorship and social fragmentation. The third characteristic of the *shabiha* is their fetishistic submission to their leaders, something facilitated by ties of kinship and allegiance. Finally, there is a powerful economic motivation, since many of the *shabiha* work as smugglers.[13] According to some of my sources, the *shabiha* prefer the *shabah* Mercedes Benz S600 model for this work because its large trunk is big enough to hold lots of valuable goods. It was also rumoured that the cars themselves were smuggled in from Lebanon. Their hallmark was a battered appearance, despite their relative newness, since the *shabiha* would treat them recklessly and take pleasure in squealing their tires, perhaps because the cars were a stolen luxury that had come easily to them.

The *shabiha* used force to seize goods or gain control over valuable resources: for example, ports. Yet while their leaders reap staggering personal fortunes, the majority of the *shabiha* are of much lower income and have no other way of making a living. It is suspected that the entire coastal region has been kept intentionally underdeveloped, and its Alawite residents purposely impoverished, in order to ensure a constant supply of cheap labour: undereducated, unqualified muscle to defend the regime, the mark of a cost-effective ruling system.

A typical *shabih* is a lowborn, uneducated person, while 'highborn [Alawites] would never work as *shabiha* for anyone,' as one of my sources put it. It used to be that a typical *shabih* was also burly and Herculean, with a shaved head and long beard, usually dressed in black.[14] However, with the expansion of the *shabiha* phenomenon—or rather, with the growing generalization of the term—there is no longer such a thing as the typical *shabih* 'look.' These days, a *shabih* is just spare muscle clutching a firearm or a stun gun.

For the regime, then, sectarianism has been a useful political device that enables the ruling elite to mobilize certain individuals and apprentice them to defend it, without necessarily requiring them to have any express interest in doing so. This is precisely what makes sectarianism such a dangerous and irrational phenomenon: merely by appealing to religious and sectarian ties held in common, the poor and disadvantaged can be deployed as fanatical defenders of a wealthy political elite who disrespect them and care nothing for their well-being.

Sectarianism, however, merely facilitates the ultimate goal of loyalty to the leader's persona. With this, the *shabiha* phenomenon transcends the restrictions of its infancy and steps into very powerful circles indeed, privileged with ties of personal loyalty, patronage, and duty to the president.

3

There is no question about the *shabiha*'s loyalty to the president and to the regime. For its part, the regime has only rarely disciplined or confronted them. Basil al-Assad, for example, led a campaign against them in the early 1990s in preparation to succeed his father. Some *shabiha* were arrested, while their leaders (close relatives of the ruling family) were obliged to exercise greater restraint in dealing with the public.

Yet the regime has never crushed them, nor has it shown any real intention to do so. The few confrontations that have taken place were the result of the regime's desire to guard its own interests at the expense of particular *shabiha* groups; in other words, there were no clashes between the regime and these *shabiha* groups until there was a conflict of interests, and even then, clashes emerged only when the basic interests of the regime were compromised. Even in these instances, mind you, the *shabiha* were not eradicated; rather, they were put in their place and then set aside. In 2006, for example, Numir al-Assad (Bashar al-Assad's cousin) and his followers were transferred back and forth between the prisons of Adra and Saidnaya, but they were still able to intimidate the inmates and warders without anyone daring to control them.[15]

All of this is hardly a consequence of any incompetence on the regime's part, but rather of the two parties sharing the same basic structures and goals. The *shabiha* phenomenon is the political unconscious of the regime, shaping its ingrained actions and responses. It is the regime stripped bare, revealing the sovereignty of a privileged, unrestricted, arbitrary brutality propelled by a combination of violence, kinship, and despotism. This political unconscious was triggered during the uprising, as the regime's avowed consciousness (Arab nationalism and socialism) gradually ceded ground to its deep political instincts. Moreover, the *shabiha* came in handy as a reserve army, enthusiastically volunteering to shield the regime from the threat of the revolution.[16]

The 'state' had first absorbed the *shabiha* into its structures, particularly into its security apparatus, and then discharged them in the form of generalized, organized, and legitimized violence against society. Yet no matter how accommodating one tries to be, it is still difficult to describe the violence of the Syrian security agencies as 'state' violence—as legitimately organized—in the same way that one cannot describe the infamous Tadmur Prison as a 'state' facility. Because in fact, the security agencies are more like an occupying army, one that has thoroughly penetrated society with violence, hostility, and an almost racist supremacy. They have paralyzed society, making resistance impossible outside the context of a full-blown revolution, as seen today.

The following tragic account by the late Mamdouh Adwan, from his book *Haywanat al-Insan* (The Animalization of Man), encapsulates the organic relationship between the *shabiha* and the regime:

> A man stopped his red car at a red light. When the lights turned green, he began moving forward, but suddenly a motorcycle driven by a *shabih* appeared from the side road, driving straight through the red light. A collision almost occurred, but was luckily avoided. Despite the fact it was the *shabih* who had broken the traffic laws, he still got off his bike and started cursing at the driver of the car for not paying attention. 'Brother,' the driver said, 'the light was green; I had the right of way.' As he kicked him in the face, the *shabih* answered, 'the right of way is yours? Don't you know that this whole country belongs to us?!'

The 'us' in the *shabih*'s response was a blend of power and sectarianism, a mirror of the humiliating *taballi* (false accusation that damages the accused) so widely practiced in the 1980s that the Alawite accent itself became a weapon of intimidation: non-Alawites would sometimes use it for the domineering effect and the material profits it reaped.

A striking feature of the *shabiha* phenomenon, related to its sectarian aspect, is the brazen, excessive use of foul language in public, and the pleasure taken in the humiliation of perceived enemies. This verbal and psychological abuse is characteristic of Assad's security apparatuses in general, especially of the staff at the notorious Tadmur Prison. The warders amused themselves by asking us about the colour of our mothers' cunts, for instance. Some prison guards, who were standing above our heads and watching us from a panoptic window in the roof of the cell, pleasured themselves with a 'verbal intercourse' concerning an inmate's sister: they fantasized about that intercourse such that her head was placed on her jailed brother's shoulder, and he was supposed to enjoy the fact that the jailor was fucking his sister. The whole sick phantasm was meant as an insult to the honour of the jailed. Brutal violations of this sort apparently aimed at emphasizing the disparities in status and degree of humanity between the governing and the governed. Humiliation and hatred are two constant features of the constellation of security functions within the Assad regime. The demand of dignity—heard very frequently in the discourse of the Syrian revolution—therefore refers directly to bitter experiences of humiliation and degradation at the hands of the regime's core, its security apparatus. In this context, dignity means rejection of physical and verbal humiliation and degradation, and, even more, a rejection of the masculine, patriarchal, sexist constitution of the *shabiha* and their state.

4

During the Syrian revolution, the concept of *shabiha* expanded, and began to refer to the unofficial militias unleashed by the regime against protestors in all regions across the country. As the term became more generalized, it grew detached from its roots and original meaning. In Aleppo, the *shabiha* was comprised of the members of extended local families. The most famous of these is the Berri clan, which is known for smuggling goods ranging from drugs to arms and its close ties to the regime, as well as occasional clashes with the 'state' (courts, police, and the local administration) that have resulted in a mode of coexistence with it. These families and their drones enjoy autonomy and almost full sovereignty over their neighbourhoods; in turn, they act 'responsibly' toward the regime, sharing their profits with its local representatives.

The groups that are referred to as *shabiha* in many Syrian cities are cast from the same mould: violent ex-offenders and outlaws with a complex relationship with the *mukhabarat* and police officers, who use their services and who also share in the profits of criminal enterprises. Leaders of smuggling and prostitution rings are looked after, though this does not guarantee blanket protection from the occasional beating or detention. The worst treatment is reserved for novice or rank-and-file *shabiha*, while their leaders enjoy the greatest deal of immunity when disputes over the division of profits require some to be sacrificed.

The original *shabiha*, along with these more recent formations, have one thing in common: powerful ties of loyalty to the extended family and tribe, which is a common characteristic of organized criminal networks of smugglers and drug dealers more generally. In Aleppo, these networks issue from large families who live in suburbs that operate without any other form of real jurisdictional control. But even under different circumstances, these networks continue to be loyal to the *mu'allim* and resemble both Italian mafia organizations and the Syrian security services.

The commanders of the latter demand great personal loyalty from their personnel, a sectarian trait which has evolved into networks of patronage based on ties of kinship, either real or imaginary.[17] Above all, such forms of organization link these groups to the regime, which is, in turn, structured around allegiance and loyalty to the president. As of the second half of the 1980s, the president became known as 'the leading father,' and everybody was compelled to treat the president the way a child treats his father. The structural similarities across these phenomena are what bind them together, allowing them to be placed on the same political and social scale.

Just as the regime is organized around a political-securitarian nucleus, the *shabiha* have a nucleus composed of a blend of sectarianism, privilege and violence, in which the regime's political unconscious is embodied.[18] The *shabiha* and the regime are more closely related to each other than the regime is to the state, on the one hand, or than the original *shabiha* are to the more recent, post-revolution *shabiha*, on the other. Were the regime to fall, it is very likely that the regime's security apparatuses would finally turn into *shabiha*, in which case the regime's official mask of statehood would drop, revealing its essence as a special force of shameless and unrestrained violence, both random and discriminatory. The progressive erosion of boundaries between the various security agencies and the *shabiha* is proving this beyond doubt.

5

One might ask: are the majority of Alawite *shabiha* willing to defend the regime to the end? As I mentioned before, sectarian affiliations ensure that the Alawite *shabiha* are easier to recruit. Yet even the loyalty of said 'authentic' *shabiha* cannot be taken for granted: there is also a 'rational' economic factor that must be taken into account. There are many who fight gallantly for the regime, not only because they have a predisposition to support it, but also because doing so costs them little and earns them much. Today, it is said that members of the *shabiha* make between 7,000 and 10,000 Syrian liras (about $100–135) for working on Fridays, and at least 2,000 liras (roughly $30) for the weekdays, which is high above the minimum monthly wage.[19] Given the generally peaceful nature of the uprising, the risks involved are also very low.[20] However, if the *shabiha*'s wages fall and the risks increase, it is very likely that some would quit.[21] Indeed, there were claims that in July 2011, the *shabiha* went on strike following a decrease in their wages, with some returning to their villages and districts in the coastal region.[22] This example allows us to envision the *shabiha* as a kind of proletariat, selling their repressive force to the 'capitalists' of power.

Yet, there is abundant information that suggests the *shabiha* have resorted to funding themselves through plunder as the regime's financial resources are being exhausted. An important report published by the Local Coordinating Committees in October in 2011 says that *shabiha* militias in the city of Tal-kalakh had engaged in acts of 'destruction and the theft of citizens' possessions, such as jewelry.'[23] In the al-Rastan area, 'the *shabiha* and state security have plundered shops and stores, stealing valuable appliances and carrying them away in their trucks,' the report stated.[24] In other words, the property of ordinary citizens is considered by the *shabiha* as booty obtained legitimately in the regime's war against society.

There have also been reports of random arrests in other regions (Idlib, in particular), aiming to extort money in return for the release of detainees.[25]

6

This overview would undoubtedly benefit from more detailed information from the field, but based on what's available to me, it seems clear that *tashbih* is an innate characteristic of the Assad regime, a practice to which it reverts in times of crisis, akin to a public *shabih* (singular of *shabiha*).

This was particularly evident in the 1980s, when the majority of the country was governed through *tashbih*. The *shabiha* remained active in Latakia, but similar phenomena and practices were witnessed in other regions of the country. The *shabiha* were the ghost haunting the Assad regime, growing stronger and darker the closer we are to Syria's true centre of power.

There is a direct relationship between the rule of *tashbih* as a mode of governance and the spread of the *shabiha* phenomenon and its practices. The more the regime acts as a *shabih*, the greater the number of *shabiha* willing to work for it and to give their undivided loyalty in exchange for certain privileges: immunity, promotion, exemptions, preferences at schools and universities, in addition to the direct wages and booty now to be had from combating the revolution.[26]

From the mid-1990s up until the outbreak of the uprising, however, the *tashbih* mode of governance had gradually declined, as did the activities of the *shabiha* themselves. But this was only a retreat into dormancy, a time during which they were unseen but ever present, ready to awaken and pounce at any moment. This is precisely what happened: as soon as the revolution broke out, the *shabiha* and *tashbih* instantly resurfaced.

The practical ramification of all this is the following: if the regime wins its confrontation with the uprising, the government system in Syria will be run by *tashbih*, the country will be ruled by the *shabiha*, and we will witness levels of brutality and discrimination even more severe than those of the 1980s. If the revolution is crushed, it will not be followed by 'reform' of any kind, but by a return to the fascist *tashbih* for years to come. The present regime knows no other way to govern: when people submit to it, it enslaves them; when they rise up against it, it kills as many of them as it can. The elimination of the *shabiha* phenomenon and its practices can only be achieved by toppling the thuggish regime.

In August 2011, demonstrators in the Talbisa district of Homs chanted: 'We want a civil state that governs us, not a *shabiha* state that murders us!'

7

In the manner touched upon so far, *tashbih* is significant because of the way it signals a broader approach to politics and political behaviour characteristic not only of the regime of Hafez al-Assad, but also of Baathist rule from its inception in Syria in 1963.

As their popular legitimacy was always very thin, the Baathists resorted to what we might call 'ideological *tashbih*': flinging accusations of treason in every direction and working hard to foster an atmosphere of collective paranoia, putting the majority of the population permanently on guard against the many conspiracies allegedly being planned against them. Under such circumstances, the patriotism of every citizen can be questioned at any instant, and the world around him is an evil and dangerous place to be guarded against and distrusted.

This ideological *tashbih* has been a primary contributor to the weakening of critical thought and political dissent in Syria, but it is not a Syrian invention, nor is it a Baathist concoction. But under the Baathists, the hyperbolic discourse I have described was elevated to the rank of a state policy that systematically uncoupled public discourse from reality. The policy of outdoing everyone else in radical opposition to Israel led to the terrible defeat in June of 1967; it demanded that everyone continually assert their true patriotic spirit while tearing Syrian society apart, abusing the Palestinians and the Lebanese, making the Baathist rulers wealthier, and causing one of the most advanced societies in the Arab world up to 1960s to become backward and stagnant.

Moreover, ideological *tashbih* corrupted the Arabic language—and political discourse in particular—as the language became more dishonest, and as the uncoupling of signifier from signified and meaning from experiences became normal. The hyperbolic discourse of ideological *tashbih* deprived the population of their chief tool for voicing their complaints and demands, making the language of the regime the only acceptable mode of expression—a language that was designed first and foremost to deprive the governed of an independent means of expression. This deficit in available means of expression may have played a role in the physical protests that emerged as the main language of the uprising. Verbal protest in *fus-ha* (Formal Arabic), which carries a high risk of blending with regime discourse, has always been the traditional opposition's preferred mode of expression, and this accounts for its fundamental weakness and impotence, at least in part. Many of those within the traditional opposition have been detained and tortured, something that separated their physical bodies from their struggle against the regime. Their generation—my generation—have nothing but words, and our opposition has rebounded as a show of ghosts: souls detached from bodies, weightlessly accosting a muscle-bound regime and equipped only with many chattering tongues. Because of their ghost-like nature, not one member of the traditional opposition has been killed since the revolution started, and only a few have been detained.[27]

The new opposition, embodied in the uprising youth, takes the risk of pushing the revolution forward with their bodies. They have put their bodies on the line. Over 5,000 of these bodies have been eliminated so far.[28]

The regime's appropriation of the national language (*fus-ha* Arabic) has also played a role in the way the demonstrators distance their placards and chants from its rhetoric and clichés. One cannot separate oneself from the regime unless one breaks with its language and symbolism—this is invisible to those who call for the Syrian revolution to adopt overtly 'Arab nationalist' positions and slogans. These calls also overlook two important points.

First, the regime's slogans are *tashbih* in essence: they murder the very concept of truth by limiting public debate to a range of ideological preferences that are all equally divorced from reality and which transform communication among the people into something entirely subjective and arbitrary. As soon as the Arab League announced on 12 November 2011 that it was barring Syria from participating in its meetings, spokespersons appeared on Syrian state TV channels talking about 'backward U'rban' (Bedouin Arabs) and declaring that Syria was a fully-developed nation-state that had nothing to do with 'Arabs'. Outside in the street, supporters of the regime chanted, 'Screw Arabism!'

The second point is that the revolution is an attempt to achieve a complete disassociation from the regime. This disassociation is inevitable, and it is destined to bring about a more genuine and sincere understanding of the Syrian social world.

8

The Syrian regime, which relied heavily on the *shabiha* to govern its interior, itself acts as a *shabih* on the regional stage: a colossal thug that uses crude power to terrorize those around him, just as it does inside Syria. Consequently, representatives of the regime (especially in Lebanon) were genuine *shabiha*: violent, corrupt, thuggish, and dedicated to *tashbih*-ify Lebanese politics and the Lebanese state. In other words, they sought to clone themselves in Lebanon and thereby rule forever, just as in Syria. The most recent of these representatives was the terrorist Rustum Ghazaleh, who earned his position as head of Syria's 'anti-terrorism unit' after 2005, in accordance with traditional practice and the use of Orwellian language.

The most important thing about *tashbih* was the accumulation of wealth by force. This phenomenon transcends the specific tactics of the Syrian *shabiha* (old and new) and has resulted in an economic system based on plunder, extortion, and forced labour. In other words, force is an economic resource. The newly wealthy Syrian elite who transformed the Syrian economy into a 'social-market economy' in 2005 were no different in this respect from their fathers, who had accrued their fortunes through the abuse of political power. Their so-called 'development and modernization' policy is but a new scheme to achieve the same goals: vast wealth and absolute power, albeit via less punitive methods. Nevertheless, in times of upheaval, these modernizers return to the tried-and-tested tactics of their fathers' generation, developing and modernizing them to effectively kill more people.[29]

In fact, the 'new bourgeoisie' who control the Syrian economy today have made their money through what we might call 'major *tashbih*', as opposed to the 'minor *tashbih*' from which the junior *shabiha* earn their living. As mercenaries who fight for the regime, these junior *shabiha* assault their opponents and the revolutionary masses in exchange for wages and loot. Their senior counterparts use the state, run the regime, and make billions from it. They are the ones who are fighting the revolution with unrestrained violence. The 'major *shabiha*' are the ones who rule Syria.

Around eight months into the revolution now, they do not show the slightest indication of changing their approach (subjugation by force) or reconsidering the way the regime is structured. The *shabiha* state follows the description of the state described by Ibn Khaldun: it has a lifespan, flourishing and then perishing. This 'natural' state does not negotiate or practice politics, and it is incapable of reforming itself. But perhaps its lifespan will be shorter than the three-generational states of Ibn Khaldun.

9

The use of raw force to govern, both domestically and regionally, without any proper form of democratic representation; outdoing everyone else in the capture of language and rhetoric; the illegitimate accumulation of wealth through the state—what do all these forms of *tashbih* have in common?

The answer is separation.

The separation of gain from effort, of words from their meanings, of positions from qualifications and competencies. Essentially, *tashbih* negates the value of work, as well as the laws that link work to income and production to wealth. It also inhibits the production of an intelligible discourse, in which the coupling of signified and signifier yields meanings discernible to everyone. And it prohibits the practice of a politics that would foster a type of social representation that would bind private interests with those of the state.

In another sense, such separations are an assault against representation in general: the representation of citizens in political structures; the representation of the value of work in income; the representation of meaning in words.

The *shabiha* phenomenon is a model of material production (appropriating rather than producing wealth), a system of political governance (practicing repression, not politics; coercing not convincing), and a construct for signification (producing no new meanings, using profanities, and effectively consuming language), all at the same time. It is 'production' without work, rule without representation, and signification without any distinct referent.

Against this, the Syrian revolution strives for the following: to redefine work as the primary source of material and moral values; to make representation and the administration of society's interests the basis of a government's legitimacy; and to ensure that ideas and ideologies are assessed on the basis of their relationship to reality. In other words, the revolution has to restore the value of production: material, moral, and political. It is a grand re-establishment project, in which all three of these components—not just the political—must be given equal attention.

3

THE DANGER OF A 'STATE OF NATURE'

DAMASCUS, SEPTEMBER 2011

As it enters its seventh month, the Syrian revolution is starting to regress into a primordial condition; a 'state of nature.' This trend may signify a second chapter within this historic process, one whose beginnings may be traced back to August 2011, the month of Ramadan, when Hama and Deir ez-Zour (two cities that witnessed huge demonstrations) were occupied by tanks.

In this context, 'nature' designates all that clashes with forethought, deliberation, 'culture' and 'politics'. It refers to all that is driven by existential self-defence, desperation, and the survival instinct, rather than by considered estimation of the means through which issues of the general interest—and demands for democracy—might be introduced into the process of revolution. The state of nature is characterized by social dispersion, direct reactive responses, violence—all characteristics of a society losing its self-control and its ability to act uniformly, and traits that the Syrian revolution is increasingly displaying. This state of nature is not yet a reality, but it is a general trend, and the result will be a politics of subsistence, focused on survival and self-protection. As the survival instinct kicks in, the more abstract demands for democracy and self-determination will be seen as unnecessary luxuries. And while the revolution identified itself with goals that were civic-minded and public in spirit during its early stages, today these are barely discernible within what has become an extremely desperate struggle against a brutal power.

I

This trend toward the 'state of nature' appears in different forms:

First, there is an tendency—increasingly apparent—toward direct self-defence and meeting arms with arms. Although it remains local, sporadic, peripheral, and a long way from overtaking the main achievements of the revolution so far, such a tendency would be capable of eclipsing what has been a key dimension of the ever-changing Syrian situation: peaceful demonstrations. There is a growing anger toward the ritualistic emphasis on the peaceful character of the revolution, an emotion that sometimes leads one beyond merely accepting armed confrontation to the point of even embracing it.

The second sign of the proximity of this 'state of nature' is the increasingly religious emphasis present within the protests. Religion and religiosity is closer to 'nature' than modern ideologies, and become a vehicle for many of the same impulses in our politically impoverished society over the last few decades. The role of religion in society predictably grows more powerful during major crises, when groups tend to identify themselves through their inherited identities. During its earlier stages, however, the revolution was more worldly, civil, and inclusive. Without the need for any 'steering' from the traditional (and mostly secular) opposition, the demonstrators were keen to deny any religious or ideological aspect to their protests, particularly when it came to slogans acknowledging the diversity of religions, sects, and ethnicities that make up Syrian society: 'No Salafism and No [Muslim] Brotherhood/Our Revolution is a Revolution of Freedom!'; 'A Peaceful (*Silmiyya*) Revolution, not a Salafist (*Salafiyya*) One!'; 'No Salafism, No Terrorism/Our Revolution is one of Young People!' (the lines rhyme in Arabic). Two months in, however, with violent suppression and casualties on the rise, other chants entered onto the scene: *takbir* (the chanting of *Allahu Akbar*, or 'God is the greatest'), along with similar slogans, such as 'To Heaven We Proceed/Millions of Martyrs!' Over time, demonstrators embraced another refrain, posited as a call for help: 'O God/You are all that we have, O God!' This development was rooted in distress over the lack of protection and support in face of the regime's brutality. However, up to this point the general character of the protests remained civil, emancipatory, and humanist. The social base of the revolution was initially diverse because it enjoyed overwhelming support from Syrians of different backgrounds, but its public face began borrowing terms from the language of Islam.

Third, the clarity of the Revolution's goals has become increasingly fractured. After a massive wave of violence that coincided with the month of Ramadan [in 2011], voices began to rise in demand of 'international protection,' naming Friday 9 September as the 'Friday of International Protection.' Not a single day of that Ramadan nor the following three days of Eid, and all since, passed without casualties; protests and murders were daily occurrences. Views of the type of international protection required varied: demands for international observers; requests that human rights organizations and/or independent media outlets monitor the situation in Syria and the behaviour of the regime; calls for no-fly zones and safe areas, as well as appeals for international military intervention. But even choosing 'international protection' as a name for a Friday was replacing a symbol of presumed consensus (the naming of the Fridays) with a politically divisive demand, and this is in itself is one of the growing indications of our 'state of nature': divisiveness in opinion, reactive attitudes, along with a minimum of forethought and assessment. However, the abstract logic of national sovereignty that collided with this particular Friday was a contemplative luxury in comparison with the 'state of nature' that increasingly pressured broad sectors of Syrian society.

Fourth, there has been an increasing tendency—worthy of further comment—toward valourizing 'direct field activities' over any other kind (including political and cultural activities), and a related increase in verbal and written expressions of anger. We are now seeing more passion, stress, and consequently, less calculation. Our abhorrence of—and psychological estrangement from—the regime and its apparatus increase steadily. During the early stages of the uprising, the slogan 'The People Want to Overthrow the Regime!' was not heard. Later, that slogan became a focal point in the uprising. Today, the main slogan is 'The People Want to Execute the President!', along with many other chants that 'personify' the revolution's object of protest in one man and one family. Hatred is drawn to such figures: it 'personalizes'. By contrast, calm and composed deliberations about current conditions, relations, and processes are becoming luxuries.

These transformations are on a collision course with the conscience of the Syrian uprising, which can be formulated in terms of three 'No's: no to violence, no to sectarianism, and no to outside military intervention. At the same time, there was a major implied 'Yes' for an inclusive, democratic transformation, based on citizenship, ensuring freedom, equality, and dignity for all

Syrians, and enabling avenues for peaceful political differences among them.

2

Before assessing the possible consequences of this 'natural' transformation of the Syrian uprising, it is necessary to look at its causes and origins. The core of this 'natural politics' is the appalling abuse practiced by the regime against its tormented populace. Its methods of aggression and abuse are known worldwide thanks to the uprising's own coverage: nails being ripped out; skinning; electrocution of the genitals and mutilation with sharp objects or lasers (in public hospitals, no less); eye gouging; throttling; in addition to the more traditional methods of corporal punishment (foot whipping, electrocution, and sleep deprivation); stripping of prisoners and insulting them individually or as groups—not to mention the insults specifically directed against women and children. Certainly, the widely-announced figure of 3,000 victims falls far short of the truth, and many times that number are wounded, in addition to the tens of thousands of detainees. And there is the looting of houses and private property, the wholescale destruction of immovable property, and premeditated humiliation on an enormous scale. Repeated instances point to a consistent, orchestrated approach. Added to this are sectarian provocations directed at the uprising, which reached a crescendo with the bombings and attacks on mosques' minarets, and the deification of Bashar and his brother Maher (for example, forcing religious people to say 'there is no god but Bashar [or Maher]')—both of which are elements of a policy aimed at stirring up sectarian strife in Latakia, Jableh, Homs and other religiously diverse regions. To top it all, repression has been steadily transformed into a business; for example, random arrests have given families of the detainees no choice but to pay ransoms that can amount to hundreds of thousands of Syrian liras. As it happens, this practice was already a flourishing business during the 1980s, and intelligence officers and prison superintendents made fortunes from it.

Riddled with hatred and resentment, and utterly lacking any legal objectivity or discipline, the oppressor does not shy away from his 'natural' subjectivity; instead of following a general code of ethics like a proper public official would, he brings all his personal origins, all his connections, prejudices, and passions directly to the table. In turn, he binds the oppressed to his or her origin, home city, religion, parents, family members, and relatives. 'The action of political abstraction' (the Lebanese historian Ahmad Beydoun's formulation) by which a government and its agencies deal with a citizen as citizen, regardless of that citizen's particulars, has been long absent during normal times in Assad's Syria, and is far more absent today. Perhaps the sectarian dimensions that condition this absence can explain the frequent desertions from the army.

Six months into such conditions there is more than sufficient evidence to conclude that the regime is practicing a war of annihilation against rebelling Syrians, both politically and symbolically, and is resolved to exterminate the participants in the uprising in an effort to destroy the rebellion completely.

This is the real lived experience of hundreds of thousands of people, not something they have read or heard. They have experienced it directly for months, and still live with it.

The Syrian condition today is a desperate one, in which a lethal force is being faced. The psyches of desperate people are being reduced to anger.

In the face of this colonial aggression, hundreds of thousands of Syrians feel they are left without support, abused by a blind, fanatic force that is unrestrained by any human, national, or legal principles. How long are they expected to follow the dictates of revolutionary conscience, instead of responding instinctively to protect themselves and preserve their lives? When the regime is an agent of unlimited violence, is it possible to endlessly continue speaking of peace? If the regime has killed your son, looted your house, and insulted your family, who could blame you for taking up arms against it? When you are vulnerable, unable to ensure your own safety let alone that of your loved ones, when you are standing alone, unsupported and unprotected, why wouldn't God, the presumed protector of the vulnerable, be your last resort? If you are standing before a junta that knows nothing but the language of power, one that has carried on killing for half a year, how could you continue to reject the protection of a more powerful party?

What do arms, religiosity, and the request for international protection have in common? A predisposition toward shelter: for the sake of self-protection or self-defence, one seeks refuge in the Almighty, and seeks shelter from the most powerful.

Two prerequisites for this process are the weak influence and structural fragility of the traditional opposition, and the truly popular and local character of the Syrian uprising. The current inauspicious situation is only underscored by the rare possibility of a convergence between two elements: on the one hand, the direct field activities of the revolution in its numerous hotspots; on the other, politicians and intellectuals whose attitude is governed by more abstract general principles, and who can turn experiences into expertise, ideas, and programmes.

Moreover, the more mature, broad-minded, and young leaders of the revolution have been subjected to detention, death under torture, and targeted assassination, which has opened the way for a takeover by the unrefined, the territorial, the muscle-bound and the narrow-minded. These people veer closer to 'nature' in their outlook.

3

Arriving at the 'state of nature' is avoidable, but if we capitulate nonetheless, we face being governed by the 'inevitable decline' described by Ibn Khaldun, and the country will be dragged into the gutter. The primary responsibility for such a transformation would lie with the regime, but it seems unlikely that it will change its policies. For the regime these policies are extremely 'natural' and instinctive: they are violent, grounded in *asabiyyah* ('natural' intra-communal solidarity), and premised on a network of regional and international connections that bring it political and security revenues, all while leaving the people without shelter, insecure, and lacking any form of self-determination.

One may not pass judgment on the people who are tormented by all of this, for there is no principle of justice that could justifiably be used to blame them. Those whose life is endangered cannot be expected to remain peaceful. And without international support, remaining committed to a secular logic is impossible—a luxury cast aside under conditions of desperation and reliance on survival instincts. Those who are helpless and set upon by a powerful, unscrupulous enemy cannot hold on forever to the political principles that would underscore an independent, national state, especially when there is no trace of this so-called state in any other aspect of their lives, and their deaths.

But the persistence of physical and psychological abuse, and the desire for outside support (divine or 'international'), will cause the situation to veer in uncontrollable directions. Stating this is not a matter of blame or merit, but an attempt to escape even greater evils.

We have, then, the following complex situation: a disdainful, cliquish regime that hates its people, accuses them of treason, and murders them; and a diverse population that has begun to practice self-defence, come what may, in the manner of a desperate survivor.

A powerful, unscrupulous offender, against whom a weak defender will not embrace high-minded principles that compromise the capacity for self-defence—under such conditions, conscience is a luxury, and so are culture and politics.

It is a fateful situation, predisposed toward destruction.

4

The transformations described above are still in their infancy, and as we speak the future is neither decided nor inevitable. For half a year, Syrian society has displayed positive characteristics that surprised detractors and supporters alike. There is nothing to prevent one from expecting more welcome surprises in a revolution that no one saw coming, much less expected to endure.

Yet it is unreasonable to rely on mere speculation regarding a society in which large segments are subject to political and symbolic extermination, and are driven by relentless brutality into this 'state of nature.' At this juncture, the actions of political oppositionists and activists can make a difference.

It is important to establish a political framework that enjoys a reasonable degree of consensus and trust, which can orient political initiatives and attempts to influence the course of the uprising, to lead it in directions compatible with the aforementioned 'conscience.' Such a framework has been unattainable in previous months, and it may be impossible to create one that is all-inclusive. Even so, an umbrella group with broad representation would likely achieve more legitimacy, along with a greater ability to lead and take initiative, and it would help ensure better relations with external powers, in contrast with the present conditions of forced dispersal. Such a group could set out on a progressive path toward acquiring legitimacy, and be a powerful influence on the course of the uprising with respect to ensuring its compatibility with the public interest. It could reduce the risk of slipping into a 'state of nature,' and create an opportunity to return to politics, culture, and the common good. It may prove possible to then encourage the sketching of a more detailed and complex conception of a future Syria, and to prepare an inclusive programme for democratic transition following the anticipated fall of the regime.

The biggest stumbling blocks facing such an effort are the physical dispersal of the Syrian opposition, along with its various political and ideological divisions—which are also expressed as social divisions when class intersects with the sectarian and the regional. Syria's regime has ruled by making such divisions permanent, and sponsoring crises of confidence among communities. If Syrians are unable to overcome these ruptures, they effectively grant the regime an undue and unfair license to rule: which is to say, a form of legitimacy by default, resulting from the absence of an alternative.

THE DANGER OF A 'STATE OF NATURE'

5

But what if this never happens, and the regime's killing machine continues to claim Syrian lives at the current rate, or even surpasses itself by expanding its murderous activities? We would fall into our state of nature, propelled by a sense of inevitability. We have seen parallel examples in Iraq and, earlier, in Lebanon. A state of nature is the equivalent of a civil war—a sectarian war, in which murder leads to murder, *asabiyyah* activates *asabiyyah*, and hatred animates hatred. This is the supposed 'natural condition' of mankind, in which everyone is at war with everyone else, much as Thomas Hobbes described in his *Leviathan*, during the middle of the seventeenth century. But the state of nature is not in fact a 'natural' condition; it is a historical conjuncture.

One very specific characteristic of such a situation is that one cannot do anything about it so long as the primary perpetrators follow their instincts, their fancies and neuroses; their madness. At the core of the continuing Syrian ordeal is the so-called 'regime': insane and extremely aggressive, its character increases the probability that its opponents will be pushed into acting unreasonably.

Under such Khaldunian circumstances, in which inevitability rules, there is no place for policy and forethought. The most that a sane individual can do is expose the reigning imperatives. This amounts to adopting an observer status, with no effect on the course of events.

The Syrian uprising initiated an effort to rationalize and discipline the regime: it shall not detain children and punish them by pulling out their fingernails; its apparatuses shall not be permitted to infringe upon the rights of the governed through enjoying full immunity and remaining exempt from any political, legal, and moral responsibility. The Syrian Revolution (and the Arab revolutions more generally) broke out primarily as a protest against indulgence, irrationality, and excess, against states of disorder and psychopathy.

The revolution will have achieved its objectives when it sets limits on the authorities, imposes controls, and establishes standards for what is inviolable. It will have achieved its objectives when conscience replaces the eternal rule of absolute power, and when edicts premised on the lust for power and a natural right to the throne are rejected. There is no room for real politics under eternity, absolutism, personified power, or 'nature'. Politics is only possible where there are terms and boundaries—that is, in a place where any ruling power has been delimited and restrained, and thus raised above the level of bestiality, instinct, and nature.

4

ARMS AND THE REVOLUTION

APRIL 2012

Between its eruption on 15 March 2011 and the point at which international observers arrived in the context of Kofi Annan's mission thirteen months later, the Syrian Revolution went through three phases.

The first phase extended from 15 March to early August 2011. This was the phase of growing popular protests that culminated in the demonstrations at Hama and Deir ez-Zour, in which hundreds of thousands participated. The second phase covered the period from early August 2011 until early February 2012. During this period, the regime switched from handling the revolution primarily as a security matter to launching full-blown military operations against it. February of 2012 marked the transition to a third phase, of outright terrorism and a scorched-earth policy, of mass murders and the destruction of neighbourhoods and towns, especially in Homs, Idlib, Hama, and certain areas of Damascus.

The three phases overlap. From the very beginning, the regime has dragged the army into its confrontations with the revolution and has carried out daily murders. The initial phase also witnessed many army defections alongside the beginnings of armed resistance.

The earliest defections, which occurred in the first few weeks of the uprising, were most likely driven by protests of conscience and refusal to shoot peaceful civilians. But armed resistance emerged chiefly during the second phase.

Throughout the thirteen months that encompassed these three phases, demonstrations remained the key tool for political expression and protest.

On 9 June 2011, Lt Colonel Hussein al-Harmoush defected and formed the Free Officers Movement. (In the autumn of that year, al-Harmoush was lured back from his hideout in Turkey, then arrested, tortured, and forced to appear on national Syrian TV to make pro-regime statements. It is likely that he has since been executed). Seven months into the uprising, the Free Syrian Army (FSA) was formed under the leadership of former colonel Riad al-Asaad: the FSA functioned as a general framework encompassing various dissident groups, including the Free Officers Movement. The 'FSA' umbrella included other civil society groups, many of whom were incensed by the regime's brutalities and looking for an opportunity to oust it. Some of these groups were ideologically Islamist, while others were rooted in families from Hama and Aleppo who were mourning relatives lost thirty years previous at the hands of the regime.

The emergence of the revolution's military component was certainly not anyone's first choice, nor was it the application of a ready-made ideology of militant action. Rather, the military component emerged primarily as a by-product of the regime's militarized confrontations with the popular protests from the outset. As this reaction grew, it gradually began to draw justification from ideologies already available to Syrians, including the idea of 'jihad'. But the strongest and most legitimate justifications have always been self-defence and the protection of civilians from regime brutality.

The first phase reached a crescendo during the mass demonstrations in Hama and Deir ez-Zour, which were similar to the protests in Egypt's Tahrir Square. The regime hesitated in confronting the protests, particularly in Hama, perhaps because of its status in the Syrian national conscience as a city that lost something like 30,000 of its inhabitants in the massacre of February 1982. The American and French ambassadors also arranged to visit Hama on Friday 7 July 2011, which provided the city some level of protection. However, the regime then occupied the city with tanks at the beginning of Ramadan, in early August, and did the same in Deir ez-Zour, Homs, Idlib, and some areas of Damascus, not to mention Daraa, the cradle of the uprising. These occupations were accompanied by exceptional forms of torture and many cases of death under torture, of the sort that Syrians thought they had bid farewell to by the end of the 1980s. During this first phase of the revolution, there was an average of twenty casualties per day.

After the military was deployed and occupied the rebellious cities and towns, accompanied by the escalation of abuse against the population, Arab initiatives emerged to address the Syrian crisis. The most important of these was the dispatch of Arab observers in late December 2011 to monitor the regime's commitment to the cease-fire. Sadly, this, and other initiatives, yielded practically nothing.

The combination of systematic aggression, a sense of abandonment and loss of support (especially after Russia and China blocked Arab and international efforts to condemn the regime on 4 November 2011) resulted in voices being raised against the heretofore peaceful approaches, with calls to respond to violence with violence. In the fall of 2011, chants resounded across Hama and Mount Zawiya, saying: 'No to "peacefulness" or any such nonsense/ We now need bang and boom!'

Yet the general character of the revolution remained peaceful. Elements from the FSA took up the task of protecting demonstrations. They provided a degree of deterrence against regime force, but the extent of this is difficult to determine because of a lack of consistent records. According to the coordinators of demonstrations in Deir ez-Zour around mid-April 2012, it seems that the presence of armed men among demonstrations was at times an additional risk factor. Still other direct informants from Deir ez-Zour stated that all demonstrations in and around the city were protected by the FSA. One distinguishing characteristic of the Syrian revolution's self-coverage is the intermingling of reliable information with personal views, due to the difficulty of obtaining information from direct sources and the near impossibility of predicting real-time events.

As the Syrian protestors were left to their own devices, their chants and placards increasingly began to express their bitterness. A placard appeared in autumn 2011 that became well known throughout Syria, which read: 'Down with the regime and the opposition, down with the Arab and the Islamic nations, down with the Security Council, down with the world, down with everything!' While the mentality suggested by such a slogan would usually connote merely negativity or passivity, in the Syrian context it seemed to be an endorsement of armed confrontation. Kafranbel, the town in which the placard appeared, is in the province of Idlib in the north of the country; it describes itself as 'occupied' and is one of the most active hotbeds of the revolution.

That the opposition was mentioned by name on the placard referenced above is significant: it took much too long to form a political framework in support of the revolution and its cause. When such a formation finally appeared on 2 October 2011 in the form of the Syrian National Council (SNC), it was neither unifying nor dynamic enough to win the trust of Syrians and lead their struggle. The SNC's internal structure, pace of work, and public activities all contributed to its failure to become a credible popular force. There were also other organizations in the opposition that were even less potentially representative, getting more involved in conflicts with the SNC than with the Syrian regime.

As a result, the range of Syrian opposition groups was poor and unimpressive, and this was another factor that shaped the recourse to arms. The absence of a tried and tested political leadership often pushes people to take matters into their own hands: no one offered material support to Syrians or promised them aid; and meanwhile the regime continued its daily atrocities.

During the second phase of the revolution, there was no major breakdown within the Syrian Army, but rather a series of small defections that continued over many months. This disordered, unpredictable rate of defections created a difficult situation as there was no institutional framework capable of accommodating the new cadres and unifying them. The many civilians who joined the ever-expanding military groupings made such efforts even more arduous. Throughout, the FSA remained weak, created under the demands of necessity by founders whose only legitimacy was their seniority.

It appears that the rate of civilians taking up arms has been quicker than the trend of defections from the army, and this has resulted in tension between civilians and the army defectors. It appears the former, who are more familiar with their local environments, more religiously strict, and, perhaps, closer to political and religious trends, are more likely to rise to higher ranks within the FSA.

Signs of armed chaos appeared towards the end of the second phase. There was a spate of serial kidnappings for ransom in several locations in Idlib province last winter: abductions were followed by exchanges of prisoners with the regime; and sectarian reprisals in Homs. Current and former criminals are potential beneficiaries of the prevalent state of chaos across the country. Local activists argue that the regime may have exploited this through incitement, in order to blame rebels for their own operations and ultimately to push people to pine for the good old days.

However, at least one Salafist formation appears responsible for cases of kidnapping and ransom: the al-Nour Group, also active in the northern parts of Idlib governorate.

Moreover, reports from Mount Zawiya in Idlib suggests that there are four types of armed group. First, there are the FSA: defectors from the army, police, or the security apparatus. Most of these people used to be officers and soldiers, and carry small arms such as PK machine guns and RPG launchers. They have wireless devices to communicate with other FSA personnel. Occasionally, they conduct operations against military checkpoints and patrols, which is how they obtain most of their arms.

Second, there are the armed groups of young revolutionists that began to form as the violence against protestors increased. They carry small arms, and their main role is to guard the entrances of towns and villages, and to provide cover for demonstrations and small operations. Some of them prefer to work under the leadership of the FSA, while others continue to work independently. Some of these groups are led by Islamists or relatives of Muslim Brotherhood activists killed during the 1980s. They receive financial support from prosperous families, and their better funding is reflected in their high levels of discipline.

The third group of armed men is comprised of crooks and con artists, smugglers of antiquities, and ex-offenders. These people take advantage of the revolution: they conduct kidnappings for ransom and steal vehicles or power cables. The number of these groups multiplied after area sweeps by official army forces during the revolution's second phase.

Finally, there are armed robbers who predate the revolution.

The past few weeks have witnessed important developments that may address some of the problems outlined above, such as the identity of FSA members, the integration of independent groups, and confrontations with groups of swindlers and scammers.

There have also been legal and political efforts to develop a code of conduct that would direct the work of the FSA, but these efforts are often stymied by the its weak command structure and its intellectual and political inadequacies.

The third phase of the Revolution began on 3 February 2012. It grew from the Baba Amr district of Homs, a hotbed of the armed opposition. The district fell into the regime's grip in early March, after nearly a month of siege and daily shelling by tanks, cannons, and missiles. The regime then implemented the same strategies it had used in the other rebellious districts of Homs and committed massacres along a sectarian logic, the most notorious of which was the massacre of Karm el-Zeitoun on 11 March 2012, which claimed the lives of forty-seven women and children, many of whom who were raped before being gruesomely murdered.

Yet more than two and a half months following the successful conquer of Baba Amr, the regime remained unable to build any momentum on their victory.

The policies of mass terror and scorched earth were extended to areas in Idlib, Aleppo, Daraa, Deir ez-Zour, and the countryside around Damascus, where activists' homes were demolished and burnt (after they were plundered, of course), and where some of the victims were burnt as well. During this phase, the daily average casualty rate ranged from seventy to a hundred.

The escalation that marked the third phase of the revolution came one day after Russia and China blocked a UN Security Council resolution on Syria for the second time, and after the Russian Minister of Foreign Affairs and the Director of the Foreign Intelligence Service paid a visit to Damascus. It seems that these two men encouraged the regime to take advantage of the political cover provided by the Security Council to resolve matters on the ground.

Up to this point, the military and civilian components of the revolution were for the most part interconnected in each region, except for limited areas on the Turkish border. With their small arms, limited resources, and humble backgrounds, most of the soldiers who had defected remained in their hometowns to defend their own people and live among them while trying to resist the regime as much as possible. The same is true, to an even greater extent, for the civilians who took up arms.

But the regime worked to destroy these interconnections via the destruction of the rebels' social environments, taking advantage of the Russian-Chinese political cover as well as Russian and Iranian military support.

With modest resources and limited environments, the rebels received aid from relief groups that raised funds from sympathetic citizens. These groups were formed all over the country and became essential components of the revolution.

Worth noting also is that up to this point (April 2012), the revolution has largely remained popular, civil, and peaceful—the same way it started. The revolution has not developed into a confrontation between two armed parties (a regime and an opposition), contrary to regime propaganda and to the sensationalized media coverage by some Arab and international outlets (including Al-Jazeera). Many media outlets are by default more interested in news of violence and death than in the daily events of a popular revolution in the context of which the military aspect has remained secondary. The Syrian Revolution is not an armed insurgency: it is a peaceful revolution with an armed component.

* * *

Toward the end of the second phase of the revolution, and still more during the third, voices within the Syrian opposition began to express reservations about the military section of the revolution, claiming it was responsible for provoking the regime's brutality, and articulating a sense of nostalgia for the revolution's early days. These arguments speak to a widespread, peaceful orientation among revolutionists, and a concern over the risks involved with armaments—concerns justified by current and potential complications. However, the stakes of the debate are often distorted: instead of maintaining connection with real events and discussing questions of efficiency and suitability, disagreement about a given issue becomes a dogmatic exercise in labels that identify those adopting them instead of clarifying the issue discussed.

But on its own terms, the argument against the military dimension is faulty in three regards.

First, it ascribes the emergence of a military component in the revolution to political choices made by individuals or groups. This is entirely false. The military component was an inevitable and even 'objective' response to the regime's brutal violence. Some try to bestow virtue on what emerged out of necessity, whether through chants such as 'God bless the Free Army!' or dubbing 25 November 2011 the Friday of 'The Free Army Protects Me.' Such responses are quite understandable when people try to come to terms with responses that were forced upon them.

Second, this argument betrays an attitude of withdrawal that would deprive people of the chance to have an impact on an increasingly complicated reality. For instance, one would not expect that those who advocate this position would under any circumstances be interested in joint work directed at trying to organize the activities of the FSA, to ensure its monopoly over arms, to regulate the behaviour of its groups, or to co-ordinate the operations of its fighters so as to be guided by the general interests of the revolution. These issues are in themselves very difficult and efforts made in these directions remain frustratingly piecemeal. But if we were to reject these efforts, abstractly, the outcomes would only lead to uncontrollable chaos.

In addition, there are thousands of fighters—militants and former civilians—who have been moved to protect their fellow citizens in full awareness that the fate awaiting them at the hands of the regime is gruesome murder. Hundreds or more of them have fallen already. The question is, what do we do with them? Do we deprive them of any moral or political protection? Do we hand them over to the regime? There is no alternative but to help them organize their military actions, to link those actions to the public cause, and to secure their physical means of support. The discipline of fighters is commensurate with the availability of the resources that guarantee them a decent living.

I have supported, and always will support, the regulation of fighters at the administrative, political, ideological, financial, and ethical levels. This is the option that protects the revolution's peaceful nature. Whenever opponents of the military component have been compelled to have a serious discussion about the best approach to this matter, they have always ended up with something close to this option.

Third, those who argue against the military dimension suggest nothing but moving backwards to the early days of unarmed revolution, which implies that the armed resistance has caused the retreat of civil and social opposition. This is not true: both retreats were caused by the regime's maniacal violence. Note that the activities of peaceful protest only declined in areas that were exposed to the regime's brutal crackdown. On the other hand, some of the biggest demonstrations in Aleppo and Raqqa, and even in Damascus, took place during the third phase. Earlier hotbeds of protest rose back up as soon as the regime forces eased the pressure on them. Protests did not decline due to the existence of fighters. Quite the contrary: those who stopped protesting resorted to arms or looked for arms; this was a typical response to the regime's violence and citizens' feelings of fragility and vulnerability.

I believe that the role delineated for the military component helped the peaceful revolution. Contrary to widespread belief, those who took up arms did not replace the peaceful revolution but rather contributed to its expansion and resilience. An approach limited to peaceful protesting would have weakened the revolution in confrontations with the regime, whatever the unquestionable moral superiority of a purely peaceful protest.

A wider view of the revolution would see that peaceful protesting and armed resistance went hand in hand. It is incomprehensible that the revolution should be asked to give up its military component without the slightest sign of change in the general political atmosphere across the country, and without the slightest glimpse of willingness on the regime's part to do without or even to limit its militarization, or to limit the extensive involvement of pro-regime civilians against a rebellious population. (The *shabiha*—Assadist thugs—are pro-regime civilians, many of whom are criminals and ex-offenders.) If the regime continues to escalate its militarized confrontation with the revolution—and there is not the slightest indication otherwise—then we will see an escalating tendency toward armament and military confrontation on the part of the opposition. And perhaps we will also see the FSA, originally a loose umbrella for armed resistance, replaced by jihadist groups. The latter do not have a national cause but rather a religious one, and they rely instead upon nihilistic violence, or 'terrorism'.

The only practical question that is posed by the emergence of the military component concerns the best way to organize its activities to support the cause of the revolution. It would be useless to sit around and hope that it will magically disappear, or to merely object to its existence without examining its roots and causes.

Today, Syrians cannot choose between the existence and non-existence of the military component. They do, however, have a choice about whether the military component should exist with or without order. There is no question: the former is preferable.

As has been pointed out, there is a risk that organized armed resistance could to some extent transform into nihilistic jihadist violence. The armed resistance came into existence in response to the regime's rejection of politics and its decision to engage in armed confrontation against the revolution. If the regime carries on with its escalation of violence to the level of state terrorism, circumstances will become even more accommodating to terrorist-style jihadist violence.

* * *

There are, however, serious complications in the militarization of the revolution that must be immediately considered and problematized in order to find ways to remedy them.

First, there are the human and material losses resulting from militarized conflict, which are naturally higher than those caused by peaceful protest. Moreover, internal armed conflict is more likely to attract a variety of external interventions than is peaceful protest.

Second, militarization and the use of arms could limit identification with the revolution. There is no doubt that a purely peaceful revolution appeals to broad demographics—various genders, generations, religions, and confessional roots—and also gains more sympathy from abroad. Debates over militarization and armament among activists in public affairs have always referred to this reality. During its early stage, the Syrian revolution did not provide anyone with reasons to oppose it. Later, the rise of a military component handed to an overwhelmed audience a cause for confusion: some became passive observers; others even came to oppose the revolution.

The third complication that results from the rise of the military component concerns the aftermath of the revolution itself. The issues that would confront the (anticipated) post-revolutionary Syria following a peaceful toppling of the regime would be incomparably easier to handle than the issues that would follow an armed ousting of the regime. The history of previous revolutions from France to China to Algeria shows that conditions following a violent revolution remain volatile for many years afterwards.

To say that the revolution was compelled to take up arms should not prevent an immediate discussion over ways to confront and mitigate the potential complications that may follow from having taken up arms.

In fact, the integrity of the Syrian revolution and the justness of its cause is evidenced by its largely defensive militarization, which did not compromise the many forms of peaceful struggle. The revolution seems to possess self-correction mechanisms that can address some of its transgressions, which is more important than setting the impossible goal of having a faultless revolution, and certainly more beneficial than a holier-than-thou attitude.

* * *

In the end, the military component of the revolution faces four challenges today. The first is the development of a self-organized military doctrine and code of conduct. Second is resistance to various attempts by individuals or regional parties to finance certain groups, i.e., creating militias that are subject to the agendas of funders and not to the cause of overthrowing the regime and building a new Syria. The third is the challenge of terrorism, whether self-produced or regime-induced. And finally, of course, there is the challenge of ensuring an effective and adaptive confrontation with the forces of the regime.

Each of these is a serious challenge; taken together, they are enormous.

We have fallen like prey into the jaws of the beast—of history, that is. Our only saviours are good insight and thoughtful policies.

5

THE ROOTS OF SYRIAN FASCISM

APRIL 2012

To the memory of Hamza Al-Khatib[1]

One day, it will be necessary to conduct an extensive, comprehensive examination of the social and cultural roots of the fascist violence practiced by Bashar al-Assad's regime throughout the past thirteen months across Syrian cities and villages. As of today, the violence has resulted in the deaths of about 12,000 of the men and women of Syria, among them some of the most courageous. It has also resulted in immense destruction for dozens of cities and towns; the internal displacement of over a million people; and over 100,000 refugees seeking asylum in neighbouring countries. The regime's brutality has been accompanied by flagrant bigotry and incandescent hatred towards the rebels.

This essay will examine three possible social and cultural structures that nurtured, justified, or enabled the development of this appalling violence: absolute Arabism, or the Baathist version of Arab nationalism; sectarianism, along with its related cultural, political, and ideological structures; and the new bourgeoisie, a class that formed under the first Assad regime and which has occupied a dominant position, politically and ideologically, during the reign of Assad the son.

Before beginning a general examination of these roots, let us be clear about the intended meaning of 'fascism' here. It refers to: violent aggression against civilians and disregard for their lives; the use of punitive campaigns in response to any objections; and shelling towns, locales, and villages—all at the hands of a wealthy ruling clique, immune from any accountability, acting under the pretext of 'defending the security of the homeland.' On examination, one may not find a systematic fascist ideology or distinct fascist social organizations, but rather a mixture of unrestrained violence and an ideology that at best overlooks violence, at worst justifies and encourages it, and which continues to oppress the people in any case.

We also need to start a discussion regarding this new fascism. We Syrians have given insufficient thought to the state of our country, and this paucity of intellectual theorizing matches the scant attempts the regime has made to offer even the veneer of democratic representation.

Absolute Arabism and its Conceptual Framework

The first root of Syrian fascism is buried in the Baathist brand of Arab nationalism, or what I call the doctrine of absolute Arabism. 'Absolute' here stands in opposition to constitutional.

This doctrine states that Syria is an 'Arab country,' and that Syria along with the other Arab countries comprise the 'Arab Homeland.' It also claims that the Arab identity of these countries is essential, definite, and entirely defining of all residents, land, and states. The preamble to the constitution of the Baath Party, issued in April 1947, reads: 'The Arab Homeland constitutes an indivisible political and economic unit. No Arab country can live apart from the others.' It also adds: 'The Arab nation is one cultural unit, and all the differences among its nationals are external, superficial, and erasable by the awakening of the Arab conscience.'[2] This dogma is central in the political and historical curricula taught in Syrian schools.

According to this narrative, Arabism was neither historical nor contractual, and Syria did not become an Arab country through complex historical processes that led to a majority Arabic-speaking population over the centuries. Rather, the Arab essence of Syria required all inhabitants of Syria to be 'Syrian Arabs.' The appellation was worked into descriptions of everything Syrian: The Syrian Arab Army, Syrian Arab TV, the Syrian Arab National Anthem, the Syrian Arab citizenry... and so forth. Failure to conform to this definition could result in forced Arabization or exile, based on Article 11 of the Baath Party Constitution: 'Any individual who calls for or joins a racist block, or migrates to the Arab World for colonialist purposes, will be exiled from the Arab homeland.'[3] This conception laid the foundation for a nationalistic assimilation that failed at assimilating anyone—rather, it was successful in 'exiling' the Kurds in Syria from Syrian public space, though not from Syria itself. By the time the rebellion began, there were some 150,000 Kurds who had been deprived of citizenship for about half a century—the justification for which was directly dependent upon the alienating effect of absolute Arabism. Kurds were unseen and unheard in Syria, a situation that led to an understandable exasperation that has manifested itself in an animosity toward Arabs. This will inevitably lead to much ethnic and political upheaval in the near future.

Yet the most prominent feature of Baathist Arabism, or absolute Arabism, is seen in its project of complete political and intellectual homogenization that was undertaken inside Syria, which aimed to create uniformity among all Syrians and to position Baathism as their profound truth, the Baath Party as the carrier of their 'eternal message' as Arabs. This is the root of the extreme circumspection that surrounds regional and sectarian distinctions within Syria, and that extends to differences of opinion and thought, all of which have been denied entry into public space under the regime's iron fist. Moreover, absolute Arabism built insurmountable barriers between Arabs and 'the outside.' The borders of the Arab Homeland are 'natural': according to Article 7 in the constitution of the Baath Party, the Homeland is 'the terrain inhibited by the Arab nation, extending over the Taurus Mountains and those of Bishtekwih to the Gulf of Basra, the Arabian Sea, the Ethiopian Highlands, the Sahara, the Atlantic Ocean, and the Mediterranean Sea.'[4] It is as if nature itself has worked in tandem with culture to separate Arabs from the rest of the world. By contrast, the borders between Arab countries are artificial according to this view, created by colonial powers and guarded by their collaborators from among our own countrymen.

Like their language, the culture of the Arabs is one and the same. The existence of other cultures or languages is inconceivable. The fact that there are various, divergent Arabic dialects and that speakers of one may find it difficult to understand speakers of another has always been downplayed. Arabs are necessarily united in their ambitions and aspirations: when that is not the case, it is because 'Arab consciousness' has not been properly awakened.

The geographical and cultural separation of Arabs from the rest of the world has laid the foundation for a mistrustful international outlook, particularly toward the West. This scepticism extends to neighbouring non-Arab countries, and even to most other Arab countries, the governments of which are viewed as conspirators or double agents. Conspiracy theories are rampant all over the globe, but in Syria they are central to the regime's political doctrine and worldview.

In fact, absolute Arabism floats on a sea of doubt about the world. It thrives in an atmosphere of war, of psychological and intellectual conscription, of hostility toward strangers and suspicions regarding infiltrators at home. The ruling elite, the intelligence services, and the armed forces are keen to maintain such a tense intellectual and psychological atmosphere in order to position themselves as the guardians of the nation. Such an atmosphere makes it possible for transgressions on the part of the rulers not only to be rendered invisible but also unimaginable: it eliminates all barriers that limit the ruling elite's fascist domination of the ruled, and institutes the justification for a violated society, one that is continually suspected of betraying the homeland.

Under these conditions, the army acquires a sanctified status: any criticism of it is unthinkable. In fact, there has not been a single paragraph of Syrian commentary that criticizes the Syrian Arab Army, despite its enormous corruption and transformation into an institution that trades only in sectarianism and humiliation. It is an army whose track record of 'victories' have been over Syrians, Palestinians, and Lebanese during the years of Assad's reign. Criticizing the army is viewed as an act of treason, and a costly one. From the beginning of the uprising, the forced obeisance to the army turned into sanctification of the military boot. Online one can find many images of individuals carrying the military boot on top of their heads or even kissing it.[5]

In general, the structure of absolute Arabism is geared toward the prohibition and criminalization of internal dissent on the one hand, and toward the isolation of Syrians from an aggressive and conspiring 'outer world' on the other.

Mingling with foreigners in Syria has long been grounds for suspicion. Foreigners are thought to be either spies or sources of cultural pollution. It is not customary for ordinary Syrians to apply for a passport or to travel to foreign countries: both processes are extremely difficult, especially for opposition figures. Driven by an imperative to protect our purity from any perversion or infection from 'outside,' this policy of isolation is typical of fascism everywhere.

The criminalization of internal dissent, whether political or ideological, is exemplified in the basic prerogative of the authoritarian: political arrest. This was a feature from the very beginning of Baathist rule, and for decades this foundational act proliferated through a mix of multiple security forces, undifferentiated in power and equivalent in brutality. With a name like Damascus' 'Palestine Branch,' (also known as Branch 235) this particular security service is emblematic: it is a bridge that connects the Arab nationalist doctrine in its absolute form (in the context of which Palestine occupies a central place) to the brutal quelling of internal dissent. The branch is part of Military Security and was originally formed to prosecute potential Israeli spies. But the parallels constructed around the notion of patriotism functioned to narrow the gap between dealing with the national enemy and the handling of any opposition activities. According to the doctrine of absolute Arabism, Syria is necessarily in a constant state of war with the 'Zionist enemy': any form of internal opposition is framed as an attempt to emasculate the nation or to collude with the enemy. Both incur the heaviest of penalties. The forms of severe punishment to which thousands of political prisoners were subjected, including many Palestinians, testify to the Palestine Security Branch's status as a veritable monument to Fascism.

Absolute Arabism serves as a foundation for expulsion from the nation. By casting political opponents outside of the realm of patriotism, it deprives them of any legal, political, and social protection. The political opponents of the regime are put on the defensive: they have to justify themselves and plead their patriotic innocence; thus, their cause self-destructs through their professions of allegiance to the very doctrine their politics were formed to oppose.

Unfortunately, and despite being the first victims of this doctrine, very few Syrian opposition politicians and intellectuals allowed their criticisms of Baathist ideology to tackle its foundations in absolute nationalism. More specifically, they failed to criticize the relationship between this doctrine and the belief that the governed are potential enemies who need to be constantly humiliated and subdued. A serious attempt at criticism would reveal that our societies are compounds that owe their Arab attributes to multifaceted historical factors, and would point out that we are not separate from the rest of the world by any imaginary fences or 'natural borders'. A worthwhile criticism would also uphold the rights of individuals and groups in the face of the state and the nation—Arab or Syrian—and would emphasize the concrete historical existence of our societies against the imposition of any presumed essence.

The general intellectual and political effect of the Baathist doctrine is reflected in the paranoia that has plagued Syrian society, and in the mindless condemnation of one another that makes it impossible to have free discussions and build networks of trust among the people. If the 'outside' is evil, then we should isolate ourselves from it and refrain from trying to emulate it or learning from it. A perspective of that sort naturally belittles the freedoms and achievements of the 'outside' world—the Western world in particular—while it perpetuates the status quo. It is not uncommon to hear talk of 'imported theories' or foreign 'cultural invasions,' particularly with reference to the West. Such a tendency toward segregation and the resistance to 'cultural contamination' is typical of absolute nationalism and fascist ideology.

It is noteworthy that anxieties about cultural invasion arose during the early 1990s simultaneously with three events: the wave of democracy in Eastern Europe that followed the implosion of the Eastern bloc; the peace negotiations with Israel, which violated the doctrine of absolute Arabism (alongside cultural invasion, 'anti-normalization' with Israel became the topic du jour); and the emergence of satellite broadcasting, which broke the state's monopoly over the media. Immunization against cultural invasion became a matter of utmost importance to counter the declining value of official doctrine in the context of growing openness to the world. It was crucial for the regime to combat the possibility of losing its main pretext for controlling the Syrian people, i.e. the narrative of confronting the enemy, in particular Israel.

During the 1960s and 1970s, absolute Arabism drew upon communist ideology and its tactics for combating Western imperialism, illustrated in its hackneyed and essentialist hostility toward the West. The West is offensive, morally corrupt, and should be avoided like the plague. In the 1980s absolute Arabism got additional support from the rise of Islamist movements by virtue of their shared cultural and political hostility toward the West, and their promotion of cultural particularism, which bestowed a degree of legitimacy on the Syrian status quo and, consequently, reduced public interest in learning from the West. With their bent toward self-sufficiency, Islamist movements can isolate the governed politically and culturally, and can grow into explicit fascisms, as can be seen in the Salafist-Jihadist currents.

The establishment of the Israeli state in the Arab Levant, followed by the West's peculiar, unfair, and wholesale support of this armed stronghold, reinforced absolute Arabism's aspirations of internal homogeneity and segregation from the outside world. Strong, domineering, and armed to the teeth, exempt from international law by the special immunity granted it on religious grounds by the world's greatest powers, Israel facilitated the militarization of thought and of public life in our countries, and greatly complicated the questions of any political and cultural change in our societies. There is no doubt that Assad's Baathist regime exploited the Palestinian cause, but Israeli colonialism gave its claims real foundation. The Palestinian issue has shaken confidence in the West and its organizations. It provides fertile ground for calls for segregation, and has been accompanied by cultural and political paranoia (which is at once ever-boastful and ever-complaining).

The doctrine of Baathist absolute Arabism has not been a functioning ideology since the 1970s. To remain effective, it underwent structural and functional alterations in ways that guaranteed absolute safety for the governors and continued to spread an environment of suspicion and mistrust among the governed.

Because of its abstraction, its isolation from changing reality, and its ideological stagnation (along with its evergreen paranoid emotional content), Baathist ideology—which was rhetorically poor from the beginning—became entirely centred on the ruler: Hafez al-Assad in Syria, and Saddam Hussein in Iraq. The glories attributed to the 'one Arab nation' were intensified by the Baath Party and staged to perfection in the two faithful men who led the parties in each country. The two were guardians of national purity against any alien or foreign infection. By definition, the party was supposed to be one unit, like the Arab nation, and required one leader. Therefore, each of the leaders, and their regimes, saw the other as a traitor.

Eventually, Baathist revolutionism devolved into a Sultanic-style dynastic rule. The transformation came with a high price that the people of Syria are still paying, while Iraqis have already suffered to get rid of a tyrant who had planned to bequeath his position to his family.

This Sultanic shift was not surprising. The inclination of absolute nationalism toward homogeneity devolved onto an organic relation—a large family—dominated by a great father and 'master of the homeland', as the two Assads are described by their followers in Syria. If we are all siblings and all alike, we can accept a reduced or summary expression of ourselves in the 'Leading Father,' 'The Great One of the Nation'. According to the standard definition of national unity in Syria during the rule of Hafez al-Assad, our unity is when we 'stand behind his wise leadership in one line.' This national unity is spoken about in mystical terms: people are expected to sacrifice their souls and blood for the beloved leader. Some of us are lost souls, however, and refuse this sacrifice; these are the traitors and conspirators, the spiteful or the deluded, and it is a national duty to punish and exterminate us.

In conclusion, the doctrine of absolute Arabism, standing upon its twin pillars of mistrust and conspiracy, has been used to criminalize dissent and opposition and, of course, protest and revolution. These doctrines make it permissible to crush all the above with a clear conscience: their structure was retained in Syria after the personification of absolute Arabism in Hafez al-Assad.

Although absolute Arabism is not the ideology of Bashar al-Assad's rule, its intellectual mould has remained in place (local homogeneity, foreign conspiracies, accusations against traitors, and so forth). Nowadays, there are a few sectors of what I call the new bourgeoisie—descended from religious and sectarian minorities in particular—who incline towards an 'absolute-Syrianism'. This is a reformulation of absolute Arabism with a single distinction—the term 'Arab homeland' is replaced with 'Syrian homeland'.

The regime has never advanced a clear set of ideas and values in its confrontation with the revolution. It attacks Arabs in the name of Arabism, even as a big portion of the regime's middle class are anti-Arabist, absolute-Syrianists who denounce both 'the Arabs' and Arabism across public media outlets. Slogans like 'Progress and Socialism' (which first appeared during the early 1980s as the regime was contending with Islamists and communists) have been replaced by an emphasis on stability and security; such values elevate the status of a class that has reaped the profits of its association with the regime in the form of wealth and prestige.

To summarise, it is necessary to clarify that absolute Arabism is a peculiar form of Arab nationalism. While this is one basis for Syrian fascism, this analysis does not concern the Arab people as an ethnic group. Absolute Arabism says nothing about Arab cultural bonds, or even about Arab nationalism as a political movement. A fascist structure is possible within any national space, and is entirely imaginable within absolute Syrianism.

Sectarianism and the structure of hatred

What is important to understand with respect to sectarianism is not that there is a multiplicity of primordial confessional communities or 'sects' that date back to the days of yore. In this regard, Syria is analogous to many other countries in the world, with the difference, perhaps, merely in quantity. Rather, what is important to understand is the peculiarity of the prevailing political and legal systems in the country, and the extent to which these specific structures allow for the neutralization, the nurturing, or even the antagonism of these differences. Contemporary systems of this sort may invoke elements from the past in order to build or solidify communitarian identities, but potential clashes of identities are not orchestrated by heritage and folklore: they are fuelled by current policies and polarizations, and by present-day narratives.

Early on, the Assad clan relied on its sectarian loyalists to secure their position. It seems that Hafez al-Assad, shortly after his seizure of power following a military coup, attached great importance to the prolongation of his reign over a country well known for political instability and frequent military coups. Perhaps it was clear to him that the biggest challenge in Syria was not how to seize power, since many had preceded him in doing so without great difficulty. Rather, the challenge was retaining power. In this regard, the main source of anxiety was the politicization of the army, and so it needed to be isolated, even before the coup, from the influence of politicians and, in particular, from his fellow Baathists. Hafez held a strong position in this respect as defence minister for the four years preceding his coup of November 1970. He established independent military units led by handpicked relatives and faithful friends who showed enthusiasm for defending the regime. Over time, the army was thoroughly planted with security and sectarian minefields, so that if a military unit commander belonged to sect X, his deputy must belong to sect Y, and the unit's security officer must be a member of sect Z. There were many variants of this tripartite arrangement, always engineered to ensure an environment of mistrust within a unit and to make united action impossible.

Political opposition forces and organizations were another source of anxiety. Hafez witnessed their conflicts and skirmishes during the 1950s, and the solution he arrived upon was to pay greater attention to the security forces, where he appointed reliable relatives and others from his inner circle to critical positions. Similarly, networks of informers and spies infiltrated political parties and broader civil society. These networks expanded the Baath Party's security functions, which eventually morphed into an invasive organism that spread throughout Syrian society in its entirety. Moreover, security checkpoints were distributed throughout towns and cities, and intelligence agencies were set up in every university, government department, and economic affairs division.

Members of the Assad family topped the list of confidants. Rifaat al-Assad was commander of the Defence Corps, the Alawite-dominated and best-armed elite formation in the Syrian army. His wife's first cousin, Adnan Makhlouf, was commander of the Republican Guard.

This structure was unprecedented in Syria's modern history and was the main source of sectarian tensions. During the pre-Assad and the pre-Baath eras, Syrian society had been moving toward diminishing community-based disparities.

Under these circumstances, a dramatic decline in academic freedom, independent political and cultural activities, and the rule of law was inevitable. The abstract nationalist ideology, along with the principle of national unity (which we previously defined as: 'Standing in one line behind the wise historic leadership of Mr. President Hafez al-Assad'), drew a heavy rhetorical curtain over the chronicles of sectarianism, and a thick veil of prohibition over any attempt to address the issue.

The holy figure of the president was the centre of political allegiance and the pillar of homogeneity. Arabism was no longer a pillar because it had turned into a political party—i.e., the Baath Party—and so it was doomed to deteriorate as the basis for collective identity, even among Syrian Arabs.

It is worth mentioning that the regime of Hafez al-Assad was relatively pragmatic in its policy toward the Kurds, despite its maintenance of absolute Arabism. In general, the policy of 'bringing hearts together' was fruitful. However, this policy sprang from the regime's sceptical view of the Arabs of the 'Jazira', the north-eastern region of the country where the majority of Kurds also live. Many of those Arabs were thought to be more loyal to the previous Iraqi regime, detested by the Assad regime. The regime showed exceptional skill in attracting the Kurds politically, even as it continued to deny their existence as a distinct nation and culture. This is a complex story involving many details, but we are only concerned here with the regime's continuous reliance on pitting segments of the population against one another and on exploiting any inherited distinctions so as to disintegrate the unity of the ruled.

The regime's top priority was to remain in power forever. Everything else—including national integration, the restoration to Syrian control of the territories occupied by Israel, social openness, the development of education and of fair judicial systems—had to be lower on the list of priorities and subject to sacrifice in situations of conflict with the primary imperative.

The only constants were a forced political immobilization, the disruption of political and social movements, and the limitation of supreme power to the president and his entourage.

On its own, the disruption of political mobilization could have activated and politicized sectarian ties, with or without the explicit use of sectarian tools. But one can easily see the outcome of using sectarian tools within a process of general political immobilization. While addressing Syrian Druze and Christians, the men of the regime claimed that their job was to protect them against the attacks of Sunni fanatics.[6] On another occasion, an Armenian Syrian activist was asked, 'You are an Armenian Christian. Why do you oppose us?' The question implies that 'you' and 'us' are fighting on one front against the common enemy, i.e. Sunni Muslims.[7]

This situation endured for decades and lead to a multivalent crisis of national trust. Syrians of the previous generation distrust and fear one another. They only trust their own ethnic or sectarian groups and feel safe only with their relatives. There is an intimate degree of trust particular to the family, while a broader and more general degree is accorded to the ethnic or sectarian group. Christians rarely act naturally in the presence of a Muslim, and the same applies to Sunnis in the presence of a Shiite or Kurds in the presence of an Arab, and vice versa. This is a lived experience known to many Syrians, especially those living in the most diverse communities. Because of these sectarianizing dynamics, the 'Syrian people' can no longer be constituted in a typical national sense, based upon a wide-ranging and general degree of trust. This amounts to saying that the Syrian people do not exist.

Each group has developed its own narratives of superiority and victimhood that combine ancient and modern reference points. Each group views itself as superior in their manners, modernity, reason, secularism, or religion. Everybody thinks of themselves as victims of the other's bullying (with 'self' and 'other' defined in terms of ethnic and sectarian language). The other is the most backward, heretical, wicked, fanatical, aggressive, or self-centred. Moreover, each group views itself as the most persecuted, the one exposed to the most extreme form of discrimination, accused of the most despicable charges, and the one whose rights have been flouted the most.

For example, there is a girls' school in Latakia, whose female students come from Sunni, Alawite, and Christian backgrounds. A teacher there told me a familiar story during the summer of 2010. A majority of Sunni students are veiled, while the Alawite and Christian girls are not (an outcome of identification with different manufactured ideal types over the last three decades). Typical Sunni girls describe their Alawite and Christian classmates as 'promiscuous'. On the other hand, Sunni girls are described as 'backward'. Such judgments harden the heart and diminish mutual sympathy among the 'promiscuous' and the 'backward', and could even tempt them to hurt one another. Within the school system as well as on a more general, national level, there has been no effort to counter such dangerous stereotypes, or to advocate acceptance and respect among different groups.

This is no mere social matter, nor is it irrelevant to politics: it is the outcome of forty years under the rule of the Assads, and it is the result of the suppression of all independent cultural and social activities. It is also indicative of the crisis of bonds of trust, and illustrates the prevalence of victimhood and superiority narratives among Syrians, in addition to the absence of any vital, dynamic content within the official ideology.

In 1981, a group of female teenager parachutists from Rifaat al-Assad's Defence Corps attacked Damascene women on the streets and ripped off their headscarves. The incident was fuelled by a combination of politically motivated hatred of the women's social environment and a cultural contempt for their presumed 'backwardness'. Sectarianism informs all of this. Considering the sensitivity of the issue, Hafez al-Assad apologized for the incident on TV in an effort to make amends with the Damascenes.

The spread of stereotypes and narrow-minded representations coupled with a context characterized by the absence of mechanisms for social, cultural, and political change work together to diminish possibilities of collaboration and sympathy among members of different groups, which in turn trivializes the freedoms and the lives of others. Since 'the others' are evil or backward, fanatics or promiscuous, why should one hesitate to persecute or even kill them? Such are the psychological prejudices shaped by oratorical devices that pave the way for collective violence and genocides.

Another mechanism mobilized in the service of atomizing the people was the spread of the belief that if we do not kill them, they will kill us. This was an odd, baseless fear in Syria's modern history during the pre-Assad era. However, this phobia has become the staunchest basis for sectarian uniformity and drawing decisive distinctions between 'us' and 'them'. Kill or be killed also provides the most solid foundation for a kind of 'absolute sectarianism' parallel to the Baathist absolute Arabism, and it has similar goals: pure interior homogeneity; complete exclusion of the other; and the distrust of dissidence. There is nothing better than the phantasm of 'identity-based killing' to provide a ground for absolute sectarianism.

Like absolute Arabism, such narratives set the stage for widespread paranoia—for seeing every outsider as an evil conspirator, and every insider as a good friend. In the Baathist nationalist doctrine, any group's dissent is the equivalent of treason. During the revolution, some of the cruellest judgments were voiced by members of one sect against other members of the same sect who chose to dissent from the presumed consensus, particularly when that consensus involved support for the regime.

Because of its excessive political impoverishment, and prohibitions against forming or joining independent associations or parties, Syrian society lacked corrective mechanisms such as youth rallies, cross-denominational political parties, or frameworks for public debate. Parties capable of representing a unified Syrian nationalism cured of such particularist afflictions were crushed. It is true that many Syrians today introduce themselves as 'Syrian'. even though their Syrian identity is rooted in the idea of absolute Syrianism or derived from slogans such as 'Syria First' or 'Syria is

Above All'. Like absolute Arabism, absolute Syrianism functions to conceal Syria's diversity, and to separate 'us' from 'them'. Its policy toward sectarianism might best be called 'sectarian chastity'—it remains deliberately reticent about publicly discussing sectarianism, and is therefore incapable of installing any barriers against it.

Just as the Palestine Security Branch embodied the fascist utilization of absolute Arabism, Tadmur Prison in Palmyra was the place where sectarianism joined with organized fascist violence during the last two decades of the rule of Assad père (1970–2000). The regime was keen to recruit Alawites to fill most positions across the prison; most of the prisoners were Islamists. The characteristic practice of consistent torture in Tadmur Prison throughout those two decades, especially against Islamists, makes it the Assads' true dynamo; it is the shrunken soul of the regime, and its core hellish aspect.[8] The notorious detention centre was reopened after the beginning of the revolution, its political wards having been closed in 2001.[9]

Sectarianism is connected to one of the most striking, and most fascist, phenomena of the Syrian revolution: the *shabiha*.[10] The *shabiha* consist of civilians who were armed during the revolution, and they are likely responsible for the most atrocious crimes, especially those of a sectarian nature, such as the massacre at Karm Al-Zaitoon in Homs on 11 March 2012, and the Houla massacre of 25 May 2012.

The connection of sectarianism and ethnocentrism with hatred and massacres is not unique to Syria. Similar calamities were seen in Rwanda, the former Yugoslavia, Nazi Germany, and in neighbouring Iraq and Lebanon. Syria is now merely ripe to host this recurring pattern.

Again, Syrian intellectuals who never criticized the military were also too timid to tackle the political role played by sectarianism, or to spark discussions about the far-reaching implications of this fatal epidemic. Quite the contrary—many were even aggressive in attacking those who tried to do so. The regime's nationalist ideology, though unpalatable, has always been hegemonic, and hegemony has saved the regime from open suppression of the (non-existent) voices of intellectuals.

Even though sectarian biases have been used as political tools from the beginning of Assad's rule, it is essential to break the taboo of sectarianism and expose it along with all the related ways in which the Syrian people have been manipulated. Doing so can be a first step towards constructing a politics of trust, solidarity, and brotherhood.

The new bourgeoisie and its cultural world

This section traces the formation of a new bourgeoisie in Syria, a class consisting primarily of 'officials' sons' and their associates whose fortunes have been accumulated under the auspices of the regime through advantageous access to contracts, deals, projects, and public resources within Syria (and previously in Lebanon).[11] The iconic figure of this class, the embodiment of wealth-meets-power, is Bashar al-Assad's cousin Rami Makhlouf, the owner of the Syriatel Mobile Network provider, and the man who, two months into the uprising, declared that they (the regime) had decided to fight until the end.[12] But Makhlouf is only the most prominent of dozens of tycoons. Together, they form a private club whose main establishments are Cham Holding, with Rami Makhlouf as the vice president, and its sister company, Syria Holding.[13]

The ideology of this class is the 'Development and Modernization' line, the very slogan that Bashar al-Assad chose to brand his reign. Anyone familiar with the history of this slogan recognizes its conservative, retrograde implications. 'Development and Modernization' first began to circulate during the short 'Damascus Spring' (2000–2001) as an explicit rejection of the opposition's demand for political reforms. As the slogan indicates, the main concern was to develop existing systems by updating their external appearance, to present the regime in a more modern light. Another, ideologically parallel slogan emerged around the same time: 'Stability and Continuity.' It was widely disseminated during the early days of Bashar al-Assad's rule. Development and modernization are necessary for stability, which is of crucial importance for the new class. But stability is in turn dependent on continuity, i.e. on the person of Bashar, the heir to his father. The ideology summed up in these two catch-phrases complements the portrayal of President Bashar and his wife Asma Al-Akhras as a 'modern', elegant, bilingual, computer-savvy couple who keep up-to-date with Western music.

I speak about this new bourgeoisie because its key figures are closely tied to the Assad regime. But the class is also seasoned with a significant portion of the old bourgeoisie, recycled and integrated into the new class as political dependents.[14] Members of the new class are brought together by the centrality of family in its projects, and by their strong attachments to political power.[15] From this follows the ferocious loyalty of the new bourgeoisie to the regime and its extreme animosity toward any opposition. This virulent animosity is particularly evident in the group branching out from the core of the regime. Although *Al-Watan* newspaper and Al-Dunya TV are private media outlets owned by Rami Makhlouf and others, they have outdone the Syrian official state media in their bigotry.[16] After Syria's forced withdrawal from Lebanon in the spring of 2005, this new class needed a

Syrian Lebanon; a domestic market for its activities. The solution was the announcement of a shift toward the so-called 'social market economy', which inaugurated a policy of economic liberalization that worked in favour of the new bourgeoisie and against all political or legal reform. Neoliberal development formulas were applied that catered to the interests of a self-centred and avaricious caste.[17]

Neoliberalism is compatible with political authoritarianism all over the world. In Syria, add to that an inherited tyranny with totalitarian traits, and explicit fascism will be the response to any public uprising. To use Marxist terminology, the regime of Bashar al-Assad is merely the 'general staff' of this class. For over a year now, the general staff has led the fight against the population of Syria, which obliged Rami Makhlouf (the supposedly private investor and 'fighter till the end') to appear on media outlets and announce his turn to 'philanthropy' in early August 2011. Makhlouf's claim was 100 per cent deceptive—but the merger of power and wealth to which the claim spoke was precisely correct.

In conjunction with these class transformations, the regime of Bashar al-Assad tested an imitation of 'liberalism.' Travel abroad became easier.[18] Similarly, transportation across the country was facilitated, and the arrival of foreigners more frequent.

At no time was the regime able to establish a firm grip over virtual public space. And with the corresponding changes in the economy and information circulation, the significance of the Baath Party and its affiliated 'popular' organizations declined in favour of the new bourgeoisie. Instead of a Baathist staff (usually of rural origin with thick moustaches and wandering eyes) working in party 'popular organizations', trade unions, and universities, we now have a new generation of wealthy and professional people from the new middle class, 'developed and modern' and resembling Bashar al-Assad in appearance and attitude (young, foreign-educated, elegant, polished etc.). They teach in private universities, or are employed at new banks, or run independent newspapers and magazines, or own posh new restaurants and cafes. But, despite their psychological openness to the world—chiefly to the West—the new staff of Assad the Younger remain very cliquish and insular: they are either ignorant of or hostile to the deteriorating neighbourhoods and brutalized sectors of Syrian society, who eventually would start the revolution.

Today, there is a partial privatization of the violence against the revolution that is proportionate to the emergence of the new bourgeoisie and its position of public authority, not only in terms of its *chargés d'affaires* (i.e. the *shabiha*) but also in terms of its funders.[19] This phenomenon is closely related to the decline of the 'popular organizations' (Baath Party and security controlled organizations of students, labourers, youths, and others) since the 1980s, when those organizations played a significant role in revolt suppression.

In addition to reflecting the rise of the new bourgeoisie, the features of modernity that surfaced during the reign of Bashar al-Assad were shaped by a modernist ideology that spread regionally and globally after the fall of the Soviet Union. This variant of 'modernism' refers to supposedly modern lifestyles, behaviours, and mindsets by means of contrast with older and apparently outmoded lifestyles and mindsets. In the process, this modernism provides no clear ideas concerning values, but tends to attribute both modernity and traditionalism exclusively to culture. In turn, culture is reduced to its fixed or inherited components (in contrast to its acquired components, a trend that was conceptually dominant up to the 1980s). Inherited culture is reduced again to religion; religion is reduced to Islam; and Islam is reduced exclusively to Sunnism.

This modernism has three fundamental traits. First, it entirely neglects issues of values (such as freedom, equality, human dignity, mutual respect among people) in favour of morally amorphous categories such as 'secularism', 'rationalism', 'enlightenment', and modernism itself. Second, it neglects fundamental social issues related to poverty, unemployment, marginalization, life conditions, illiteracy, women's status, and gender relations. Third, the advocates of this modernism are politically conservative. They are close to the regime (and to regimes in general): they evince an outright hostility toward democracy, describing it as a 'numerical democracy' (a stance common to all fascisms) that masks the tyranny of the majority and persecution of minorities. They also present democratic activists and intellectuals as an anti-state movement (statism too is a constant peculiarity of fascism). This doctrine involves a political theory of no subtlety whatsoever that blames our political and social problems on a 'ruined' or 'antiquated' mindset, or on a retardation that is defined in terms of culture.

It is not surprising that this doctrine is well-suited to the regime and its security apparatus. Any problems stem from people's minds and society's failures; its bigotry, irrationality, or perpetual violence. According to this view, social problems have nothing to do with the tyranny of a corrupt junta, nor with the brutal intelligence services, nor with the monopoly of national resources by one privileged class—none of this leads to poverty, low levels of education, or unemployment. A perspective of this sort is undoubtedly compatible with the devaluation of the life and freedom of people whom they cast as backwards fanatics. This is not to say that these are the only reasons that protesting civilians are being murdered in Syria today—but a better representation of the people, one less suffused with contempt and hostility, could have provided them with some protection.

In Marxist terminology, this modernism is the ideology that enabled the new bourgeoisie to take the offensive in their struggle to gain hegemony: power, influence, and wealth, to the exclusion of the general public. The new bourgeoisie see the people as backward, illiterate, ignorant fanatics who are responsible for their own living conditions, which are a function of attributes rooted in their beliefs. Again, the conditions in which the people live have nothing to do with social or political factors. This modernity is an ideological supplement to the violence carried out by the intelligence services against backwards riffraff.[20]

Modernist ideology reflects the consolidation of a new bourgeoisie from within previous circles marked by a social alliance of the rural and urban petit bourgeoisie, whose shared ideology was a mixture of absolute Arabism and statist socialism. Justification of the privileged position of the new bourgeoisie required a new, privileged ideology: modernism. A real social war was required for the alliance to prevail. During the 1960s, this older 'petit bourgeoisie' justified its rule by making real gains on behalf of a demanding audience in what was a young and small nation (about 5 million at the time): they did not rely solely on pompous rhetoric against the official enemy (Israel). But today, a parallel social war has solely benefited a narrow segment of the wealthy, and it justifies itself by deploying the fight against Salafism and al-Qaeda in ways that make it marketable to the 'First World.'

By substituting Arab nationalism with modernist ideology, we arrive at an explanation for the current paucity of Baathist regime defenders. Before and during the revolution, the regime's apologists were mostly non-Baathist professionals, contemporaries of Bashar al-Assad and 'absolute Syrianists' (not absolute Arabists), free of Baathist intellectual controls and values—as demonstrated for example in the extensive references to the *u'rban* (a derogatory term for Arabs), and in the public expressions of racism against Gulf Arabs. The regime's ideologues belong to the world of Al-Dunya TV, which is owned by members of the new bourgeoisie.

A perfect example of 'New Bourgeois Social Thought' can be found in an article written by a Syrian engineer about overpopulation on the Syrian Jazira (the north-eastern part of the country—my comments in brackets):

> Let's be frank, we are not going to give our money to uncivilized people who care for nothing but to have 8–15 children or more, as long as they do not act reasonably, logically and wisely with their resources. They cause their own poverty due to their lack of wisdom; if the year brings a good season, they squander their money and wealth on over breeding. As long as the government is going to provide food assistance [to the hungry residents of the Jazira, an area always treated like an internal colony, and plagued by four droughts in a row between 2006 and 2010], it will do so by spending our money, which gives us the right to interfere, not as a favour towards our brothers and countrymen, but in the spirit of reform. Every donation must be conditioned by them changing destructive and wasteful behaviours.

Not surprisingly, the writer equates the reproduction rates of the population in the north eastern regions of the country to a 'lack of awareness and culture.' He then concludes: 'I do not want our beautiful land and country to become poverty-stricken and plagued with a crowd that does not work, and that will eventually turn into a bunch of thugs and tramps on the streets and beggars on the roads...We call for firm actions, free from any religious, tribal, clannish, or regional sentiments.'[21] This contains all the elements of a fascist view of the general public. It blames them for their misfortunes; it imputes their presumed slowness to a lack of awareness and to ignorance; it calls for firm action. It is shot through with the Social Darwinism typical of the fascist Right everywhere.

The anti-democratic formalist character of modernism is demonstrated by total accord with the 'Development and Modernization' ideology peculiar to the regime of Bashar al-Assad. Blaming the oppressed for their oppression and deteriorating social conditions is very convenient for the new bourgeoisie and intelligence services. It appears that some senior intelligence officers (especially those holding the title of 'Doctor') are on very good terms with the intellectuals who advocate this type of modernism. One such advocate wrote about one of the doctor-generals, Fouad Nassif Kheir-Bek, saying that he 'is worthy of the gratitude of real intellectuals, being the first to sponsor an actual democratic, secular, cultural growth in Syria.' The article in which this appeared was entitled 'The Disturbing Silence of the Intellectuals: In Defence of Truth and Syrian Security!'[22] The writer brought up this 'democratic, secular, cultural growth' in an extremely anti-Islamic context. It is unfortunate and embarrassing that some notable Syrian intellectuals participated in that ideological security cohort, brought together by an obsession with 'Islam' and an object-oriented, inhumane modernism that is socially rightist and morally empty.

The reactionary nature of this modernist ideology was not unknown before the 'Arab Spring'—but its fascist side was decidedly revealed after the uprisings, especially after the Syrian revolution.

This third root of fascism in Syria shares with the previous two a predilection for devaluing the lives and worth of the people, who 'breed like rabbits and live in filthy slums and distort the civilized public appearance of the country' (so it was put in a Syrian TV talk show on 12 April 2012).

Behind the coalition of the new bourgeoisie, the intelligence services, and modernist ideologues stands a fear of change and an impetus toward sustaining existing conditions. The new bourgeoisie serve to raise the value of stability and security, which are ensured protection by the intelligence services, and the ideologues constantly warn against the dangers of democracy and the 'tyranny of the majority' which emanates from ballot boxes. In order to avoid this impending tyranny, one of the main modernist ideologues proposed that illiterates be prevented from voting in any free elections, since the problems of our society reside in the heads of the people and not in the absence of ballot boxes.[23] This theory prevailed in the years that followed 11 September 2001, and became the standard ideology for a significant number of Syrian intellectuals, most of whom occupy positions close to the regime, if they do not support it openly.

In the current Syrian context, 'modernism' provides a ready-made pretext to oppose the revolution because some of its early protests came out of mosques. Using phrases like *mutakhallifun* (literally, 'retards'), 'Salafists,' and 'Aroors,' all revolutionists were elided into a single negative image, making it seem necessary to treat them harshly without giving the matter a second thought.[24]

Perceptions shaped by labels like 'retards' contain a combination of elements related to class and to sect, under an apolitical regime that is at the same time sectarian and a guardian of an absolute, monstrous form of capitalism. Modernism is the ideology that blames the 'retards' (the Sunni poor), praises the civilized (non-Sunnis), and defends an absolutist capitalism. The label 'retards' in particular carries with it a cultural component shaped by this modernist ideology that is linked with various social terms that are also ideological, such as 'degradation,' 'slums,' and 'humble education'. Other descriptions of the rebels as 'scum' and 'mobs' direct our attention via different routes to the same classist-sectarian amalgam.[25]

Thanks to the intersection of modernist ideology with classism and sectarianism, we see a special kind of racism in our society today, one that uses false cultural terms to provoke hostility against the general public. It is no secret that racism has always been accompanied by a devaluation of the lives of 'others', and a desensitization when it comes to persecuting or murdering them.

Conclusions

The bottom line of this discussion is that the absolutist formula of Arab nationalism functions as a basic mould that shapes the innermost layers of justification for Syrian fascism. Sectarianism provides an emotional supplement that charges Syrian fascism with sentimental passion, and establishes the need for segregation among the people. The class privileges of the new bourgeoisie are the guarantees of protection.

Politically, what can be built on this analysis is the following: a strike against the pillars of fascism must involve a shift toward a constitutional conception of nationalism. This shift requires that we recognize the plural character of our society and its real and necessary connections with the world, as well as recognizing individual independence and freedom. The slogan 'Syria First' is ineffective, while 'Syria is Above All' is rooted in explicit Nazism.

It is necessary to disarm the mines of sectarianism, to keep the issue a topic for public debate, and to build institutional, legal, and intellectual fences to prevent sectarianism from leaking into the state. Moreover, it is of utmost importance to develop an anti-sectarian culture, which above all requires putting the issue on the table, instead of taking the head-in-the-sand approach that most Syrian intellectuals adopt when addressing the regime's taboos and sensitivities.

The regime has not ruled Syria for more than four decades by force alone. It has also ruled by ideological hegemony. Built around a condescending nationalism, this hegemony has prevented public confrontation with—and handling of—sectarian issues. Our resistance to the regime is vulnerable unless it attacks this hegemony, exposes its function as a guardian of fascism, and addresses the taboos it has imposed.

Fascism in Syria is not exclusively linked to the rule of Assad, nor is it connected solely to the privileged position of the Alawites in the regime today. It may seem so for the time being, but a similar scenario can occur on any religious or sectarian basis, and might regenerate on Sunni—particularly Salafi—grounds.

Thirdly, it is necessary to attack the correlation between power and wealth, and to move toward a competitive and productive economy, one that is coupled with a labour force capable of protesting and developing the democratic public spaces that allow society to organize its forces and to defend itself in the face of capital.

Culture and critical thinking must re-establish their political role through resisting tyranny and aligning with the vulnerable, as well as their necessary ethical role within the lives and actions of intellectuals.

6

THE RISE OF MILITANT NIHILISM

DAMASCUS, MAY 2012

I will here consider the emergence of elements—borne of the preceding fourteen months of struggle—that may be leading to a 'nihilist' complex within Syria. The characteristics of such a complex would include extreme violence, strict religiosity, and the withdrawal of trust from the world. A confluence of these three elements could generate a nihilist Islamic movement similar to al-Qaeda, and the chances of this happening increase in accordance with the long-term presence of conditions favourable to these elements, combined with the weakening of possible forms of social resistance to nihilism.

The remarkable thing about the Syrian context—and the Arab context in general—is that nihilism 're-forms' Islam as its base (*qaida*, in Arabic) of struggle, with a constant tendency toward negating the world and ordinary life. I will attempt to explain this point.

The withdrawal of values from reality is characteristic of revolutions, all of which have exhibited a nihilist aspect. Consequently, we can refer to both 'revolutionary nihilism', which aims at a radical change of the present reality, and 'militant nihilism', which relies upon armed force to effect change.

THE IMPOSSIBLE REVOLUTION

I

Over the past fourteen months, three ongoing processes have contributed to the emergence of a propensity toward nihilism.

The first process is the continuous, aggressive violence by the regime: the killing, torture, random shelling, massacres, expulsions, burning of houses, rape, arbitrary executions, and burning of people. This induces intense feelings of shock and anger, particularly among Sunni Muslim communities, which feel targeted in a discriminatory way by the regime's most extreme violence, a violence that has been profoundly destructive to their basic living conditions throughout the country. Such feelings reinforce the conviction that such a violent regime cannot be overthrown without violence. A year into the revolution, and having faced continuous, horrifying violence, Syrian society has become a classic example of a brutalized society—one that has been abused for so long that it no longer trusts anyone, and in which the most abused groups are likely to meet violence with violence, murder with murder. Such reciprocity is not just a fitting punishment for the aggressor, nor is it simply retributive: it is a welcome opportunity to regain honour and pride.

The second process relates to the deeply divided and ineffective Syrian political opposition. The problem does not lie in the multiplicity of views and positions, the divisiveness of having so many parties, or even with the overall weakness of the opposition spectrum and its consequent inability to realize change in the country. Rather, the problem lies specifically in the unnecessary, unjustifiable, and persistent infighting, which is most likely driven by attempts at self-promotion; and the deeply mediocre standing of most opposition spokespersons, manifest in their lack of discipline and a clear, shared vision. Consequently, trust in the broader opposition has collapsed, resulting in a nearly indiscriminate public repudiation. The opposition has been found ineffective and worthless at best, disrespectful and despicable at worst—and this is when they are not considered the regime's double agents, an epithet not uncommon among some activists. Such judgments have gained credibility to the extent that local revolutionaries have become self-sufficient. For a year now, the path of the Syrian revolution has seen local communities speaking publicly and taking over 'politics' and public space to confront the regime. It is therefore not unusual for local revolutionaries to refer to this shift using expressions that condemn politics, calling it dirty and corrupt, and describing politicians as dishonest, power-hungry opportunists.

The third process is the regional and international paralysis regarding the Syrian crisis, which has persisted for over a year. Some Arab countries and world powers initially made clear statements that blamed the Syrian regime for killing its people, statements that reassured Syrians that they were supported in their struggle and their sacrifices, and that the days of the Syrian regime were numbered. Today, however, almost fifteen months into the revolution, these countries and regional powers have done nothing. Their statements have simply not been borne out by action. The regime has concluded from such posturing that it has a free hand to decide the fate of Syrians. This has led to a widespread feeling among Syrians that they have been left to their own devices, and that the world is indifferent to them, if not actively conspiring against them. Syrian collective memory is replete with episodes that justify such scepticism, especially toward the Western powers.

2

The combined effect of these three processes has been enough to finish off Syrians' trust in all organized powers around them. The resulting, increasingly negative outlook was evident in some placards and chants. On 17 February 2012, during the siege and bombardment of Baba Amr in Homs, residents of 'Occupied Kafranbel' raised a placard that read: 'Do you think we are fools? Our blood flows in rivers, while you play and exchange the roles of good and evil! The world is a lying cheat!' The word 'occupied' became commonplace on protest signs elsewhere. The term is psychological as well as political, seeing the revolution as liberation from a foreign occupation, and implying an endorsement for confronting such occupiers with force.

The famous chant, 'Oh God, you are all we have, Oh God!' appeared during the summer of 2011, months after the revolution began. It signalled a profound feeling of isolation and lack of support. On 17 March 2012, during a funeral procession for those martyred the day before, demonstrators in Raqqa shouted, 'Your people are defenceless, Oh God!' In one sentence, they had announced they were God's people, who were also helpless and targeted by an armed, aggressive force. The combination of God and arms affords 'God's defenceless people' a way out of their vulnerability.

Earlier, on 14 October 2011, Occupied Kafranbel raised a placard that later became well-known for its combination of originality and cynicism: 'Down with the regime and the opposition! Down with the Arab and the Muslim community! Down with the Security Council! Down with the world! Down with everything!' Like most small towns in Syria, Kafranbel was generally unknown even among Syrians; its people (and those of Idlib governorate in general) typically considered rather conservative and religious. In its call for an all-inclusive, radical, levelling collapse of everything, the placard showed no bias toward any party: they are all evil, plotting, or ineffectual. One year into the revolution, demonstrators held up another devastating placard in Binnish, a town socially and culturally similar to Kafranbel. This time, however, despair and radicalism replaced originality: 'Down with the coordinating bodies and councils! Down with the traitors in the [Syrian] National Council! Down with the official page of the Syrian revolution [a famous Facebook page in which there had been a regular poll to choose a name for Fridays for more than a year after the beginning of the revolution]! Down with the union of coordination committees and the General Organization of the Revolution!'

What distinguished that sign was its declaration of a radical withdrawal of trust from the opposition, including those groups established under and connected to the revolution.

This is not submissive and despondent despair, but that of an angry and desperate fighter—it is not a declaration of withdrawal from the struggle, but a withdrawal of trust from those who were once thought reliable. Reliance might indeed be dispensable, but anger and struggle are not so easily cast aside. Many reports from active anti-regime strongholds have indicated that those who stopped demonstrating did not simply retreat to their houses but took up arms or tried to acquire them. The combination of desperation (marked by anger and a final resort to arms, *istimata* in Arabic) along with weaponry could lead to a nihilist struggle—an absolute contest of kill-or-be-killed. The regime itself has embraced such a mindset from the very beginning.

3

The extremely decentralized nature of the Syrian revolution stemmed from nearly half a century of regime-enforced seclusion and isolation of Syrian society. It was also occasioned by the regime's forcible domination over all social interaction—and so a divide-and-conquer strategy was used by the Assadist oligarchy to confront the revolution right from the start. Such strategies made any protest activities in central squares obviously impossible because this would have permitted the gathering of Syrian society's diverse groups, and perhaps would have also allowed a degree of discussion, exchange of opinions, and general building of trust. Keeping this in mind, it becomes clear that the extreme, forced fragmentation of the revolution's activities is an additional factor that has facilitated the spread of the nihilist synthesis of complete distrust and a propensity for violence.

A third element must be added to this synthesis, one rooted in religiosity. 'Islam' either accords an absolute status to the conflict, or adds a positive value to an inescapable, extreme struggle. Moreover, Islam legitimizes a violent response to violence by describing it as jihad ('holy struggle') and possible death as martyrdom. To be able to perform these roles, Islam itself is 'reformed' in ways that respond to escalating desires for purity, for desperate but virtuous struggle, and for *takfir* (judging someone as being-infidel).[1] Jihadist Salafism provides a version of Islam that perfectly meets all the requirements for making those tendencies concrete.

The fragmentation of militant groups in the Free Syrian Army, along with their lack of a unified framework, effective leadership, and a self-sustaining doctrine, is likely to act to the benefit of extremist groups within the Syrian revolution.[2]

In addition to problems of distrust and the fragmentation (or multiplication) of revolutionary strongholds, there is also a fragmentation of vision. There is a continuous lack of clarity regarding both the path and fate of the revolution, as well as the future of the nation. This state of affairs certainly reflects the general impasse that has been the Syrian situation for about a year now—

but it also reflects the ineffectual role of cultural and political elites. Such criticism is quite justified, given the poor performance of politicians and intellectuals, and their constant quarrels and disputes. The present state of confusion and uncertainty about the future only substantiates a more 'action-oriented' trend: one that scorns intellect, politics, programmes, plans, politicians and intellectuals, and that would settle for a mixture of 'subsistence intellect' and pure action, both of which aim to alter reality through direct violence. This combination is exactly what Islamist hardliners possess. I speak of a 'subsistence intellect' because the extremists' version of Islam looks like a heap of practical prescriptions, with hardly any added intellectual value. As is well known, jihadist Islam is hostile even toward many aspects of Islamic cultural heritage.

Arabism pays the price incurred by its status as the official doctrine of the Syrian regime: Islam alone captivates those who have withdrawn their trust from the regime, from Arabs, and from the rest of the world. A placard seen in the town of Tafas in Daraa on Friday, 4 June 2012, read: 'To hell with all the Arabs, the Lord of the Worlds [Allah] is with us!' Arabs lampooning Arabs is nothing new, but doing so in a context based on the 'Lord of the Worlds' is novel indeed. Mind you, that Friday was entitled, 'He who equips a fighter for Allah is as if he fought himself'—a saying attributed to Prophet Muhammad, which appears to secure the link between religion and violence, i.e., jihad—while also seeking financial support from the wealthy inhabitants of the Gulf States.[3]

Syrian people shouted in anger and screamed in horror until they were blue in the face: 'Where are the Arabs? Where are the Muslims? Where is the world?' Eventually, large segments of the population came to distrust everyone: all political powers are inadequate, conspiring, or corrupt; all Arab and international parties are complicit or simply powerless. Similarly, the regime is an unprincipled, armed savage: the only way to confront its violence is through violence. Perhaps armed violence is not always in fact exercised, but belief in its necessity is now rampant.

Additionally, the mocking of all politics is now prevalent, a circumstance congenial to violent elements and, naturally, to dictators.

The ridicule of politics inevitably resulted in praise for arms. Toward the end of last year, 2011, a chant was heard from Hama: 'No peacefulness or baloney! Bang and boom is what is needed!' The same slogan was also seen on placards in Mount Zawiya, in the northern part of the country.

This tendency is expanding across large segments of the Syrian population, chiefly among Sunni Muslims. It grew from an insignificant constituency: it was not anyone's first choice and certainly no-one's basic ideological or political predilection.

Note, however, that I am not equating all armed resistance against the regime with nihilism. Indeed, the dominant form of violent resistance against the regime is not nihilistic: it is not linked to the systematic withdrawal of sense and value from the world; nor is it linked to any particular religious belief. Rather, it is defensive violence: one that is organized to a degree and guided in its general intellectual orientation by Syrian nationalism, even though most of its practitioners are thought to be believers. The Free Syrian Army is the loose framework for this kind of armed resistance. It is not a nihilistic organization, and does not resemble one in any way—not in its leadership, nor in its battalions and their current basic orientations. Moreover, I believe that recognition of the Free Army's legitimacy, along with efforts to organize it politically and ideologically, would make it a bulwark against increasingly belligerent, nihilistic tendencies and formations. Defensive resistance is being carried out today under great hardship. But if it stumbles, or if the Free Syrian Army disintegrates, the result will be a growing proclivity toward al-Qaeda and its fellow travellers. Nihilism does not flow from violent, organized resistance against a violent regime, but rather from the possibility that such resistance will fail.

4

Nihilist tendencies can comfortably coexist with religion, especially in their most extremist versions, which are most obstructive to normal life. A religiously-tinged form of nihilism is most likely to be found in a society that no longer trusts any available social mediations: politics, culture, laws and institutions, or the 'international community'. The repudiation of mediation in favour of abiding by God along with an insistence on the most literal interpretation of the divine word: radical Islams throughout the ages have borne these hallmarks. Wahhabism (which is a radical repudiation of all mediation—including customs, traditions, arts and all the different forms of religiosity that Muslims developed across generations and centuries), becomes increasingly attractive in proportion to a growing distrust in the surrounding world.[4] The Islamic concept of the infidel, *kufr* (which is easy to invoke in Islamic thought, especially within Salafist currents), offers a religious basis for the withdrawal of trust and values from the world, and provides it a deeply rooted Islamic, even cosmic support. Modern Islam (and, to a certain degree, Islam in general) is very susceptible to nihilism, having already internalized the notion of worldly negation, with the Muslim world having been introduced to 'modernity' from a passive and weak position.[5] From that time on—and even before—the Muslim world has tended to belittle the value of real, present-day life during times of constant change, instead favouring what is believed to be the fixed essence of Muslims, embodied in the strength and grandeur of past golden ages. Belittling the value of present-day reality typifies all nihilist movements.

I suggest that our Islamic nihilism be called the 'nihilism of an overabundance of meaning,' in contrast with the nihilism drawn from a scarcity of meaning in the world, from which contemporary European nihilism was apparently born. Our version, however, is ultimately more conducive to a complete disengagement between meaning and the world. This contemporary world is a *dunya*—the lower world—in contrast with the upper world or Heaven. For many of our fellow citizens, the immediate as well as international realities of Syria today cannot be coherently visualized, represented, or endowed with meaning. These realities are burdensome; consequently, moves to reject them, to justify their overthrow and act to destroy them, are logical and straightforward. Such a mindset is advantageous for power-hungry Islamic ideologues, who claim to monopolize meaning because they claim sole proprietorship over the correct definition of Islam and use it as a basis for their mandate to rule over contemporary society.

Our nihilism is nevertheless akin to every modern nihilism because it shares a common root: the fundamental meaninglessness of the world. While an Islamic ideology is characteristic of contemporary Arab nihilism, it exists alongside a tendency toward outright violence or 'terrorism' in a way that resembles Russian nihilism before the end of the nineteenth century.[6] In general, what distinguishes contemporary Islamists—I refer here to the devaluation of all contemporary cultural and political agencies, as well as the restriction of their actions to instrumentalities and procedures, all while ascribing meaning to 'Islam' alone—is actually an enduring aspect of the nihilistic view. God has become distant from the modern world and has abandoned its territories. But Islamic thought still has not seriously reckoned with this major historical process—the independence of the *dunya*. From this perspective, Islamists who, by definition, identify themselves with an 'Islam' that negates the world are generally inclined to violence, because violence is closely related to their method for stripping meaning from the world. Through violence they want to bring Him back, closer to the world, or to destroy a Godless world.

Because jihad brings together violence and religion, God and arms, and because Islam provides the intellectual basis for distrusting the world, Islamic nihilism is best represented by the jihadist movements. With its extreme withdrawal of meaning and value from the world (a world that is alien and marked by inveterate alterity, configured as a world of 'Jews' and 'crusaders,' or an age of corruption from which Salafism is distinguished and to which it is superior), al-Qaeda is the purest embodiment of jihad (i.e. Islam and war) as well as of Islamic nihilism.

For these reasons, the emerging nihilist tendencies in Syrian society play to the advantage of Islamist hardliners in general and Salafists in particular, but not to the advantage of the Muslim Brotherhood, who (like others) are mistrusted. In any case, the Muslim Brotherhood's denial of worldly mediation is much less radical than that of the Salafists and Wahhabis. Consequently, the Muslim Brotherhood could find itself in confrontation with the rising Syrian nihilism, and be targeted by it. Salafi-Jihadists are known to regard the Muslim Brotherhood as a secular movement.[7]

5

Rising nihilism has met with resistance in Syria. This new nihilistic tendency both contrasts with and is limited by the active, influential, and humanizing traditions of local society. Popular Islam, the basis for these traditions, is more widespread and more closely tied to people's lives and lived experience than the more austere and extreme forms of Islam.[8] Contrary to popular Islam, the latter have expansionist inclinations. They also rely on provoking a sense of guilt and religious delinquency among the faithful, undermining people's resistance to them and, ultimately, pushing them toward the nihilist orbit. Open to life and reconciled with the world, the traditions of local communities are those most exposed to disintegration in Syria today, as are the communities themselves.

Rising nihilistic tendencies have also been limited by the vitality of Syrian society and its dedication to protesting the regime in a variety of ways, primarily in a civil and peaceful manner. The general spirit of the Syrian revolution is open to the world and oriented toward liberation and dignity, and is in itself a warranty against nihilism, despite the likelihood that most Syrian revolutionaries are believers.[9] The opportunities for the expansion of nihilistic tendencies look set to remain limited as long as the revolution continues. Only the defeat of the revolution, including its military component represented by the Free Army, can lead to the predominance of Islamic nihilists.

The spirit of the revolution can accommodate and uphold a range of principles, including non-violence in general, non-violent Islamism, and secularist activism. All of these have something to contribute in opposing nihilism. The contribution of secularists to the Syrian revolution is both broad and crucial (in terms of its size and role) even though it has been affected by the dreadful disarray of the secular communities and the serious intellectual and moral deterioration of 'hard secularism' because of its association with the ruling regime, even prior to the revolution.[10]

Today, our nihilism remains shallow and reversible, so long as a *détente* is conceivable and so long as daily scenes of bloodshed decline. Yet if the three processes observed at the beginning of this article continue (i.e. the unrestrained violence of the regime, the inadequate performance of the opposition, and international indifference to the Syrian ordeal) any constraints on the rise of nihilism will grow increasingly weak, especially given the geographical and intellectual fragmentation of the revolution. If these constraints disintegrate, nihilism will become unstoppable.

6

One might ask: why speak of a militant nihilism instead of using the common concept of 'terrorism' or 'Islamic terrorism'?

The truth is, the Western handling of the concept of terrorism (both before and after 11 September 2001) has discredited it as a serious topic of discussion to a considerable degree, by means of two interrelated moves. First, the West denied that there might be reasons for terrorism: causal explanations were rejected, because they were taken as amounting to justifications or legitimizations. Consequently, terrorism had no rationale outside of the terrorists' own personal constitutions or their moral degeneracy. Such a view required no inquiry into the social and political roots or the international context of this fundamentally evil practice. The second, supplementary claim was for an intrinsic connection between terrorism and Islam, so that an unjustifiable terrorism simply issues involuntarily from the Islamic faith. The expression 'Islamic terrorism' is heard so often in the West that it is really just a matter of time until a rigid, permanent connection between the two constituent parts is formed in people's minds.

Such a formulation, premised on bigotry, does not permit an adequate understanding of this historical phenomenon—terrorism—which has been practiced in the West and by Westerners more than in any other place or in any other political-cultural context. Additionally, such premises are entirely unsuited to the task of effectively confronting nihilistic trends. If we are to develop effective policies to challenge terrorism, then an honest explanation of the basic phenomenon is essential. I suspect that the absence of such an explanation is symptomatic of the state of profound denial in mainstream Western thinking, and is part of an attempt to remain absolved of any possible responsibility for the current situation. When Arabs and Muslims highlight Western responsibility to restrict blame to the West, excluding all else, or to hide the domestic responsibilities of tyranny and corruption across Arab and Muslim territories, it does not change the fact that Western powers have been enormously destructive for the Arab and Muslim worlds. And while many topics along these lines are open for discussion, the fate of Palestine and its people continues to embody an enduring Western crime.

Sunni Islam has incurred the greatest burden as a result of the linkage of Islam and terrorism. It is the most common denomination among Arab Muslims: it has been historically hegemonic, and is identified with the history of Islam and its global spread more than any other Muslim group. At the same time it is Sunni organizations, especially al-Qaeda, that are the most prominent embodiments of Islamic nihilism and the Islamic rejection of the world.

If we work to rethink and clarify the concept of terrorism by using it to describe the practice of non-discriminatory, politically motivated violence, one driven in particular by a deep sense of injustice, discrimination, lack of support, hostility toward the world, and self-righteousness, then, and only then, would it be possible to speak of nihilistic or terrorist tendencies in Syria today. Seen against the backdrop of the regime's suppression of the revolution with unrestrained, terrorizing violence, the issue at hand is the arbitrary violence that is likely to increase. This violence is based on Islamic ideology, the sole credible reference point for a society that has lost faith in the contemporary powers that be, whether local or international.

By contrast, it is no mistake at all to describe the terror of the regime as nihilistic, or to say that the regime itself is the most nihilistic force in Syria—not because of its expanding use of indiscriminate violence against the civilian population across the country, but rather because of its siege mentality, based on a fundamental withdrawal of trust in the outside world. This withdrawal originated in the Baathist version of Arab nationalism, or what I have called 'Absolute Arabism'.[11]

Withdrawing from the world affords the regime the most psychologically and politically suitable environment for its sovereign legitimacy. If the world is wicked, the internal opponents must be double-agents working for nefarious global powers, and so it becomes a matter of public interest to rid society of internal enemies and isolate it from further, global contamination. Such isolation need not to apply to the country's rulers, however, because they are the incorruptible incarnations of pure patriotism.

The regime's nihilism shares with every nihilistic tendency a devaluation of immediate reality in favour of some momentous concept (like 'Arab identity') that is extraneous to the daily lives of the people. By such means, the ruling oligarchy aims to control popular opinion and isolate those who are ruled from the real conditions that shape their lives, and to deprive them of the ability to influence their circumstances in the process. In this the oligarchy has been successful, partly due to Syrian intellectuals' failure to publicly criticize the regime's essential philosophy through appealing to the material conditions of Syrians. Freedom cannot be based on an essentialized perception of the self, be it Arab, Islamic or anything else.[12]

The theatrical, debased nihilism of the regime nevertheless lacks an impassioned belief that the world, either as an international sphere or as a lived reality, is indeed degenerate, or that political opponents really are double agents, or that the governed society truly is bad or backward and intolerant (according to the unwritten doctrine of the Syrian intelligence services). None of these apparent judgments is based on a sincere belief: their sole value is functional, as strategies to aid governance. In this, the regime's nihilism is unlike contemporary Islamic nihilism or any of the historical currents of nihilism, whether practical (i.e. terrorist) or philosophical. Be that as it may, the content of the regime's nihilism is explicitly revealed in the chants of the regime's intelligence services and militias (the *shabiha*): 'Assad or no one!' or 'Assad or we burn the country!' The regime's terrorism is fascist and fundamentally reactionary; it is a pure expansion of the executions, annihilation, and destruction that it uses to preserve its grip on power. Practical nihilists—the Russians of more than a century ago and the Islamists of today—have a strong sense of the self-righteousness and justice of their cause; their beliefs are heartfelt, unlike the Assad family and regime.

7

The fact that there are reasons for terroristic resistance (i.e., militant nihilism) does not grant it legitimacy. Terrorism is indiscriminate violence: not only does it cause the loss of innocent lives, it also tends to spare those who may in fact be deserving of punishment or sanction on other grounds. Terrorism may or may not punish the guilty, but it necessarily hurts the innocent, owing to its arbitrariness. Therefore, terrorism possesses a criminal dimension, regardless of its reasons, motives, or justifications.

Furthermore, terrorism never achieves its stated goals. Never. In fact, it never has goals—contrary to the common Western understanding of terrorism, which defines terrorism as targeting of civilians for certain political ends. By its very nature, the practice of terrorism emanates from intense feelings of subjugation and denial of justice in the present world. Consequently, the 'goal' of terrorism collapses into the very act of rebellion against this condition and into the elimination of enemies without ever achieving anything greater, such as 'liberty, equality, and fraternity', or national independence, or ending poverty, or even punishing criminals among the rulers and their collaborators. There are no examples of liberation or achievement of any political goal by means of terrorism.

Were a nihilist organization to somehow come to power in a country, the result could only be brutal despotism. Not only are nihilist organizations accustomed to indiscriminate violence: their radical withdrawal from the world encourages the cultural and psychological conditions necessary for prohibiting dissent and uprooting any alternative or distinctive voices—as we have seen in North Korea, in Syria under Baathist rule, and in the Soviet Union and its successor states. These regimes have all embodied the degradation of revolutionary tendencies into terrorist rule during the twentieth century.

Islamic nihilism is oriented toward the establishment of terrorist rule of the greatest magnitude: a people-crushing machine that sacrifices human worth on the altar of an absolutist doctrine, and isolates people from the world. Afghanistan under Taliban rule was a perfect example of such a venture. The justification for the brutality of Islamic jihadists, in their own view, is the essential sameness of all finite means at their disposal in the face of their sublime infinite cause and its imperative, absolute necessity: applying the rule of God on earth. What is important is the absolute end, while the means are all relative instruments, none of which is more legitimate than another; no means are unthinkable so long as they serve the end, although the means with the quickest results are given preference. Absolute doctrines are quite compatible with theories of efficiency, and lean toward the application of pure force to change an unacceptable reality. Machiavellianism, in the conventional sense, is not a characteristic of unprincipled ideological and political groups, but it is precisely a characteristic of those groups that value abstract principles over human life, history, and actually existing society.

Jihadism constitutes a grave danger to Syrian national interests because it imposes a supranational structure centred on the imaginary concept of the 'Islamic Nation.' Jihadists have no qualms about demolishing the state, in Syria or elsewhere. They even see it as desirable.[13] Jihadists also seek to fan the flames of sectarian conflict whenever possible, and are hostile to culture, or any modern social and political organizations.

8

In the face of the regime's unrelenting fascistic terrorism, the likelihood of militant nihilism spreading in Syria has increased in tandem with the revolution's propensity to define itself in contrast to the enemy (i.e. the regime) and its fervour to dispose of its foe.

Militant nihilism will not prosper because of the revolution's alignment with a positive goal (i.e. a new free Syria) but rather in accordance with the extent to which the revolution has become desperate.[14]

We may try to rationalize its origins or explain it causally, but we cannot attribute positive outcomes to militant nihilism. This point contrasts with the dominant Western understanding, which attributes political goals to terrorism based on statements made by contemporary militant nihilists, while denying the validity of their cause. The opposite is in fact the case: terrorism may have reasonable causes, but it cannot possibly have reasonable ends. Terrorism demonstrates, but does not deliver.

Beyond soliciting support from heaven, another motivation for militant terrorism to anchor itself in Islam is the former's 'intransitivity,' by which I mean terrorism's demonstrative quality as well as its sterility, which is essentially an inability to deliver. 'Islam' provides terrorism with presumably loftier and more legitimate goals not just for the political struggle, but for human life itself. Under this pretext, contemporary Islamic nihilists are exempted from defining their specific goals because goals become impossible to conceive of within the desperate conditions that foster their militant nihilistic tendencies.

One should therefore object to militant nihilism in the context of the Syrian revolution, in the context of contemporary protests in the Muslim world, and in the Palestinian context. It does not achieve anything, but instead causes a lot of harm to each of these communities, and seldom brings the promised reckoning with its perceived enemies. It cannot bring justice.

In 'revolutionary' nihilism, then, there is a lot of nihilism and little revolution.[15] It affirms the murderous and destructive aspects of revolution to a degree that distorts its most vital aspects: those connected to the freedom of a tired people, and to their everyday lives.

9

I prefer using the concept of militant or even revolutionary nihilism, rather than the concept of terrorism, not only because of the Western distortion of the latter (where it has been used as a pretext for costly and aggressive policies in Afghanistan, Iraq, and, for much longer, in Palestine), but also because I want to underscore that there is no particularity to our contemporary terrorism. It is of a piece with perhaps the most legitimate political tendency in the modern world: the revolutionary tendency that regards the present social and political institutions as corrupt, unjust, and illiberal, and works to change them. However, this sort of revolutionary nihilism systematically failed to achieve its general goals, whether after the revolutions in France or Russia, in Palestine either between the 1960s and 1970s (when it was practiced on a nationalist and Marxist basis) or in the 1990s and 2000s (when terrorism was Islamized). Militant nihilism fails because of its enchantment with the essentialized and the abstract at the expense of reality, being, everyday life. Islamic nihilism, in particular, fails because it is attached to an idealized past and defends an imaginary Islamic essence, one in which the majority of Muslims would not recognize themselves.

Islam itself hardly privileges Islamic nihilism. The issue is not with a self-identified eternal Islam, but with a newly manufactured Islam that has been moulded in response to contemporary conditions and demands, in the same fashion as the major modern political ideologies (nationalism, and especially communism). This version of Islam is an ideologically driven attempt to deprive the world of meaning and values amid conditions that could justify such a deprivation—as during the Syrian Revolution. The more radical the deprivation, the more suitable this version of Islam becomes as a support—even though, in the process, Islam itself is restructured to become a justification for the withdrawal of trust and meaning from the world. Naturally, the more fundamental this withdrawal, the lower the chances are for post-revolutionary political development, and the greater the possibilities for terrorism. Both the French and Russian revolutions stand as testament to this.

In Islam itself, there is an easily-activated nihilist tendency based on three elements: the devaluation of the *dunya* (worldly life); the extreme centrality of 'oneness' at the expense of a diverse, plural world; and the centrality of the foundational era (the earliest periods in Islamic history) at the expense of subsequent history. The last element has been reinforced by historical developments and a (mainly Western) modernity that have both muddied the waters of Islam and made it an ideological source for opposition to the modern world.

However, from the beginnings of Islam onwards, one quality has limited any nihilist tendencies: namely, the reality of Islamic morality and its acceptance of the world. The world is the *dunya*, but it is not essentially corrupt; a true Muslim should not forget to partake in and enjoy his share of the *dunya*. These non-nihilistic predilections surface every time relations between Muslims and the contemporary world improve, and always in those circles that reap the benefits of an accommodation with the world as it is (the wealthy or upwardly mobile classes).

10

With respect to the Syrian context, I avoid the concept of terrorism for an obvious political reason: the regime has used this concept to stigmatize the revolution, thereby categorizing its confrontation with it in a global context that brings the regime closer to the rest of the world, especially to Western and Arab countries. This has been fundamental to the regime's characterization of its struggle today: 'These are mere terrorists, without legitimate grievances, without a cause,' accompanied by frequent references to al-Qaeda. Outright violence is the only way to deal with terrorists. It is no surprise that the regime conflates cause and effect, a practice of authoritarians everywhere.

I have additional reservations about using the concept of terrorism because it is a matter of a nihilist complex, comprised of three elements whose convergence is still limited and reversible, and of which violence is only one, as previously stated. In Syria, there have been operations that could be described as terrorist, but there were also strong, plausible suspicions about the regime's involvement in organizing them to look that way. While there is no doubt about the expansion of the use of violence by agents opposed to the regime, most of that violence is not nihilistic; it is instead defensive and deployed within the revolution, along with peaceful protest. Even up to the present, the violence that has been deployed is largely discriminate, directed against the regime and its apparatuses. There have been examples of unfocused, chaotic violence, unacceptable from the point of view of justice and human rights, which have prompted warnings both from international organizations and from voices inside Syria who have been observing and documenting. However, these violations remain limited in comparison with those committed by the regime, according to Amnesty International and the Independent International Commission of Inquiry on the Syrian Arab Republic at the General Assembly of the United Nations: they constitute a limited part of a social resistance movement that is fully legitimate, in both the political and ethical sense.[16]

Elements of the nihilist complex (withdrawal of trust, indiscriminate violence, and a neurotic, extremist Islamism) are nonetheless still capable of a more extensive convergence in accordance with the regime's terrorist violence and the persistence of the crisis—the social environments of the revolution are under brutal attack, and people are being killed daily, without any countervailing trends that might repair Syrians' trust in the world or open windows of hope for them. So far, social violence has remained disciplined by resistance to the regime, the guidance provided by the revolution's cause, by local communities, and by connection with other activities (demonstrations, self-defence, political opposition, relief activities, etc.). By contrast, the distinctive feature of terrorist violence is its increasing alienation from local communities as it becomes more rooted in its own ideology. Eventually, terrorism will end up fighting society itself, declaring opponents 'infidels', breaking with the cause of the revolution and working instead to subjugate it. There is preliminary evidence that religious groups appear to be more loyal to their ideology than to their ties to the revolution or to local communities. It has been reported that one of these groups, in Mount Zawiya, began to practice random kidnappings for ransom.[17]

It is also possible that there are jihadist groups similar to al-Qaeda acting in Syria, such as the al-Nusra Front, which announced its responsibility for operations in al-Maidan on 6 January 2012 (supposedly targeting a gathering of security officers), two explosions at the Air Force branch and the Criminal Security Directorate in Damascus on 23 February 2012, as well as the operation in Qazzaz in Damascus on 13 May 2012. That the regime's narrative has lost credibility does not justify denying the existence of this group, and Syria today offers an environment that is increasingly fertile for its growth. There is nothing to suggest that such a jihadist group is a fabrication by the regime.[18]

11

Some practical conclusions, to which I have already alluded, can be derived from this analysis.

One is that the longer the revolution and its violent confrontation with the regime persists, the more likely it is for nihilistic and extremist tendencies to proliferate and expand. This hardline, world-rejecting propensity is not an automatic result of an extremist gene in Islam; rather, it is a response of a brutalized society in the presence of an Islamic ideology that offers a justification for violence by elevating it to the status of 'jihad'.

Another is that the possibility for nihilism is a local Syrian product that is directly connected to the conditions of the revolution and the regime's handling of it. It is not an outbreak of an exotic virus of terrorism, as the regime would have it. The revolution's victory would reduce the chances for a convergence among the various nihilist elements, or would at least drive them in different directions—however, the prolonged brutalization of Syrian society increases the chances of convergence. If the regime were to regain control, it is likely that nihilist groups, most certainly with an Islamic ideology, would emerge from among the thousands (or even millions) of activist cadres involved in the revolution today.

Consequently, there is a general interest—Syrian, Arab, and global—in liberating Syrian society from its state of brutalization and stopping the activities of organized terrorism. If this had happened earlier, it would have been possible to stop further violence. However, if it is further delayed, the possibility of nihilist violence will separate entirely from the revolution and gain its own momentum, making it unlikely to disappear as a matter of course when the terrorist regime falls.

The Syrian opposition can play a role in reviving trust and resisting nihilism. This role does not necessarily require unity; instead, it requires avoiding meaningless disputes, repairing their tattered appearance and remedying poor performance, and achieving a degree of credibility and humility. The problem with the Syrian opposition is neither its deficiencies nor its divisiveness, but rather its failure to give an impression of seriousness and dedication. This does not inspire a sense of respect among the public.

International and Arab powers could also play an important part in reversing this nihilist trend in Syria by helping Syrians end Assad's terrorism. The form of this assistance could be negotiable. The problem today is not in the unwillingness of international powers to intervene militarily in Syria. Rather, the problem is this tendency to portray assistance as either direct military intervention or nothing. This is unreasonable, if not patently ridiculous, and it excuses international powers from helping in other, less costly ways. What is needed is a complete political boycott of the regime, and the imposition of an effective embargo that would guarantee cutting the supply of arms while directly helping Syrians overthrow the regime on their own. This is laborious, but is still easier and less costly than military intervention, and better suited to the interests of Syria and Syrians.

We live in an interrelated, universal world, which makes it impossible for the growth of nihilism in one country to remain contained within its borders, as we have seen in Afghanistan. Arab and international powers would therefore be doing themselves a favour by helping Syrians rid themselves of their nightmare once and for all. This does not in any way conflict with the idea of national self-interest, though it does require states to consider more inclusive and less parochial global and historical horizons.

But it is unlikely that we will see this sort of generosity in the near future. All states are selfish, the world order encouraging this vice to be regarded as the highest virtue. Yet it is clearly an unfair, imbalanced world from the perspective of the vulnerable and from the viewpoint of general human development.

It seems that nihilist groups, regardless of their ideologies but particularly including those active in terrorism, are the preferred partners for intelligence agencies across the world. On the one hand, security agencies rely upon violent nihilist groups to justify their actions, operations, and large budgets. This is true in dictatorships and democracies alike. Yet, these groups—from the Russian nihilists and the Red Brigades in Italy to the Abu Nidal Group and al-Qaeda—can always be easily infiltrated by intelligence agencies (including Syrian intelligence services), and redirected as seen fit. The attraction between these apparently opposite poles of the underworld requires an explanation. The pole represented by nihilist organizations is characterized by a complete renunciation of reality, coupled with a strong attachment to death and a fixation on a mysterious past or distant future; the pole represented by the intelligence agencies is one of extreme worldliness, materialism, and engagement with the present. Each have a constituent relation to violence. For al-Qaeda, several factors facilitate either entrapment within the orbit of the intelligence services or their actual penetration: their weak relationship to society, their hostility to normal life, their alienation from the world of work and production, and their parasitic nature.

Perhaps the various intelligence agencies (Arab, Western, Iranian, and Turkish) are also encountering a suitable environment for their work in the rising nihilism in Syria, using it as a means to settle old scores with their enemies.

12

Ultimately, the Syrian crisis exposes the shortcomings of the global system and all its deep contradictions. The major Western powers bear a significant share of responsibility for the suffering of the Syrian people because of their own violations of principles of justice in their support of an aggressive Israel, a country that has facilitated Syrians' disillusionment with the global order, as well as the disenchantment of wider circles of Arabs and Muslims, which in turn has reinforced the militarization of Syrian public life. The international system does not occupy a sufficiently elevated position with respect to morality and human rights from which to condemn the Syrian regime even-handedly. Granted, it is more equitable than the Syrian regime, but to describe it as less awful than a murderous regime—the worst in the world today, without equal—is a backhanded compliment.

I expect only more ineffectiveness from the international system, and more centralization around states' security policies, accompanied by a continuous structural deficit in confronting the Syrian issue. One must conclude from this the necessity of restructuring the international system in a more democratic and humane direction.

This may appear utopian rhetoric, but it is merely an attempt to address the issue at its roots.

7

'ASSAD OR NO ONE'

DAMASCUS, OCTOBER 2012

I am particularly fascinated by the slogan 'Assad or no one'. Its candour is as impressive as it is malicious. It is direct and simple, but it sums up the entire political philosophy of Assad's reign. It is a nihilistic yet existential slogan. Here, I reflect on this flamboyant mantra and the conditions under which it was implemented politically.

Until recently, the modern history of Syria hadn't witnessed a slogan as unique as 'Assad or no one!' or its twin, 'Assad or we burn the country!' (both versions rhyme in Arabic). It appeared not prior to but in the context of practice, from which it derived its power. It is a catchy slogan: shockingly honest, incredibly obscene, and strikingly extremist. It is a condensed expression of the 'theory' and practice of the Syrian regime. The spread of the rallying cry over the past eighteen months has been intriguing.

The theory of the Syrian regime assumes the existence of a territory named 'Assad's Syria', where the landlord (Assad) has free rein. He does not kill everyone, just enough people to keep everyone feeling unsafe. He does not jail everyone, just enough to haunt others with fear of detention. He does not torture everyone, just enough to frighten everyone else and keep them in check. He does not humiliate all Syrians, just enough (a bit more in this case) to induce the rest to keep their heads down. He does not corrupt everyone, just enough to implicate so many to the extent that corruption is seen as inescapable.

The owner of 'Assad's Syria' may accomplish the above because he possesses a specific tool called 'The State'. The State oversees murder, detention, torture, humiliation, corruption, and much more. It is also in charge of maintaining hegemony without necessarily affecting each and every Syrian individual. Murder, corruption, detention, and torture are all public practices that remind the ruled of the tools possessed by the landlord.

Another crucial task performed by the State apparatus is the endorsement of the landlord, the affirmation of his exceptional status and singularity. The fact that he is wise, a genius and a hero, identifies him with 'his' country. The legitimacy of the ruling landlord is based on his exceptional status: it is not based on any general rule that would position him alongside others, because he cannot be replaced by anyone else.

This exceptional authority only superficially resembles the charismatic authority discussed by Max Weber. We are not looking at someone with natural gifts or personal appeal tested prior to the seizure of power, but at the products of a post-takeover charisma industry maintained by the State apparatus through tireless coercion and indoctrination.

Not only is this legitimacy distinct from the bureaucratic, rational legitimacy of the modern state that Weber described, it is the complete opposite. The legitimacy of the regime is based on ingenuity, uniqueness, and exception. It is not based on the ordinary but on the extraordinary. It is not based on the law, but on breaking the law. It is not rooted in reason, but in miracles. It is an idiosyncratic legitimacy, closely tied to the ruling figure and to his physical integrity and particularity. Moreover, this legitimacy is an inherited obligation. Bashar's succession of his father—his extraordinary, exceptional, great father—was not just legal or expected, but was in fact the acceptance of an obligation, the standard expected by Syrian patriotism and for the safety of Syria. Before Assad became a name for the dynasty founded by Hafez and inherited by Bashar, and which will someday be conferred on Hafez Jr., it was the name of Syria itself and a token of the good fortune of his presidency.

Assad is the name of the regime. The regime is the 'homeland' of regime supporters, particularly of the sectarian security nucleus whose bonds with the regime surpass mere loyalty to resemble full symbiosis.

The predication of 'Syria' with 'Assad' in the phrase 'Assad's Syria' serves as a cover for the sectarian security nucleus, granting it a national character and, in the process, a rationale for expelling any potential dissidents. In 'Assad's Syria', to oppose the regime is to be a traitor because 'Assad's Syria' is the one and only existing Syria. That a Syria unquestionably existed before Hafez al-Assad seized power sheds light on the regime's propensity to mark the beginning of Syria's modern history by the 'Blessed Corrective Movement' and to omit everything that existed prior to that point, particularly pre-Baathist Syrian history. To acknowledge the existence of a pre-Baath and pre-Assad Syria perilously implies the potential for a post-Baath and post-Assad Syria. The solution is to deny the existence of Syria before Assad: that era was wild and obscure and does not deserve mention; those were the bad old days during which Syria was a primitive country wracked by chaos. Thus, according to the regime's media outlets, Hafez al-Assad is the 'builder of modern Syria.'

From this standpoint, the link between the general (Syria) and the particular (Assad) is neither historical nor contingent. It is necessary and rational. Breaking this link would be equivalent to destroying the homeland. A Syria that is not Assad's Syria simply does not exist. Therefore, 'Assad or no one' is not merely a warning or a prescriptive phrase. It is simply a statement of the fact that Syria and Assad are one. No Assad means no Syria. The two are symbiotic.

Yet behind the apparent clarity of the phrase 'Assad's Syria' is hidden the fact that Syria is the private property of a dynasty, and that, like any private property, it can be bequeathed. The phrase also obscures the fact that those who are close to the ruler's entourage (particularly his relatives) occupy special places in the Syria that he owns. 'Assad's Syria' is not a scheme to place obstacles in the way of tribe and sect, but rather a scheme to turn tribe and sect into the regime's hidden operating mechanisms, which are nevertheless visible for those who want to see.

If one speaks from a perspective that accepts an essential bond between Assad and Syria as a reality, then the conflict between 'Assad's Syria' and the revolution, with its promise of a different Syria, is an existential conflict. Such a perspective has been stated clearly and repeatedly by the regime. Consider, for example, the statements of Assad's foreign minister Walid al-Moualem in June 2012, when he declared there would be no negotiations before the full elimination of 'terrorists', by which he meant the Syrians who oppose the regime. Bashar al-Assad said much the same one month later: he linked the fate of the 'homeland' to that of his regime, which he predictably called 'the State.'

But neither al-Moualem (literally in Arabic, 'the teacher') nor his 'teacher' could possibly emulate the eloquence, concentration, and precision—the inimitability even—of 'Assad or no one!' or its twin, 'Assad or we burn the country!' The eloquence of both versions consists in the stark contrast with the mumbo-jumbo of the regime's spokespersons. The rhymed, catchy slogan grows even more distinctive because of its anonymity, which allows it to function like an adage that condenses a far-reaching and primitive—almost pre-historic—'authentic' experience. Indeed, it is a 'popular' slogan that one would not hear in the official media: it is the most conspicuous expression of identification with the regime, a distinctive characteristic of the *shabiha* phenomenon.

The primitive character of the *shabiha* phenomenon—in particular, its combination of violence, sectarianism, and hatred—is what can produce an existential, 'authentic' slogan of this kind. The *shabiha* are the regime's instincts, its political unconscious. They embody a sense of danger and the regime's survival reflex. They see the revolution as an existential threat and amplify that sense through this atavistic slogan. The unique character of the Syrian conflict today—the absolute and primitive nature of the regime's war against society—is in full accord with the primitive nature of the *shabiha* phenomenon.

The fundamentally nihilistic character of the slogan 'Assad or no one!' perfectly encapsulates the existential conflict between two Syrias. Here and now, the existential conflict as waged by the Assad regime is equivalent to a nihilistic conflict. It is a conflict in which an organism presumes that the opponent's life means its own death such that its existence requires the elimination of the opponent. It is a conflict that rejects politics in favour of war—not just any war, but an absolute war that aims not to change the behaviour of an opponent or to win concessions, but to wipe it out entirely. The regime has never made room for politics or negotiations, precisely because it has engaged in an existential war—i.e., a nihilistic war. The regime views the revolution as an enemy that must be exterminated. In principle, politics assumes that compromises are possible: it assumes that 'Assad' is not the 'One' against whom no one could stand, but that he is 'one' among many, and the representative of one party among others. But the slogan clearly says that there is no match for Assad, and therefore it is impossible for anyone to be his equal. Consequently, because Assad has been exposed to the challenge that we see today, the country has to be burnt so that it becomes ungovernable by anyone else. Nothing in the practice of the regime is inconsistent with this nihilistic outlook.

According to the regime, war is not a political tool or 'a continuation of politics by other means' as Clausewitz declared long ago. War is the regime's policy: the policy goals are to exterminate opponents politically and morally by denying that they have a public cause; to exterminate them physically by declaring that their annihilation is required. The violence of the Assad regime is structural because it stems from its formation, and violence is preferential—a first choice, not the last. Its violence is optional because the regime was not compelled to it, and it is pre-emptive—the regime was not attacked militarily by anyone. It undoubtedly stems from the relationship of identification and ownership between Syria and 'Assad'. Because the relationship between Syria and 'Assad' is held to be natural, it should not be surprising when its opponents are confronted with unlimited violence.

So is it possible for the Syrian revolution to face the absolute, existential-nihilistic war of Assad without itself acquiring a nihilistic outlook? The just cause of the Syrian armed resistance and its essentially defensive core still prevent the transformation of its existential struggle into a nihilistic conflict. But this has not prevented the emergence of nihilistic formations on the margins of the revolution, ones that view the conflict (they call it 'jihad') as an aim in itself: a political cause intolerant of negotiation, a historical procession to the Day of Judgement.

Here we refer to 'primitive' and 'authentic' formations similar to the *shabiha*, such as al-Qaeda, which one might describe as the 'instinct' of Islam, its political unconscious. It would be appropriate to describe members of al-Qaeda, which is both an organization and an ideology, as the *shabiha* of Islam who represent its absolute, world-rejecting, extremely zealous and nihilistic form. It is likely that the *shabiha* of Assad and of Islam have hidden links of which we know very little. But they clearly share both a violent, discriminatory nature—and a philosophy: 'It's us or nothingness!'

The *shabiha* is a fascist phenomenon that works hard to maintain its privilege. Al-Qaeda and the like are also fascist formations that could very easily transform into machines for annihilating human beings on a scale that could surpass even the Assad regime.

The revolution fights against both of these counter-revolutionary forces. Up until the time of writing, its constitution has guaranteed a counter-nihilistic outlook. In general, the revolution is popular and defensive: it is neither a quest for identity nor a doctrinal fury; it is not a call for utopia, nor is it an application of theory. The revolution is, above all, a defence of life: a realistic uprising of a realistic people.

8

AN IMAGE, TWO FLAGS, AND A BANNER

DOUMA, JULY 2013

From the outbreak of the Syrian revolution until close to the end of 2011, rebels waved the official Syrian flag. The flag consists of a horizontal red stripe on top; a white stripe with two green stars in the middle; and a black stripe at the bottom. This generally coincided with the phase of peaceful demonstrations and other protest activities by Syrians. The flag implied that the rebels were speaking for a Syria that had been seized by the regime, and that it was the symbol of a rising Syrian nation. By contrast, the images of Bashar and his father, which were fervently reviled by the rebels since the early stages of the revolution, were symbols of a privatized Syria, one that had been appropriated: 'Assad's Syria'. Raising the flag at a demonstration where the crowd chanted in favour of toppling the regime established a popular correspondence between this flag and 'the people' who have demands, and simultaneously served to disassociate the flag from the two presidential images and the 'regime' to be overthrown. During major demonstrations in Hama in July 2011, hundreds of thousands of demonstrators formed a human tapestry of the flag's three stripes and its two stars.

After this phase, the 'flag of independence' re-emerged, the official Syrian flag that was used from the late 1920s through the

Egyptian-Syrian Unity (1958–1961), and that was also the flag of 'the separatist period' (1961–1963). This flag was also used for some time at the beginning of the Baathist era (1963 onward). This flag is composed of a horizontal green stripe at the top; a white stripe with three red stars in the middle; and a black stripe at the bottom. In 2012, this flag became the symbol of the revolution and a sign of the deepening Syrian struggle. It indicated a will to bypass the Baathist chapter of Syria's history. The Syrian Revolution was dragging on in comparison to the Tunisian and Egyptian revolutions. The Libyan example, which was built on both military and symbolic ruptures with the regime, inspired broader sectors of Syrians to turn gradually to armed resistance.

In the summer of 2012, a black flag began to appear with remarkable frequency. It was emblazoned with words in white: 'There is no god but God, Muhammad is the messenger of God,' i.e. the Islamic *shahada* (declaration of faith). There were other variations, one of which had a white circle displaying the same *shahada* written in black. This is the flag of the Nusra Front, or rather its 'banner,' as those folks prefer to call it (a version that was later adopted by ISIS, while al-Nusra's banner became a black oblong that displays the *shahada* in black and, beneath it, the words 'al-Nusra Front'). The Nusra Front was formed in early 2012, and announced its affiliation with al-Qaeda in April 2013. (It pledged allegiance to Ayman al-Zawahiri in what could be interpreted as a struggle with Daesh for al-Qaeda legitimacy, so to speak). Variations of the black banner with the white *shahada* were also adopted by other Islamic groups, generally Salafist in orientation. Occasionally, these groups display a white flag with the *shahada* itself written in black, claiming that this was the Prophet Muhammad's banner during times of peace, whereas the black background is reserved for times of war. The banner used by Daesh is, supposedly, the prophet's seal.

Currently, in the summer of 2013, it seems that banners with this basic design, in all its variations, have spread across many anti-regime armed groups. I have often seen them in 'liberated zones' that I have visited or lived in for a while. It is also common to see them covering the rear windshield of a car, particularly the black banner with the *shahada* written in white.

While it may seem that the banner is therefore a symbol of a distinct and self-aware orientation that serves more or less as a partisan emblem of the Salafist movement, it is also an expression of a religious freedom that was laboriously reclaimed, and is a challenge to a regime that has aggressively suppressed all public expression of religion.

The green flag of the revolution continues to be raised in demonstrations today, but the black flag has become ubiquitous. For example, activists in Douma have remarked upon the tension between the flag and the banner. It is widely known that the green flag symbolizes the revolution and its civil component, including the 'Free Syrian Army,' while the black banner and its variants symbolize the rising Salafist currents, the armed groups associated with them, and a general religiosity that has been strenuously reclaimed.

Each of these three flags symbolizes a distinct version of Syria. The first, the red-striped flag, is that of the 'Syrian Arab Republic'. This flag appeared during the period when Syria itself was deteriorating amid the exhausting experience of unity with Egypt, before it fell under Baath Party rule and then eventually under the control of Assad—a frightful and irrecoverable fall. The 'second' Syria, with its green top-striped flag, represents the Syrian revolution with both its civil and armed components, as well as its aspirations toward social and political inclusion. The 'third' Syria is the Islamic Syria—namely, a Sunni and Salafist

Syria—and it has emerged in a remarkably intrusive manner, more than two years now into the revolution.

But there is a fourth Syria as well, to which I have already alluded. This fourth Syria is represented by the image of Bashar al-Assad, and by the images and statues of his father Hafez before him. Hardly anyone outside Syria realizes that Hafez al-Assad's image became the real symbol of the country only a few years into his rule. It was everywhere: printed on school books, notebooks, and pupils' folders; on the largest Syrian coin (25 pounds) and the largest banknote (1000 pounds). Hafez's image was carried high during 'spontaneous popular marches' and throughout a calendar cycle marked by many 'national occasions'. It appeared on the front pages of newspapers and on television screens every day. This tradition eased slightly in the months just after Bashar al-Assad inherited the presidency, but then it came back, hesitantly at first and then brazenly: Bashar appeared in the company of his father, his late brother Basil and his brother Maher, sometimes alongside pictures of Hassan Nasrallah and the Iranian President, and even with his young son, Hafez Jr.

Because they were known as symbols of 'Assad's Syria', these images were explicitly loathed by Syrians, who boldly crushed and trampled them in public as a way of declaring a rupture with the Syria that had been appropriated by Assad.

During the years of Hafez's presidency as well as those of his son, most people didn't know the colours of the national flag. That changed when they entered the flag-conflict phase of the revolution. But before that, it wasn't customary for Syrians to display the national flag in their homes, cars, or offices. In addition, the flag of the Baath Party competed for attention in schools, the military, and official government departments. That flag was also composed of three bars: black on top; white in the middle; green at the bottom, with a red triangle on the flagpole side that pointed to the centre of the white stripe. The Baathist flag weakened the distinction of the official national flag, diluting its presence.

During the years of Bashar's rule the national flag underwent two waves of opportunistic rehabilitation. The first was in 2005, following the forced withdrawal of Syrian forces from Lebanon. The regime wanted to rally the public against a segment of the Lebanese population, which had rebelled against the Syrian regime's intervention and hegemony in Lebanon. At the time, the regime launched a campaign that encouraged people to display the national flag on the balconies of their homes. The red-striped flag was then put aside for several years before rising again in the context of the 'spontaneous demonstrations' that were organized by the regime for its loyalists during the first year of the revolution. For example, a flag many miles long was unfurled in a 'popular march' along Mezzeh Highway in Damascus in late 2011. The likely purpose of these antics was to broaden public identification with the regime: those who identify with the image of Bashar are the people of 'Assad's Syria', and not the general Syrian population. It was ill-advised to display the image in marches that were meant to unite; displaying the national flag was a tactic aimed at addressing a wider audience.

However, images of Bashar were never absent from those marches. The regime's bet was to unite the presidential image and the flag, to underscore that Syria is indeed 'Assad's Syria', and that real Syrians are pro-Assad. This symbolic equivalence informed the printed images of Bashar that were brandished and the flags that were unfurled in 'popular processions.' It says something about the deeply colonial instincts of the regime, and about how unattainable they thought a separation between 'Assad's Syria' and the 'Syrian Arab Republic' or between the 'regime' and the 'state' to be.

Therefore, we have four Syrias, with four symbols:

First, there is 'Assad's Syria', whose symbol is Assad's image. Its proponents are the regime's sectarian inner circle, as well as a group of diverse beneficiaries within the army, the government, the Baath Party, and moneyed circles, all of whom identify with the regime.

Second is the 'Syrian Arab Republic', symbolized by the red flag (with the red stripe on top). This represents a wider, pan-denominational Syrian population drawn from a newly-formed, educated urban middle class, alongside intellectuals and activists from those circles, many of whom are self-identified oppositionists. However, this group lacks an independent political will, something reflected in the acquiescence of the 'Syrian Arab Republic' to 'Assad's Syria.'

Insurgent Syria is symbolized by the flag with the green stripe on top. This green flag appears to represent a broad but socially differentiated audience: many come from deteriorating cities and towns, among people who have generally lower incomes and levels of education; alongside them are a well-educated, independent segment of the middle class and a diverse group of intellectuals and political activists whose views have not been shaped exclusively by apparent social inevitabilities. The spectrum of people identifying with this flag is among the most radical in their opposition to the regime. It includes some who are keen to highlight an Islamic dimension to their opposition by adding the phrase *Allahu Akbar* (God is great) to the white stripe in the middle of the green flag.

This 'green' party of Syrians is the most diverse in social, cultural, and political terms. There is a secular division that includes some of the most prominent intellectuals and activists in Syria, alongside an Islamic component comprised of liberal Islamists and the Muslim Brotherhood movement, as well as a broad sub-spectrum of independents. The 'green' party also includes much of the 'Free Army', particularly its senior and less Islamized formations. In general, one might say that 'green' is a fragmented Syrian domain without a single centre of gravity. The political and military institutions that have ventured to represent the 'green' party have been clearly unstable and at a high risk of severe disputes that undermine their legitimacy from within. In terms of turmoil, instability, and intensity, its situation is reminiscent of pre-Baath and pre-Assad Syria.

The counterpoint of insurgent Syria is 'Assad's Syria' with its images and statues, and not the 'Syrian Arab Republic'. The red flag has not been subject to any reported desecration from the side of the 'green party.'

Finally, we have a Salafist, Sunni, Islamist Syria, which is symbolized by the black banner. This Syria is mostly rural. It is likely comprised of two distinct branches: chieftains who belong to cross-border religious networks (from Saudi Arabia and the Gulf in particular), and an impoverished majority that is attracted to the simplicity of the Salafist doctrine and the availability of discipline, particularly with respect to their immediate environments and among their groups of fighters. The 'other' that its black banner opposes is the green flag of the revolution: the black banner differentiates itself from, and defines itself against, this (especially with regards to the organized component of the movement, the Salafi jihadists). The red flag and the images of the Assads are also implicitly separated from it. On more than one occasion, the (black) banner brought down the (green) flag and replaced it: the incident at Al-Halawaniy in Aleppo on 6 June 2013 is an example.

These identifications are each relational and dynamic, rather than indicating attachments to fixed identities. A broad segment of those who associate themselves with the 'Syrian Arab Republic', will identify with 'Assad's Syria' if the presumed alternative is the 'black' banner and the Salafist dominance for which it stands. Conversely, the 'Syrian Arab Republic' demographic could come closer to those siding with the revolution: the red flag might draw near its green counterpart and move away from those who worship the Assadists and their images, provided that the black banner is banished from the revolution. Assuming the regime, or 'Assad's Syria', falls at some point, most who follow the red flag would turn to the green. Today, over two years into the revolution, there are signs that the black banner is in ascendance. There are also signs of confusion about this ascendance in the green flag's camp, especially in the context of the continuous aggression represented by the presidential image camp: it is too much for the green campers to confront the image camp and the black camp banner at the same time.

Winning the struggle against 'Assad's Syria' is likely to reveal more cleavages amongst those who follow the black banner as well, separating the rigid jihadist and Salafist groups from those whom we might categorize as occupying a 'grey zone', as well as those who take the black banner as a representation of a general Islamic identity and a regained religiosity. The only thing that obscures such distinctions today is the regime's war against all insurgent parties. To choose a white flag with 'The Banner of Ahrar al-Sham Military Brigades' written across in black font implies a desire to separate from al-Qaeda. So does writing 'The Banner of Ahrar al-Sham Movement' in green on a white background.

In general, I think that the Salafist current is more complicated than it appears to be: its growing prevalence and broad influence remain highly ambiguous. This is one of the biggest questions that confronts the Syrian revolution: solving this riddle is incontestably a top priority.

In passing, let me point to a distinction between Salafist jihadists, such as the Nusra Front and ISIS, and Salafists who talk about jihad, such as Liwa'a al-Islam (Islam Brigade—which changed its name to the 'Army of Islam' in the autumn of 2013) and other, similar groups. For the latter, the link between Salafism and jihad is less essential because these groups are comprised of local Syrians, albeit with foreign ideological and political connections. The former—the Salafist jihadist groups—are Islamist Internationalists, both in terms of organization and political vision.

To conclude this section, I must note that the symbolic/sociological juxtapositions explained above are not only schematic and approximate, but are also mobile and flexible, like all that is social. One can always find new indicators rebutting the trends we have discussed.

* * *

'Assad's Syria' reduced the Syrian Arab Republic to a hollow shell, elevating the presidential image to a supreme position and setting aside the national flag in the process. Today, the black banner is attempting to attain a similar position within the ongoing, wider socio-historical movement. It is trying to claim sovereignty by replacing the flag of the revolution.

The rebels raised the flag of the Syrian Arab Republic in 2011 and banished the presidential image of Assad, before the green flag supplanted those of the SAR and 'Assad's Syria'. This gesture indicated a radicalization and an increased psychological rigidity among the rebels. At the time, the movement was linked to significant political and social phenomena, some of which coincided with a complete departure from direct participation in the revolution by 'civil society', referring in this case to a diverse spectrum of intellectuals and middle-class activists. Most members of this current either emigrated, sought asylum abroad, or declared themselves loyal to formations that were closer to the regime than to the opposition: they began to identify with the red flag. Moreover, since 2011, many initiators of the revolution and civil society activists have been detained or assassinated, while armed resistance has been emphatically on the rise, with militants being recruited from the most disadvantaged ranks of society. A range of outside 'sponsors', mainly from the Gulf States, have also found their way to the revolution: they combine Salafist religiosity and wealth, and have used their rentier money to corrupt as many as possible.

All these factors should be considered against the backdrop of 'Assad's Syria' and its expanding war against insurgent Syria, the heightened intensity of the Syrian struggle, and the deadlock at which peaceful protests arrived after the regime's military occupation of Hama and Deir ez-Zour in August 2011.

It is not clear who prompted the adoption of the green flag of the revolution (also known as the independence flag), nor is it clear when it made its first appearance (though it is possible that this was during an early conference held by the Syrian opposition in Antalya, Turkey, in June 2011). But the process by which it gradually superseded the red flag reflected, on the one hand, the real psychological and social entrenchment of the revolution and, on the other, a return to the icons of a previous historical era in a manner not unlike other revolutions. The re-emergence of the green flag today indicates a diverse and more desirable image of Syria, one with more freedom and, undoubtedly, more political vibrancy.

At the opposite end, the Islamic banner seems to clash with images of the Assads and their deeply sectarian allies who, unlike the Salafists, conceal their sectarian character. But, from the revolutionary viewpoint, the black banner has the same alienating effect as the presidential image: both are united by their exclusion of dissent.

In both cases, we are confronted with a privatized Syria that would impose itself on a more public Syria: 'Assad's Syria' on the Syrian Arab Republic; a Salafist Syria on a rebellious Syria fighting against tyranny.

Nothing reveals these shared exclusionary and authoritarian structures more than the fact that Assadist slogans have been modified and turned into Islamic ones in many areas. For example, a new chant filled the air in early 2012: 'Our Leader Forever/ Prophet Muhammad!' This is a cheap alteration of an Assadist slogan that circulated after the 1982 Hama massacre: 'Our Leader Forever/the Faithful Hafez al-Assad!' I have seen other examples written on walls around Eastern Ghouta. One was a 'corrected', albeit poorly-spelled, version of 'al-Assad or No One!' that turned it into 'al-Aslam or No One!' Apparently, the graffiti was converted by adjusting the letters of 'al-Asad' but it was done in such a sloppy way that it read 'al-Aslam' instead of 'al-Islam'. Another Assadist slogan, 'al-Assad or We Burn the country!' became 'al-Aslam or We Burn the country!'; 'al-Assad's Men Were Here!' turned into 'al-Aslam's Men Were Here!'; 'Long Live al-Assad!' became 'Long Live al-Aslam!'; 'al-Assad Forever' became 'al-Aslam Forever!' I also once watched a video of the commander of a Salafist military formation, Zahran Alloush, in which he said, among other things: 'al-Islam or No One!'

These alterations speak not only to a lack of imagination, but also to a desire for absolute power in their haste to degrade the revolution and replace 'Assad' with 'Aslam,' i.e. one Syrian minority with another minority. The so-called 'Aslam' that this current is so eager to see replace Assad is in fact the rule of a specific Islamic current, which is one part of Islamism, which is one part of Sunni Islam, which represents a (big) portion of Syrians.

Extremism (*tatarruf*, in Arabic) stems from this social aspiration of one party (*taraf*, in Arabic) to occupy the place of everyone else (*atraf*, which is the plural of *taraf*). Assadists are but one small party imposing itself upon the public sphere. Likewise, 'Aslamists' are one small party aspiring to control the same. I think 'Aslamists' is an appropriate label for this current, both because the term allows for a distinction to be made within diverse Islamist groups and also because it links this current to the political and intellectual extremism and sectarian structure of the Assadists. Aslamists are those Islamists who desire Assadist power for themselves.

On a few walls I saw a poster that struck me as another example of the similarities linking these two formations. The poster said: 'One Nation, One Banner, One Country.' The black banner with the *shahada* in white appeared above it. The slogan itself is reminiscent the Baath party's 'One Arab Nation.' Above all, the poster's insistence on the kind of 'oneness' marked by the banner negated the revolution's green flag.

It is well known that the leaders of these two extremes, the Assadists and the 'Aslamists', have strong ties in foreign political quarters: the Assadists are part of a regional sectarian axis led by Iran that also includes Hezbollah and Iraqi and Yemeni Shiite groups, among others; the 'Aslamists' are either linked to a Saudi-Gulf axis or to the global jihadist movement. In both cases, we are confronted with exceedingly tyrannical, foreign-affiliated and unpatriotic sectarian forces.

But structural symmetry is not proof of equivalent responsibility. Symmetry is not a good guide for better policy, but is rather a significant intellectual and moral indicator. In reality, we have an aggressor and a victim: an actor and those who are acted upon; a strong party and a weak one. In fact, to treat the two sides as somehow equivalent only serves to support the powerful initiator of aggression—the Assad regime and its allies.

At the same time, we now have a victimized party that acts dictatorially, absolutely, and narcissistically, and that contributes to the weakening of the rebellious social spectrum from which it emerged, which is a spectrum that struggles to resists an aggressor far stronger than itself. This Salafi party and its leaders bear political and moral responsibility for many of the internal and external difficulties that the Syrian Revolution faces today.

Nevertheless, it is important to recognize the high degree of fluidity among the 'Aslamists' themselves (and the revolution as a whole). Many fighters are leaving Salafist military formations for 'normal' ones or vice versa in a continuous dynamic. It is likely that we would see many 'Aslamists' deserting their current positions and moving toward more moderate ones if the regime were to fall. This is indeed what many are saying in East Ghouta.

While this social fluidity contrasts sharply with the cohesive, resilient, and determined regional Assadist camp, the implementation of social policies that address the needs of the less-advantaged segments of society has the potential to re-involve the 'Aslamist' elements in national life and to strengthen their connections to the Syrian body politic. The ascendant Salafist current of 'Aslamism' draws its strength from the widespread marginalization that plagued many Syrian towns, cities, and neighbourhoods over the last twenty-five years. It is a type of 'informal' religiosity, so to speak, prevalent in environments in which other possibilities for organization are denied and in which people do not participate in the general life of the nation, leaving them feeling alienated and disenfranchised in their own home. The black banner, with its sacred verse displayed in white, is compatible with the simplified worldview of a socially enraged and deprived demographic that lacks any positive ties to Syrian territory and society and which has found an alternative homeland in 'Islam'. The black-and-white worldview is well suited to the aspirations of demagogic and power-hungry political and religious leaders. But it is also closely related to the abject living conditions of marginalized sectors of society.

* * *

The socio-symbolic approach adopted here could be useful in charting the best way out of the Syrian war which, two years and four months into the revolution, has progressed beyond the danger of merely tearing society apart to a complete collapse of society, state, and nation.

If we assume that extremism indeed feeds extremism, then it is essential to stop the growth of extremist currents within the revolution. Stopping this growth requires disposing of extremism's main generators—the Assad regime, 'Assad's Syria' and, of course, Assad himself. The national treason of Bashar al-Assad has been carved in stone. He has forfeited the homeland of Syrians to an ambitious foreign force—Iran—which is indifferent towards the fate of the majority of Syrians and has played a disruptive role at the regional level. Assad has torn Syrians apart on sectarian bases. He has discriminated among them in an obscene manner. He has killed about 100,000 Syrians and has 'invited' sectarian foreign mercenaries to murder still more of his rebellious people. He has not protected the country's independence, nor has he been a faithful guardian of the unity of Syrians.

What is certain is that more of Assad means more Aslamism. More of Assad means more nihilism that has to be combated, more Nusra Front, ISIS, and their ilk, and more invalidation of the political and moral bases from which one can oppose them.

Toppling Assad, his 'state', and his images would generate the space for moderate dynamics across Syrian society. It would put the national and social forces which identify with the green flag in a better position to win the battle against the black-banner extremists, and it would also speak to segments of the national populace who identify with the red flag of the 'Syrian Arab Republic'. What I mean by 'nationalism' here is a concern with the social, political, cultural and economic framework of Syria, one that gives priority to Syrian internal interactions over and above interactions with any outside parties, and one that prioritizes Syrian obligations relative to any other ones.

Today, everything is conspiring in favour of the black banner or the 'Aslamists' placing moderates and Syrian nationalists in progressively weaker positions, especially given the fascism of the regime and its allies. Supporters of the green flag feel left to their own devices. The regime has not only used fighter jets and long-range missiles against them but also chemical weapons, and it has morphed the Syrian struggle into a sectarian, regional war on Syrian soil. (Note: My reference to chemical weapons here illustrates the many tactical uses to which the regime has put them. I personally witnessed two attacks in April and June of 2013 in East Ghouta, before the chemical massacre in August 2013 that took place after this article was written).

The socio-symbolic approach I have developed in this essay endorses the general political vision of the revolution and also addresses sectors of Baathist Syrian society that are attached to 'modern' lifestyles and social roles. One must defend those lifestyles and roles because they provide an area for convergence within Syrian society, one that has been part of Syria's short history dating from the end of the First World War. I refer specifically to 'social liberties', such as freedoms with regard to food and diet, drinking, fashion, and mixing of the sexes in public and semi-public spaces; necessities in any country today. It is inconceivable to suppose that political freedoms can thrive when social liberties are threatened.

This vision would turn the page on Assad's Baathist rule while maintaining the social implications associated with the Syrian Arab Republic. More specifically, I have in mind four levels on which this would play out. First, the introduction of marginalized Syrian segments into public life in the 1960s was not a process limited to Alawites, since it also included large populations of Syrians in the countryside. A corresponding logic today would favour protests against Assad's Sultanic regime and the reintegration of rural and semi-urban areas marginalized by the regime's neo-liberal economic policies. A second level involves expanding the broader social operations of the state in the areas of education, medical care, major utilities, and national resources, since these functions will soon all be in dire straits. Third, 'social liberties' as defined above are strong candidates for serving as the cornerstones of the concept of freedom in Syria, just as they are always the cornerstones of any concept of freedom in Muslim countries. The forth level relates to Syria's ties across the Arab world, especially with Palestine and Lebanon, since severing or weakening these ties cannot have progressive implications.

Bashar al-Assad's regime has virtually eliminated the social functions of the state. His economic policies have accelerated the marginalization of rural areas, which eventually led to their deterioration.

Moreover, his regime has made Syria into an appendage of Iran and its imperial project. The regime of Assad père ended the republic by instituting inherited rule, transforming a public Syria into a sectarian, clannish and personalized centre of power. Before the two Assads, there was Baathist rule and the rise of Pan-Arabism during the 1950s and 1960s, which resulted in the Kurdish alienation without solving any Arab issues, creating a major national division that will accompany us for decades.

Just as the Baathist version of Arab nationalism destroyed the emancipatory ethos of pan-Arabism, so its more modernist, Assadist version destroyed the spirit of social liberties by associating them with tyranny and the marginalization of the social majority. This resulted in a confused situation in which those liberties became objects of social dispute instead of features defining a shared public space. From this follows the imperative that the explicit defence of social liberties should always be accompanied by a genuine struggle to end the marginalization and alienation of large sectors of Syrian society.

The 'Syrian Arab Republic' is a chapter in the country's history; a layer in the composition of Syria and its populace. While it is imperative to move past it politically, past its Baathists and Assads, we must nonetheless safeguard what is national and public within it (i.e., the four levels outlined above) after we have rooted out its privatized ideological and political formulations.

The new Syria is capable of being—and should be—the product of an historic compromise between the green and red flags to the exclusion of Assadist imagery and the black Aslamist banner. A new Syria cannot be widely acceptable based on either of these proprietary symbols.

* * *

The first step toward such an historic settlement, which would also mark the threshold to a comprehensive peace in Syria, is to get rid of a regime that was never a faithful guardian of Syria; a regime that betrayed Syria for the benefit of the Assad dynasty and foreign interests.

9

THE DESTINY OF THE SYRIAN REVOLUTION

RAQQA, SEPTEMBER 2013

Today, Syria faces grave dangers: disintegration, collapse, and dissolution as a geographical unit, as a state, and as a community. This article investigates the immediate origins of this situation.

The most conspicuous feature of the current situation is the shift in the status of 'Assad's Syria', which had been an overarching framework but is now just one among four or five Syrias that are moving towards either divergence and conflict, or hostile coexistence.

Competitors now rival Assad's kingdom for the representation of public Syria. First, there is 'insurgent Syria': two and a half years into the revolution, it is now scattered and weak, a situation evident in its political expressions, its military splits, and its level of self-awareness. Second, there is Salafist Syria, which has strangely mushroomed for over a year now. Salafist Syria is comprised of two main sub-divisions: the al-Nusra Front and Daesh (ISIS) Then there is Kurdish Syria: Rojava, or 'Western Kurdistan', as it is called by the Kurdish Democratic Union Party (PYD) and many Kurdish activists.

Each of these Syrias seems fairly mutilated politically, controlled by warlords or armed feudal masters who do not consult the population about their preferred form of government.

Today, 'Assad's Syria' is merely the instigating force for a general dynamic of disintegration and destruction, and the distortion of the idea of one inclusive Syria. The situation is similar to the way Israel has behaved so far with respect to Palestine. A monopoly on air power and advanced weapons is deeply Israeli, as is the monopoly on weapons of mass destruction, coupled with a portrayal of itself as a bulwark against extremism and terrorism.

The Syrian Trinity

Although it resembles other middle-income Arab countries, Syria is distinguished by three traits.

First, there has been a regression toward dynastic rule under the Assad family, which has made hereditary rule the basis of the regime's legal substructure or its 'true' constitution—albeit an implicit, unwritten one. The official name of Syria remains the 'Syrian Arab Republic'. No official from the regime ever announced that Syria had become a private monarchy, the Assad Kingdom. Likewise, no 'rational' ideas have been proffered to justify or legitimize this state of affairs, despite its being the most significant political transformation in the country's history since its inception. It remains a muffled reality, repressed and not discussed. Most Syrian intellectuals acquiesced to this open secret out of fear, though some colluded with it for reasons of personal interest. Both locally and globally, however, everyone is missing the fact that the Assad regime is not a dictatorship in the way that the pre-revolutionary Tunisian regime of Zine el-Abidine Ben Ali and the Egyptian regime of Hosni Mubarak were. Rather, the Assad regime is predicated on political enslavement overseen by a young, ferocious dynasty with a disgraceful record of murdering Syrians on a massive scale, as well as killing

Palestinians and Lebanese, and, indirectly, Iraqis. Instead of functioning as administrators of the state, the Assad dynasty behaves as if Syria were its private property. A better comparison, then, might be the absolute monarchies of the Arab Gulf. But at least these monarchies arose simultaneously with their countries and have declared their royal status openly—quite unlike Syria, which is ostensibly a republic but secretly a monarchy.

The second distinguishing characteristic is the transformation of sectarianism into an essential tool of governance. From the early stages of Hafez al-Assad's rule, the regime has been and remains heavily dependent on kinship in order to maintain its power. The extensive reproduction and reinforcement of inherited social divisions has always served the regime's interests. The regime's reliance on division as an instrument of power has kindled sectarian responses across Syrian society. Now, four decades later, the combined history of such strategies has created real obstacles to a general Syrian rapprochement and to the ability to fashion an inclusive Syrian nation. Additionally, the regime's reliance on division has provoked an outpouring of resentful emotions, which are a source of fascist violence today.[1]

Above all, this sectarianism has distorted politics and rationality in ways that have precluded any possibility of public discussion of societal affairs. Such discussions have been impossible not only because initiators or participants run a 'security risk', but also because segments of the population who are the presumed voices of reason (intellectuals and political activists) have made the fact of the suppression of such discussions into the only focus of their public activities and patriotic emotions. By limiting their focus in this way, they protected the sectarian taboo both directly and indirectly. The explanation for this is ultimately rooted in the formation of Baathist Syria and its political and cultural elites, which I will not scrutinize here. But this reality has deprived Syrians of the experience of using their reason and refining their arguments in the context of public debate on issues of common interest, which has contributed to transforming sectarianism into a shapeless ghost that haunts society, politics, and culture. Public debate would have allowed for sectarianism to be defined, examined, and critically assessed, and would have made it possible for society to overcome and free itself from it.

Thirdly, once Bashar took office, Syria was introduced to a form of economic liberalization, one usually referred to as 'crony capitalism'. While there is nothing necessarily extraordinary about this transformation, in our country the process reflected a Syrian peculiarity. Liberalization is spoken about only in economic terms, whereas there is a deafening silence about its political roots, as if it happens in a political vacuum and as if politics is a trivial matter. At the same time, the traditional political opposition in Syria has been constantly preoccupied with the political system. They have paid little attention to economic transformations. As a result, the traditional political opposition has not developed a thorough understanding of the regime's new centres of gravity: wealth and extraordinary privilege, along with political domination and the security apparatus. Today, the regime is a security-political-financial complex.

The liberal transformation legitimized a de facto metamorphosis that allowed the 'third Baathist generation' or the 'sons of the big officials' (as we call them in Syria) along with their cronies to move to the forefront of a new bourgeoisie, while descendants of the old bourgeoisie were relegated to subsidiary positions.[2] The formation of this new class is the outcome of nearly half a century of Baathist 'socialist' rule. The new bourgeoisie cannot break its ties with the 'state' because of the conditions under which the class was formed, and also because of the origins of its wealth. Consequently, this new class has no liberal or democratic potential. During the revolution, fascist tyranny emerged as a key trait of the Syrian regime, and on a level that remains unmatched except by the Gaddafi family's tyranny in Libya. This fascism is a political strategy above all, one adopted in defence of the extraordinary and unreasonable privileges that developed and were consolidated during the last two decades of the rule of Hafez al-Assad.

The tripartite schema outlined above suffices to show that we are nothing like a nation-state whose leading elite might move forward by coercing a 'backward' and divided society for the sake of unifying it, as some would have it; nor are we socially, economically, or culturally like a nation-state.

When we talk about dynastic rule, we indicate a regression to a pre- or sub-nation-state that is far apart from the world comprised of 'the people' and 'citizens'. Dynastic rule is the antithesis of political modernity, in which the state, political parties, intellectuals, and citizens are effective public agents. We still have a state, political parties, intellectuals, and the remnants of action ideologies (as opposed to identity ideologies), but each one of these operates in a context of increasing fragmentation and decline shot through by patron-client relations. Consequently, any of these variables are stripped of their emancipatory potential.

The basic outcome of this mutually reinforcing tripartite schema (hereditary dynastic rule/sectarianism/crony capitalism) is the collapse of the nation as a framework for social and political life, thought, and identification. What we have instead is mixed and muddled: marginalized and oppressed groups have no tools of control or influence, while 'elites' prefer to take advantage of the existing situation instead of listening to objections that might prove very costly for them.

The country breaks down, the regime continues, and the revolution stumbles

What happened in the revolution? How did the collapse of the national framework end up turning Syria into a contorted, divided country, with a population that has no control over its fate?

Four significant shifts took place in the summer of 2012, near the middle of the Syrian revolution's timeline so far. The confluence of these four, ever-expanding, has particular explanatory value concerning what was to follow.

First are the cumulative effects of incredible violence: war, arrests, torture, siege, and starvation; all signs of intense hatred and contempt. This violence has affected millions of Syrians directly, has hit everyone indirectly, and has poisoned the souls of all. The following should provide sufficient indication of this fact: airstrikes have targeted populated areas, including a series of strikes on bread lines in August of 2012; populated areas have been bombarded by long-range Scud missiles; and 21 August 2013 witnessed chemical weapon attacks that killed 1466 people and injured about 10,000 in East Ghouta.[3] A very large number of people experience daily scenes of blood, death, and dismembered human bodies. Because of death's abundant presence, and from fear of being targeted, no one attends funerals anymore except a few relatives of the victims—a phenomenon I witnessed myself in Ghouta during the spring of 2013. I think the above should be enough to indicate something of the hell in which millions of Syrians have been living for the past thirty months.

Nearly one-third of Syrians (about 7 million people) have been displaced from their homes either internally (5 million) or externally (over 2 million), in the largest population transfer not only in the history of the country, but in the Arab world as a whole.

This is comparable neither to the *Nakba* (Palestinian exodus) of 1948 and 1967, nor to the wave of Iraqi asylum seekers that followed the US invasion of Iraq in 2003. It is likely that there are 200,000 people held in detention centres around Syria: in Mezzeh Military Airport, which had never before been used as a detention centre;[4] in the detention centre of the Fourth Brigade, led by Bashar's brother Maher,[5] where merciless torture is carried out every day; and in the re-used terrorist institution of Tadmur Prison,[6] whose brutal system has now been disseminated to other security headquarters and prisons. Prisoners in security headquarters are subjected to extreme forms of torture, about which there are appalling stories.[7] According to the Violations Documentation Centre (VDC) in Syria, the most reliable source of information regarding victims of the revolution, 2,826 of these detainees have been killed as of 29 August 2013.[8] This brutality has likely played a role in the resort to armed resistance, and in the preference of many people to risk death in combat rather than detention.

Moreover, countless women have been raped in prison or in their homes by the regime's forces or by the *shabiha*.[9] Additionally, the number of those injured and disabled may be half a million or more.[10]

Violence produces uncontrollable emotions: raging anger and a thirst for revenge, hatred, ruthlessness, and an eclipse of insight. In one well-known case, a commander named Abu Sakkar reportedly attempted to eat the organs of a fallen murderer.[11] In some quarters, he became a representative for the revolution as a whole, and was mentioned on international platforms by tender-hearted leaders such as Vladimir Putin.

The ancient Arabs believed that a bird named al-Sada leaves the body of a slain man and shrieks unceasingly until revenge is taken. Today there are undoubtedly tens of thousands of al-Sada birds crying out for revenge all over Syrian skies. If jinn, demons, and ghosts are the external projections of human emotions, then this mad violence must have released armies of such ghouls from torn and ruptured Syrian flesh.

Where is cool-headed, clear thinking to be found, in a world of al-Sada, jinn, and ghosts?

The monstrous violence has also ravaged communal relations across the nation and intensified enmity among Syrians to the virtual exclusion of any other animosities or antagonisms, even those against Israel (with respect to which animosity is 'written' into the country's very identity). To extinguish the prevailing violence, by any means possible and at the hands of whomever, has become a legitimate aspiration. The abused, the vulnerable, and the humiliated cannot rightly be blamed for it.

As the conflict gradually escalated, some forces associated with the revolution committed numerous unjust and inhumane abuses, to an extent exceeding anyone's ability to control and limit them. It is possible that one can understand the motives behind some of these actions. However, when we reach the point of 'understanding' Abu Sakkar's behaviour, for example, we have left the world of revolutionary values and identification and entered into a realm of vengeance, of kill or be killed, in which everyone becomes as bad as the worst among us.

Today, there are many prisons controlled by anti-regime groups and others who have taken advantage of the regime's retreat from various areas. At these sites the treatment of prisoners (who are not necessarily associated with the regime) does not come close to complying with basic human dignity. Some of these prisons already have a disturbing reputation, such as the 'Tawbah' (Repentance) Prison of Liwa al-Islam (known today as Jaysh al-Islam) in Douma. Others have a terrifying reputation, like all seven Daesh prisons in Raqqa province. These institutions exist in addition to the common practice of 'Islamic' corporal punishment, which in some areas is carried out in a sort of parade; it does not take place in accordance with any concern for fairness or justice, but rather only enables those in positions of high authority to boast about the privilege of occupying positions of high authority. At the Tawbah Prison in Douma, prisoners are forced to learn parts of the Qur'an by heart and how to perform prayer, in a manner similar to that seen in Daesh's prisons. Those who designed this ugly penal system do not seem to have understood that they are giving the Qur'an penal connotations and are turning the presence of God in people's lives into a tool of coercion and oppression.

We are locked in a vicious cycle. The long-standing violence of the regime provokes strong emotions among the abused, causing them to act violently and unjustly when they have the opportunity, while society seems to be continually surprised by what is happening and unable either to organize itself against violations at the hands of the new aggressors or to influence their behaviour. The scope of the political alienation that originally triggered the revolution expands even further: those who are financially able to do so seek asylum in Europe or elsewhere; those who cannot afford do so resort to hiding away at home, where they embrace the orders and prohibitions of their new masters, or violate them in secret.

The problem is that as Assad's violence continues, there is very limited space for public, organized opposition to violence and arbitrariness—but it is only organized public action that might be capable of stemming the tide.

Second, the effects of horrific violence were already proliferating when jihadists and mercenary groups of various ethnicities entered the scene. Most of them are foreigners, coming from other Arab or Muslim countries and the West. But 'foreignness' is still a pertinent characteristic even when these jihadists are Syrian. The 'foreign' ideas and policies, sensitivities, and moral values in question are those that diverge from trends historically linked to our nation (or any nation for that matter) and that interpret the social and the political only in terms of the abstractions to which these jihadists aspire. Their exclusive commitment to this 'foreign' model gives them little sense of responsibility to contemporary Syrian society, to its sensitivities and memories, to its structures and modern history. Jihadists are foreign everywhere, their homeland is their doctrine.

The flow of foreign jihadists into Syria signals a widening scope for the exercise of what could be called the 'politics of the depths', or the 'political unconscious', to borrow a term from Régis Debray. Religion and politics are mixed in a way that sublimates one into the other. Consequently, any registers of thinking and any concepts or symbols that might supersede the religious depths in the regulation of interactions among people in the contemporary world—i.e. what I call 'reason'—come to be seen as layers of dust to be wiped away, or as innovations (*bida'*) that must be suppressed. These concepts include: the nation-state; the principle of citizenship; the differentiation of a religious from a political nation; the differentiation of law from *sharia*; and the priority of national memory over archaic, pre-national history.

When the regime lost its grip on border crossings in the summer of 2012, and when this was followed by a loss of control over wider areas in the summer and autumn of the same year, the flow of jihadists increased. But prior to that, in June 2011, the regime itself released hundreds of convicted Islamists, Salafists, and jihadists from jail in a cunning move that likely aimed to turn the rebellion into 'jihad' so that the regime could market itself on global political and media platforms as a participant in the 'war on terror'. Abu Abdullah al-Ansari, twenty-eight years old, is a jihadist from the Nusra Front and a former first lieutenant who defected from the regime's forces in autumn of 2011. We travelled together for eight arduous days in July of this year. He said: 'The regime was cunning [in releasing jihadis from its jails], but God plotted against it, and God is the most cunning of planners [a verse from the Qur'an].' According to Abu Abdullah, God's planning abilities manifested themselves in the rise of jihadists and their cause.

The Nusra Front is a jihadist organization that announced its existence at the beginning of 2012. It became linked to al-Qaeda after it pledged allegiance to al-Qaeda leader Ayman al-Zawahiri in April 2013. However, in recent months another jihadist organization has appeared that is also linked to al-Qaeda: Daesh, or the Islamic State in Iraq and Syria (ISIS). The two organizations are now in a dispute over the Salafist Jihadist mantle. It seems that al-Zawahiri acknowledged both the groups on condition that the 'Front' would remain in Syria, and the 'State' in Iraq. The latter (Daesh) did not comply; it expanded, despite the Front, into areas of Northern Syria—Raqqa, Tal Abyad, Manbij, Jarabulus, and some areas of Idlib. The tension between the two organizations seems largely driven by national considerations. The Nusra Front is composed primarily of Syrian *mujahideen* (*ansar*, which means local supporters). As Abu Abdullah al-Ansari explained to me, it accepts other Arab and Muslim *muhajireen* (immigrants) only when they have special competencies, but their roles are limited to non-leadership positions.

But to me, the tension between these organizations doesn't seem to be about a consistent Syrian-national orientation. Instead, it is linked to the Front's better understanding of the Syrian environment when compared with Daesh. This state of affairs, however, conflicts with the jihadists' explicitly internationalist intellectual and political models, and it is not clear how this interpretive conflict might be resolved. Will it be resolved in favour of the internationalist tendency, which would establish an absolute, more 'foreign' authority, so that the Front would come to resemble Daesh and possibly dissolve into it? Or will it be resolved in favour of interests within the Syrian framework, of the *ansar*?

Daesh is comprised of expat *muhajireen* and Syrian *ansar*. It is striking to note that Daesh has been attracting Syrians from the bottom of the social scale (smugglers, ex-offenders, street vendors of cigarettes and so on), and has been giving them both power and prestige. In return, they cling to Daesh: they owe it everything they have.

The general atmosphere now seems suited to jihadism. In addition to the extreme violence and rage of the past two years, Sunni neighbourhoods have been targeted, on sectarian grounds, by the regime. Jihadists are the fruit of a multidimensional dynamic of Islamization that has been legitimated in Syria by a Sunni narrative of victimhood that is hostile to non-Sunnis (and to Alawites in particular) and that encourages violent responses to the brutalized condition of society. Over time, the fraught conditions of the revolution have allowed for two factors to be integrated over a larger territory: a self-conscious, political Sunnism, on the one hand, and armed resistance, on the other. What is the outcome of a marriage between a politicized religious identity and armed resistance? Between religion and violence?

The outcome is 'jihad'

Jihadists are jihad personified. The broad areas of convergence between religion and violence explain the gradual shift toward an

Islamic disposition within resistance against the regime, one that is not oriented toward the Muslim Brotherhood, but instead toward Salafism—a Jihadist-Salafist orientation, to be more specific. This fact also explains the rise of the black banner of jihad over the revolution's colourful green flag.[12]

There is also a thirst for power—for absolute power—that can easily be provided with a sacred foundation and legitimation by religious extremists. Such a thirst is remarkably common, but it has yet to be critically examined among Syrians. I believe the emergence of this thirst is related, on the one hand, to the disintegration of traditional frameworks of solidarity and, on the other, to the collapse of the nation-state's social and organizational frameworks (political parties, trade unions, and voluntary organizations) under the weight of Assadist tyranny. One could add to this the effects of the deterioration of the state's welfare functions as the result of economic (neo-) liberalization, as well as the serious weakness of national identity and the lack of any unifying national project in the wake of the Assads' appropriation of Syria.

Third, there is an increasingly tangible yet subtle role played by the unseen and unknown in the Syrian conflict. By this, I mean the role of secret services that work for a variety of parties. While these agencies have always played an important role in international politics, their impact becomes much more pronounced during periods when state authority and public order have collapsed and the state has lost its grip on its borders and its interactions with the outside world. Today, Syria is an example of such a geographically penetrated state. It is a dysfunctional space, vulnerable as a society, and as bestial as the regime. Syria has become a non-homeland, exposed to every kind of incursion.

While little specific information can be found as to this development, there can be no doubt that the secret services of many countries have intervened in Syria: Israel, America, Iran, Hezbollah, Turkey, Saudi Arabia, Qatar, Britain, France, and others. It is to be expected under such circumstances. And there is no doubt that, along with the Assad regime's intelligence services, they control a multitude of Syrian groups in a variety of ways.

We encounter the same kind of unseen factors in the emergence of jihadists themselves, in their confidential and restricted activities, and in the suspicions that surround at least some of the groups about whether they have links to or have been infiltrated by some of these agencies.

The story of Michel Samaha presents a typical example of the role played by the Syrian *mukhabarat* (intelligence apparatus) in the jihad trade. Samaha is a former Lebanese minister who is currently [in 2017] serving a jail sentence in Lebanon for plotting to detonate bombs targeting some Christian figures in order to frame Islamic jihadists, at the beshest of Assad's intelligence services.[13] His example shows that the *mukhabarat* play a role that goes beyond dirty tricks: they are also adept at shuffling the cards in order to manipulate the minds and attitudes of the public. This is one of the most important aspects of intelligence work, and likely constitutes a large part of what Syrian intelligence does, alongside its Iranian and Russian partners.

In Raqqa, questions have arisen about the regime's air force. For some reason, they have never launched airstrikes on Daesh's headquarters, despite the fact that it is located at the well-known local Provincial Palace. But they have shelled other populated sites, and have killed civilians continuously. Is it possible for an 'objective' inquiry to avoid the question or the suspicion of links of some sort between the regime and Daesh?

Because they are all foreign from the perspective of the Syrian nation, these intelligence operatives and organizations (including

Assad's intelligence, in this context) are no different from the jihadists in their damaging effects on the framework of the nation.

The fourth element is linked to the three previous. It concerns the very significant role of political money and its influence on a growing number of Syrians, and on their political and intellectual commitments and options. Last April in East Ghouta, I heard a saying attributed to Ho Chi Minh: 'If you want to destroy a revolution, shower it with money!' Money has played a hugely corrupting role, and has killed (or has come close to killing) the spirit of initiative, volunteerism, and courage that arose during the first year of the revolution. This money is linked to the agendas of 'supportive' foreign parties. It is rentier money that severs the links between effort and income, efficiency and responsibility. Above all, it corrupts politics through the purchase of loyalties and points of view.

For example, let's assume that a group of masked militants posts a video in which they introduce themselves as Battalion X and claim to have carried out Operation Y in order to obtain financial 'support' from certain sponsors. Then they post another video under a different name, which also shows a group of masked men and claims responsibility for other (mostly faked) accomplishments to gain support from another sponsor. If this were true, this single narrative would be enough on its own to demonstrate the havoc caused by political money. In fact, I heard this story from a militant from Deir ez-Zour, who used to be a soldier on the Golan Front before he defected to join in the fight against the regime forces in East Ghouta. Note that, militarily speaking, such money provides a channel that links some armed groups inside Syria to funding groups from the Gulf States: most of these groups are Salafi extremists, and at least some of them are likely connected to the intelligence services of those states.

Additionally, money from both Gulf and Western states, and even Iran, seems to have corrupted an unknown—but likely considerable—number of politicians. Money also comes from Western 'support' institutions, contributing to the corruption of Syrian activists both inside and outside the country. Today, there are various training courses in Beirut, Turkey, and Europe that prepare Syrian 'activists' for what are supposed to be civil-society activities: 'needs assessment', 'conflict resolution', and 'civil peace'. While these courses and activities are not always suspect in themselves, they nonetheless create negative habits of dependence on the part of Syrian activists who 'feed' on the generous financial support.[14] Some 'activists' even make a living off their participation in such schemes. Such individuals are usually known for their incompetence and their half-hearted participation in actual revolutionary activities.

In all cases, the combined effect of money is a transformation of loyalties that channels them in directions incompatible with the interests of the Syrian revolution or any conceivable Syrian national interest.

These four transformative factors (the incessant and insane violence practiced for over 900 days, jihadists and their political unconscious, the role of invisible or unknown powers, and political money) have all contributed to the destruction of the Syrian struggle's national framework. Any attempt to limit one's focus to internal forces, processes, and dynamics has now become useless and unproductive. Syria no longer has an interior. We have quickly turned from a homeland with a suffocating interior into a land without a home.

The Assad regime has maintained the upper hand within each of these four transformations. Not only is it a likely partner in jihad and in the jihadists' trade, but it has also continuously waged its own jihad using its own version of a political unconscious, one in which politics and religious bonds go hand in hand. Sectarianism, an essential component in regime politics, is in itself a 'politics of the depths' that has consistently undermined the power of rationality and the validity of rational political views. The odds are very high that the regime's secret services play a significant role in manipulation, deception, and framing, but we know very little about such activities. If, one day, the truth were to be made public, we would probably find that we have lived in a counterfeit world that has fooled even the most sceptical among us. It is well-known that the regime's secret agencies remain very 'foreign' with respect to any Syrian nationalism of real value, because of their endless brutality and cruelty in dealing with the general population, their deep-rooted sectarian attitudes, and their ties to similar, outside agencies (Iran, Hezbollah, Russia, and others). It is also a known fact that some western governments (including the US, Germany, and Spain) sent unwanted Syrians living in their respective countries to Syria with their full knowledge that they would be savagely tortured or even killed. The regime agencies that did their best to recruit Syrians as informers were always ready to act as informers, and jailors, in the service of more powerful security agencies. One could add to this list the matter of their secret budget and the opportunities it provides for funding individuals and groups inside and outside the country.

Then there is the corrupting role of political capital. The buying of loyalties at home or among regional neighbours is an art in which the regime has excelled: consider for example the domestic parties of the 'National Progressive Front', or many Lebanese politicians and journalists. Public power goes hand in hand with private funds: in Syria, capital opens all closed doors in ways unrivalled in any capitalist country.

The Assad dynasty is unmatched in its use of unrestrained violence as well. Ultraviolence was the card played by the regime from the first day of the revolution, and it has the great advantage of stirring desire for revenge, breaking national bonds, spreading violence to Syrian society as a whole, and turning what could have been a domestic political struggle into a civil—and a regional—war. The Assad dynasty had previously killed tens of thousands of Syrians, and arrested and tortured tens of thousands more during the enormous national crisis of a previous generation (1979–1982).

Then there is the effect of time, of the ways in which the prolongation of the Syrian struggle has intensified the effects of exposure to all of the above.

The destruction of 'reason'

The results of the four factors outlined above, amplified by the passage of time, appear to converge today in the collapse of the 'modern' aspects of Syrians' lives and existence: its institutions; its language and symbols; its psychology; its ideas and politics; and its moral components. It also seems that Syrians have begun to rely on registers of thinking comprised of more primary or primeval elements (religion, sect, ethnicity, tribe, province)—elements that have become prevalent as the modern Syrian framework, or the nation-state, has deteriorated. Such elements used to be characterized as 'the other' or 'the foreign', against which our modern state was to define itself; its national consciousness, its conscience, and its use of public reason. But this was back in the days of its ascendancy, before Syria proceeded to undermine itself as a national state by turning to dynastic rule, one that is both 'foreign' and colonial.

I use the term 'reason' in a particular sense: it refers to the newest registers of thinking that are formed by living within certain social, political, and intellectual contexts of a given period, and that are capable of presenting the best solutions to contemporary issues. When these emergent registers are destroyed or disabled, others that are outdated, out of touch, and less 'reasonable' begin to resurface; they emerge as objects of political and intellectual investment for certain disadvantaged segments of society, especially those who do not find the current 'reason' a suitable medium for self-expression.

In the Syrian context, 'reason' was initially formed by categories like: the state and state institutions; the nation; the people and citizenry; class; the constitution, the laws and political parties; and the roles played by intellectuals. During the Baathist and Assad era, this 'reason' was inverted into a penal code for Syrians. This code permitted their incarceration and encouraged their distrust. Because of it, their voice was forfeited and they were deprived of opportunities to protest, to formulate collective demands, and to seek self-representation. With the collapse of an already-decayed national life in the course of the revolution, 'reason' has also been shattered. This shattering has resulted in an undermining of its possibilities for organizing our awareness and criticizing an unstable, explosive reality.

Like nature, however, human thought abhors a vacuum; it does not easily tolerate bewilderment and confusion, and would rather fill itself with the nearest perceptions available. The perceptions and concepts we use to understand reality are not 'superstructures', or the weightless manifestations of some heavy, underlying reality. Rather, they are essential tools for directing and controlling reality. When the accompanying structure of 'reason' is disabled or is turned against people and used to rob them the ability to understand their situation, they tend to use outdated and unsuitable tools: 'un-reason'.

Un-reason takes two forms. The first is 'ex-reason', and is comprised of layers that are older than immediate perceptions and out of sync with contemporary issues. This register is closest to the usage of the 'political unconscious' articulated by Régis Debray.[15] It is based on religious ties and related accounts of how society was formed, and coexists with various overlaying social structures (sect, clan, ethnicity, tribalism). These layered structures are mingled with violence that can be re-activated by a contextually-driven collapse of thought in the present, along with all its social frameworks with the results that new perceptions lose the capacity to organize contemporary life.

The other form of un-reason is creativity: the avant-garde in thinking and organization, that which has not yet taken a definite form or been solidified into a social stratum.

In today's Syria, an older version of existence and culture is resurfacing, one in conformity with atavistic structures such as the tribe, clan, sect and ethnicity. However, we also see many forms of new and creative thinking, which so far have been moving along less determinate paths.

We are also seeing substantial affective investment in un-reason, and the construction of corresponding social and political structures—particularly religious military fiefdoms, which I discuss in the next section.

Religious-military fiefdoms

In our current situation, we appear far from ridding ourselves of tyranny, but rather we are at risk of falling into the clutches of a new despotism. Today, the threat in Syria is more existential, and that threat affects the country's integrity, unity, and 'reason'—that is, our self-awareness as a nation-state. This threat has recently affected Syria's overall political prospects, which extends to its overall coherence as a country, and even to its ability to survive. We have an aggressive, Assadist emirate that occupies half of Syria's territory and half of its population in a manner not unlike the Israeli occupation. We also have fragmentation across multiple dimensions—the fragmentation driven by sectarianism is just one example.

In many areas of the country, the situation is a sort of military feudalism, one dominated by military structures which have taken over public spaces (schools, administrative buildings, security and military offices, Baath party headquarters, and banks). This new feudalism exerts nearly absolute power over its territories. These conditions do not exist everywhere. But wherever they do, a certain proportionality can be observed between the advance of this kind of military-feudal fragmentation, and the withdrawal of the other new fiefdoms' participation in either challenging Assadist feudalism or in defending communities that have come out of the Assadist grip. Daesh is the most obvious example of this kind of religious-military fief, and is the one most inclined to avoid conflict with the regime. Daesh calls itself a 'state' but it acts on the communities under its control like a colonial power without the slightest regard for the demands or preferences of the population. Other military organizations frequently enter into open hostilities with Daesh: this happened in Raqqa during the first two weeks of August with the Ahfad al-Rasul Brigade ('Grandsons of the Prophets'), which is associated with the General Staff of the Free Syrian Army (FSA), and again with the FSA during the first week of July in the town of Dana, near the Turkish border in the province of Idlib. But until now, Daesh's expansion has not been curbed.

In the absence of any larger, unifying trend, the proliferation of military formations organized against the regime present an increased risk of accelerated fragmentation: they get support from a range of external parties, from states and sub-state donors, and sometimes capture public and private property as well. The possibility of a unifying, positive role for the political opposition has been more than restricted: it has been negative, mostly because of the opposition's poor performance and its foreign dependencies.

Sunni Islamism—often in Salafist forms and, to a lesser extent, the Muslim Brotherhood's variety—is the legitimating ideology for a variety of militant groups, but it does not provide a basis for unity even in Sunni areas that are beyond the regime's control. Needless to say, it is even less capable of providing such a unifying basis for Syrian society as a whole.

I was able to closely observe some of the Sunni areas around Damascus, Homs, and Raqqa. People in these areas seem to live in deep misery. Isolated from the state except as an arbitrary, external force, and isolated from the wider and ever-changing world, as well as from culture and the arts, they live deteriorating, rural lives on the margins of the nation-state and the economy. Perhaps they are willing to settle for Islamic structures that provide them a minimum income and for 'Islam' as a form of imaginary alternative homeland. But the reality of these areas is otherwise, and this 'homeland' leaves the majority of the population out in the open: it does not provide a congenial place to live, except for a bunch of new notables and their followers. I saw no joy following the Islamists' seizure of power in areas outside the regime's authority, nor any public sense of identification with the new rulers.

The organizations affiliated with the FSA, which has been part of the armed opposition since it began, have not shown enough coherence to curb the spread of Islamic military groups, whether these are linked to various parties abroad (the Muslim Brotherhood receives support from Qatar, and the non-jihadist Salafists like Jaish al-Islam from Saudi Arabia), or to the nihilism that connects the heavenly 'outside' (the sacred) to the social 'outside' (the pariah) and which promises heavenly rewards for the most vulnerable, marginalized, and deprived. Indeed, the lack of discipline among some of the FSA groups, and the notoriety of some other groups linked to it, provide fertile ground for Islamic militant groups, which may not usurp private properties, but which certainly do not spare any public property and see it as a reservoir for acceptable plunder. The Salafist Harakat Ahrar ash-Sham al-Islamiyya (Islamic Movement of the Free Men of Syria), seized the equivalent of 6 billion Syrian pounds (around 50 million US dollars at that time) from the Central Bank in Raqqa after wresting control of the city from the regime in the first week of March 2013. No one knows how that enormous sum of money has been spent, and the movement has not provided any statement or account of the fate of those public funds to anyone.

The above indicates a complete atrophy of the moral, humanitarian, and national dimensions to the politics, behaviours, and thinking of these Islamic groups. To my knowledge, there have been no indications to the contrary. This atrophy reveals their preoccupation with their own interests and their thirst for power.

Each of these groups has its own project(s). These projects are not aligned with each other because there is no cooperation among their respective leaderships. The 'Islam' on which these many, similar organizations are based is nothing but a buttress for absolute power, one that encodes that power as 'holy' and unassailable and that legitimates the self-centred interests for wealth and power on the part of childish Islamists. Cunning and theatrical, yet effective and protected by force, these Islamic organizations use the designation 'Islamic' to mask their basic nature as schemes for gaining absolute power without any emancipatory dimensions. In every area these groups control, all 'culture' regresses to the Islamic tendencies of self-enclosure and conspiracy theory. Islamists of all types share a worldview that is much darker and more sinister than that of the old Arab Nationalists. According to Islamists, the world is an evil, corrupt, dangerous, and offensive place that is secretly controlled by Israel and the US, which use the Arab regimes as puppets or pawns. I have heard this simplistic harangue from Islamic jihadists, who take it as the one and only truth.

We have nothing much to learn from the sinister world outlined above. However, we do have an urgent need to erect barriers against it, and even to combat or to 'defeat' it. The standard accusation against opponents of the Assad regime has always been collaboration with an unidentified enemy—usually the US and Israel. But it seems that Daesh considers every independent Syrian activist to be an agent of NATO. This accusation is a legacy from al-Qaeda's experience in Afghanistan and Iraq.

The aforementioned tendencies to self-enclosure and conspiracy theory shape the (anti-) intellectual world of Islamists, in proportion to the degree of their extremism. They do not claim that everything they possess is true, but rather believe that all truths are in their possession. Even the less extreme among them are still not too removed from this kind of self-enclosure. The more educated do not have the courage to criticize this delirious worldview explicitly—conceals its intellectual and moral poverty behind trite dogma and projections of depravity on to the world.

I tend to believe that the unrelenting cultural deterioration suffered by many social environments in Syria helps to explain both social fragmentation and the rise of jihadist organizations. For about four decades now, Syrian society has been without a sense of historical purpose or a 'project' that could unite the people and align their expectations. Syrian society has been suffocated in an endless, miserable present dominated by a decadent clique. Hafez al-Assad installed himself as Syria's only project and its final destination. That project was handed down to his offspring. Today, not only is the project devoid of any national or humane aspects: it is a killing machine.

'Islam' has now become an alternative project for politically active sectors of Sunni Syrians. Today, we speak of fundamentalist Islam, interpreted literally as a series of dos and don'ts, i.e. *sharia*. The reduction of a culture to a series of prohibitions is both far-fetched and very distant from an understanding of culture as a process of learning, acquisition, and innovation. This 'Islam' lives in a state of airtight cultural subsistence, and is obsessed with imposing its power over people. Without question, it is Hafez al-Assad, obscured.[16]

In sum, these religious-military fiefs emerged as the product of a country torn apart by the incredible violence unleashed on rebel areas, and as the product of the multiple parties that 'support' the Syrian struggle. They are also the result of an earlier deterioration of culture and politics and an earlier fragmentation at the local level, processes previously concealed behind the centralized superstructure of Assad's Baathist regime. Finally, this new feudalism is a result of the unchecked, authoritarian aspirations of people and groups brought up under the Assad regime, whose ambitions expanded along with the acquisition of arms and the grabbing of land from the aggressor regime, and whose interests are served by prolonged conflict.

How many fiefs are there? The answer remains unknown because the process of their formation is still in its germinal stages. To date, there is no single fiefdom that is in sole control of a particular region of the country. But things are moving in that direction. It is likely that struggles will erupt in parts of the country and result in consolidations of power, and that the resulting rule of the strongest will include gaining control over resources. In areas around Deir ez-Zour, armed groups control oil wells: they either filter it in primitive ways, sell it as crude oil, or buy small but sophisticated oil refineries—and they reap millions in the process.[17] Similarly, the Nusra Front seized a few oil wells in Deir ez-Zour.[18] There is nothing but 'Islam' that legitimates this systematic dismantling of the nation-state and the accompanying exploitation of public resources. It is now enough to hail *takbir* (chanting *Allahu Akbar*/God is Great) over something for it to be considered booty that can be appropriated. So long as these groups suffer from extreme intellectual and political impoverishment, 'Islam' will remain a ready-made politics and culture that can be used to conceal that impoverishment and even portray it as richness and self-sufficiency. The sceptical are seen as enemies of Islam, i.e. 'infidels'. *Takfir* (accusing someone of apostasy) is the tried-and-true boundary-term that protects the authority of Islamists, and is the equivalent of 'traitor' or 'agent of an enemy state' in the Baathist dictionary.

The Assad regime has had no problem coexisting with religious-military fiefdoms. The regime was the first to speak about them, and is likely to have itself been involved in engineering some of them. Before the revolution, the regime itself was already a private military fiefdom ruled by a hereditary emir: Assad. He would have preferred to restore the status of a full emirate to his rule, but only because he cherishes his inheritance. No national considerations can ever be addressed in sectarian military fiefdoms.

Furthermore, the existence of military fiefs around the country, Salafist as well as Kurdish (the latter seized some oil wells in the province of Hasakah), confers a kind of relative legitimacy onto the regime's own fief by normalizing it and turning it into the mirror image of a fragmented, feudal society in terms of structure and ideology, to borrow the words of the regime's organic intellectuals. Under current circumstances, the Assadist fief can even appear in the guise of a continuation of the Syrian state—an impossible claim for religious fiefdoms to make and irrelevant to the potential Kurdish fiefdom. For that very reason, because of its especially high historical and symbolic status, the Assadist lord cannot sacrifice Damascus. Because it is the capital city, maintaining control over Damascus obscures a feudal reality behind the umbrella of Syria-in-general. Whoever controls Damascus has a better chance of being the 'state' as opposed to a 'fiefdom', even someone with as murderous a pedigree as Hafez al-Assad.

It seems to me that the situation in Syria is already heading toward a sort of coexistence among fiefdoms. Assad's occupies a superior position militarily and economically, and enjoys strong support from Russia, Iran, and the latter's well-known retainer, Hezbollah, in Lebanon. However, Assad's fiefdom may not regain all of its property because of internal, regional, and international balances of power. Such a situation of coexistence might well last a long time. It is reminiscent of bygone eras of fragmented emirates, known from Syria's ancient and Islamic history.

So instead of one supreme tyrant, we must deal with many smaller ones as well, as the country moves further along toward barbarism and disintegration. As the Lebanese academic Gilbert Achcar has written: 'The sooner the Syrian regime falls, the better. The longer it stays in power, the greater the risk of sinking the country in barbarism.'[19]

In fact, the indications of ongoing disintegration, particularly those that manifest as religious-military fiefdoms, are closely linked to the difficulty of toppling the Assad regime. This process will only accelerate unless the Syrian struggle finds a just and progressive outlet.

The dynamic of military feudalism is linked to all the drivers described above: violence; the emergence of jihadists; the roles played by various secret services; and political money. However, the most powerful and potentially explosive of these drivers is the continuation of the regime as an 'Israel-like', aggressive power in an exposed, 'Palestine-like' world surrounding it. There is no hope of stopping this dynamic unless its most powerful drivers are disrupted. The fall of the regime would not mean an immediate end to the process of 'feudalization'—but there is no hope of stopping this feudalization without overthrowing the regime. Perhaps the overthrow of the regime would put new counter-dynamics into play to the benefit of a new form of Syrian nationalism that could halt the creeping 'un-reason' with which religion conceals and protects fragmentation, tyranny, and the plunder of public resources. Conditions could then develop for national resuscitation and a new 'national reason' could emerge, one that is informed by perceptions synchronizing to our new situation and which is suited to addressing our present challenges.

It is clear that toppling the regime will be a strenuous process. The rebuilding of a new Syria on the ruins of 'Assad's Syria' will be even more so.

Syria above and below

The current complex situation in Syria is the greatest ordeal the country has faced since the French mandate (1920–1946). Questions about the definition of a Syrian nation-state as well as of its survival are raised by the following: the organized Iranian, Lebanese, and Iraqi interference in the Syrian issue on the side of the regime; the less-organized Turkish and Gulf interference; the discreet Israeli interference to protect the regime and ensure its survival; and the sectarian dimensions of all these interventions, including those mounted by the West under the pretext of 'protecting minorities'. There is some talk about the erasure of the Sykes-Picot borders in order to allow for something new but as-yet-undefined, perhaps a broader Levantine body.[20] But it has also become possible now to talk more openly about the actual division of the country into smaller entities, which might endure and solidify, but not consolidate into anything bigger.

In fact, talk about unity in the form of larger entities has always gone hand-in-hand with increased internal fragmentation. Particularly in Syria and Iraq, 'Arab Unity' was a slogan that disguised sectarian domestic policies and crude interventions into the affairs of weaker neighbouring Arab countries. In all cases, the weakening of our countries from above in the name of 'the Arab nation' has translated in practice into a weakening from below through sectarian discrimination and foreign dependencies. The rise of the Islamists, based on the concept of an Islamic nation, does not contradict the logic of fragmentation into emergent, competing fiefdoms. The present will not be an exception to this general pattern. Talk of the demise of Sykes-Picot and its borders can only be recommended for those who support a subservient Levant under Shiite dominance and Iranian sovereignty. The proponents of this view take no issue with Iran's politics and its aspirations for control in the Arab world.

For my part, I vote for the Syrian nation-state. I vote against the hypothetical erasure of the Sykes-Picot borders, and against the creeping feudal fragmentation as well. I do not see a conflict between the two because inherited borders are already being violated in the interest of Iranian dominance while people across large portions of Syria live in deteriorating, feudal conditions with no way out. Despite all its faults, and despite being in dispute on the battlefield, the Syrian nation-state would provide a solution for several problems.

First, there is an argument to feasibility: reviving the Syrian nation-state is more achievable than creating new ethnic and sectarian entities from scratch, each of which would be faced with the same tasks of gaining internal and international legitimacy.

Second, these kinds of entities would inevitably provide much more restricted options for political and moral advancement than a fully liberated Syria would, not least because they would be shaped by sectarian or ethnic parameters even more limited than those of 'Assad's Syria'. The difficulties of coexistence among 'post-national' Syrian entities formed by war—which would surely continue to relate to each other in a state of 'hot' or 'cold' war for the foreseeable future—would be psychologically and economically more costly than the difficulties of forging a coexistence among Syrians of different backgrounds who are fighting today.

Third, the idea of a Syrian nation can provide a consistent, positive orientation for combating the Salafist jihadist formations and other tendencies toward military feudalism, including those of Assad.

Finally, a united, post-war Syria would have fewer conflicts with regional neighbours to mend than would a divided, internally conflictual post-national Syria. Each small Syrian fief would be a regressive, subsidiary affair that would inevitably succumb to the temptations of foreign control.

Syria is a historical asset, a foundation from which all Syrians can benefit. Although it is a young country, less than 100 years old, Syria already has a history. The massive conflict witnessed during the last thirty months provides a strong motivation for reflecting on the Syrian nation's character, history, and meaning as well as on its geographic and social structures. What would subsidiary entities created by dismembering the Syrian body really be? What would be their histories and meanings?

Nothing but fear and hatred

But it goes without saying that the meaning of Syria, its identity, and its political regime have to be reconstructed on new bases—not those of the Assads' Baathist era, nor those of the pre-Baathist era. Within current discussions about this issue, there have been a few mentions of federation, of political decentralization, and sometimes of a sectarian 'joint venture'. While one might have reservations about some or all these suggestions, their shared, negative implication that any centralized state is necessarily excluded is stronger than their positive connotations.

The need to change Syria's political structure is linked to another necessity: a different perception of identity. Already a self-designated 'Arab republic', a future Syria with no ambition but to dissolve into one Arab nation has already lost the battle for survival, both politically and morally.

An 'Islamic' Syria, to which different types of Islamists look forward, is even less authentic. Its current military incarnations are primarily about land reallocation. They all share repressive intellectual, political, and social characteristics that make it impossible for them even to establish conditions of reduced sectarianism, and still less conditions rooted in substantial equality and freedom.

A Syria for Syrians remains the one and only option whose essence cannot be maintained without settling the issue of coexistence among different Syrians, with better guarantees of freedom and justice for all.

We know nothing about the course of the path leading to a new governable, livable Syria. But the truth remains that there is nothing progressive, national, or humane about 'Assad's Syria', or about Salafist Syria (already many Syrias), or about a Kurdish strip of Syria that does not care about locals' opinions and preferences and that is now a source of additional conflict and violence in an already afflicted country.

In what direction is the situation in Syria likely to develop from here?

In my opinion, the Syrian situation is likely to develop in one of four or five directions.

One possibility is that the Assad regime will triumph in its war and regain control over areas of the whole country. This is unlikely within current horizons as I see them. But such an outcome would devolve into the rule of *shabiha* (Assadist thugs) and into extreme forms of brutality, looting, murder, detention, and torture. It would also result in an aggressive Iranian domination of the country. Syrian society would be crushed economically, politically, and psychologically.

Another possibility is a victory of the revolution in the form of an uprooting of the regime by force. This takes us back to the scenario of an 'absolute revolution' that eliminates all traces of the old regime.[21] But the paradox of an absolute revolution is that once it starts the process of rebuilding, it is likely to find nothing available but the expertise and foundations of the ousted regime. This leads to the reconstruction of that very regime, albeit on different intellectual foundations and under the control of new elites. We would likely get an Islamic regime rather than a Baathist one: instead of 'comrades' ruling us, we would be ruled by 'brothers'.

Today, in areas outside the regime's control, we already see religious maxims from the Qur'an or sayings of the Prophet replacing the banal slogans of Bashar al-Assad and his father, along with their images. In both cases, the purpose is the same: to inform the population about who is the new boss or master. Nothing about the practice goes beyond that.

So far, there is nothing that would guarantee that the overthrow of the regime by force today would lead to the demise of the (proliferating) military fiefdoms. The latter are now embedded in material, moral, and political interests in areas where challenging the regime is no longer the main concern. It is possible they would deplore both the end of the revolution and the fall of the regime, because in either case they would then be held to account for their raison d'être—for what they have done and what they have gained. The most likely outcome to follow getting rid of the Assad fiefdom would be a new conflict among or against the new fiefdoms—first, the aggressive Islamic State in Iraq and Syria, but also all the other, less coherent and organized fiefdoms.

A third possibility is a peaceful, political settlement through which the regime undergoes a fundamental change and the page is turned on 'Assad's Syria.' Today, this may be the least damaging of the options, but there is not the slightest indication that it is likely to happen. The regime is incapable of giving up anything because of its composition and the structure of its extremist interests. The regime's structure is open to only two choices: remain the same or break down entirely. This explains the regime's policy over the past thirty months, during which all other doors have been shut. Today, the regime carries on its war alongside allies that have no shame in declaring their support and demonstrating it with money, arms, and men.

Additionally, the revolution's spectrum of already inconsistent positions makes it particularly difficult for consensus to be reached about any political settlement. This is due not only to the uneven political, intellectual, and emotional development of the revolution across multiple geographic spaces—but it is also due to the regime's crimes, which can only be forgiven through its complete eradication. The possibility of consensus is further complicated by the fiefdoms, the emirs of which would bet against any possible political arrangement, no matter how close to fairness, in order to protect their fiefdoms and to protect their interests, which are closely tied to the prolongation and increasing complexity of the conflict.

The fourth possibility is the persistence of current conditions: an uncontrolled, absolute war by the regime continuing alongside limited regional and international support of the armed resistance groups, support that is just enough to prevent the regime from regaining control over dissident areas but insufficient to bring it down. On 25 August 2013, the *New York Times* published an article by Edward Luttwak of the Centre for Strategic and International Studies that revealed its argument clearly in its title: 'In Syria, America loses if either side wins.' Luttwak characterized the parties in the conflict as the regime and its allies, on the one hand, and an opposition dominated by the Islamists in its ranks, on the other. Quite cynically, he theorized that a prolonged stalemate in Syria is the only outcome that would not harm US interests.[22] The political conclusion to be drawn from Luttwak's position is that both parties must lose. The actual situation in the past thirty months coheres with such a perfidious judgment. What is more, the judgment has precedents, the most famous of which is the Iran-Iraq war that lasted for eight years in the 1980s.

The conflict's persistence tallies with the disintegration of the country into fiefdoms, continued loss of lives and properties, and hopeless conditions in which the poorest of Syrians pay the greatest price.

Finally, isn't there a fifth possibility of international military intervention? Until a few days ago, this option seemed unlikely. But as of today, in early September 2013, the possibility looms again, following the 21 August chemical-weapon attack on East Ghouta. However, I expect that this potential interference would take the form of Israeli-style strikes against specific sites which would be intended to punish and discipline the regime but not to bring it down. This would save face for the Obama administration after the Assad regime's frequent use of chemical weapons, and it would avoid embarrassment in front of Arab and regional allies. But such an approach would not have a decisive influence over the course of the conflict. Worse, it would give the regime a moral victory: it came out of an international confrontation unscathed, still able to strike and abuse. The prospect of a full-blown intervention to topple the regime seems non-existent because it would entail a double interference from the West, so to speak: it would add the Syrian regime to the list of targeted enemies alongside jihadist formations, al-Qaeda and the like. The dilemma faced by the West, America in particular, is that a small intervention would have no significant impact and may be considered as a defeat, while a more forceful intervention (to topple the regime) would entail a much greater involvement (confrontation with the jihadists). In military, political, and economic terms, such a conflict would be expensive and complex, and would not come with any guarantee of success.

Where is the Syrian Revolution?

Is it true, then, that the revolution has led to a country ripped apart and to a collapsed state, to emergent military feudalisms and to the rise of jihadist groups? This is the general trend today, as it has been for about a year. If the revolution had been able to overthrow the regime earlier, in June 2012, fifteen months after the beginning of the outbreak, when protests were at their climax of more than 700 per week, Syria would have had a much greater chance of survival. But during its second fifteen months, the revolution's subsidiary objective (toppling the regime) parted ways with its primary goal (a new democratic Syria) under the pressure of a draconian struggle. Toppling the regime became a vital demand that stemmed only from the legitimate defence of lives against a mass murderer, and from no other aspirations. Other goals gradually became luxuries, incompatible with the psychological situation of an abused society in a desperate struggle, or with the intellectual, military, and political modes that the revolution had to adopt in order to sustain itself.

Undoubtedly, there is a broad spectrum of human rights' activists, politicians, and fighters, men and women alike, who represent a continuation of the revolution's positive aspirations. But today this spectrum is scattered and voiceless. Only the fall of the regime would afford this decentralized multitude a better position to regain the initiative, even if only partially, in favour of an emancipatory, all-inclusive view of Syria.[23]

Syria today seems to be a theatre for a violent, large-scale operation of 'reform', one that affects the state—both as an identity and as a set of governing institutions—and society, population and religion. Today, Syria is neither a national state nor a traditional Sultanic one, but a shapeless country in which hundreds of military formations are fighting the regime in a way that has never seen before in any social revolution or national war. Syria today is a country witnessing the emergence of strange creatures of religious extremism. Tremendous violence now engulfs the country. It is practically a playground for ghouls and terrifying, faceless beings. We speak of a major 'reform' process, because it seems that our country is immersed in a furious process of transformation, completely losing its shape and passing through malformed, monstrous incarnations.

10

THE NEO-SULTANIC STATE

ISTANBUL, JANUARY–FEBRUARY 2015

Conventional wisdom on sectarianism holds that it stems from the existence of 'sects' in a given society, and that sects are nothing but various confessional groups, coexisting in a natural state of constant dispute, mistrust, or even war. Yet this theory fails to explain why only certain societies are prone to overt sectarian tension, even though hardly any society is free of religious and ideological diversity. I have referred to this theory as 'common', since it is a crude theory based on first impressions that seem not to have been revised or re-examined. Criticism of first impressions and the presumptions that shape them might produce knowledge that is more insightful. In what follows, I argue that sects are artificial social constructs, created under certain political conditions that I will explore below.

Sectarianism isn't a reflection of obsolete social constructs, as claimed by another supposedly progressive theory. Rather, sectarianism is a political tool and a present-day affair, not a continuation of something outdated that refused to vanish over time. The untimely continues to live when it is sustained by modern policies, organizations, and power matrices. Legacies of the past remain active only by virtue of the momentum they receive from present structures, which fix them within the status quo.

Neither is sectarianism a phenomenon of consciousness or one of its disorders—such as illusion, fantasy, or ideology—although it does manifest itself in the form of an ideology, and has been known to be a source of fantasies and illusions. Likewise, sectarianism is not a phenomenon of identity and belonging; nor is it one of its afflictions (such as fanaticism), although sects do tend to appear as exclusionary, alienating identities. Rather, sectarianism is a phenomenon of power and social privilege that manifests in political circumstances and social constructs, taking shape in practices that can at times even amount to murder. In any case, it is based on discrimination, which both expresses and perpetuates itself through public discourses and beliefs.

The following inquiry will be limited to the Syrian domain, which promises to be an ideal specimen for the study of sectarianism—not despite, but rather because of the vigilance and prohibitions that have surrounded the topic, which have been maintained both by oppression and by 'culture' (i.e. by nationalist and secularist censorship). To think about sectarianism in Syria, one needs to look beyond conventional public discourse and toward existing practices and conditions—reflecting upon society, state, and politics in Syria during the Assad era.

My approach will focus on investigating the social and political origins of sectarianism in Syria and aim at developing a wider socio-political model for understanding sectarianism, which I refer to as the 'neo-Sultanic State'. Sectarianism is not the ultimate truth of politics and society in Syria; rather, it is one of the many facets of the neo-Sultanic state. This state is based on *baya'a* (a pledge of obedience), *fitna* (civil disorder and war), and *abad* (eternity or continuity 'forever,' through dynasty and inheritance).

THE NEO-SULTANIC STATE

A new regime and its contradictions

My analysis focuses on the period after 1970, and the foundational years of Hafez al-Assad's rule. This era did not signal the debut of any issues concerning the status of confessional groups, either at the state level or in the public sphere. Rather, it marks a conventional beginning, one that is pragmatically justified because dynamics were introduced during that time that conflicted with the state of social, political, and cultural affairs in the period between independence in 1946 and the 1970 coup, during which there was a pronounced expansion of the 'national' political sphere. This era (1946–1970) witnessed a wider participation in public life by Syrians from divergent backgrounds than ever before, a broad secularization of thinking and of public life, and a decline in the significance of sectarianism on the state level. Baathist-Assadist rule would not have come into being without such an environment.

Yet such national developments were accompanied by major incongruities and conflicts during the pre-Baathist era as well as in the pre-Assad Baathist years (1963–1970). During the former phase, there was a complex tension between the inception of an independent national state with a diverse, growing population (totalling less than 4 million at the time of independence in 1946), and the existence of a dominant oligarchy that descended either from the notable urban families that had emerged during the last decades of the Ottoman rule, or from the infantry of the French Mandate Army. Additionally, a Sunni Islamic apparatus was in charge of defining Islam—what it is and what it is not—and its religious authority extended over non-Sunni Muslims. Although this authority possessed no sovereignty and had no access to means of coercive enforcement, it enjoyed a nearly universal jurisdiction in the fields of religious education, civil status, and public religious festivities. Its range was not limited to possibly non-consenting Sunnis, but extended as well to non-Sunnis such as Alawites, Druze, Ismailis, and Shiites, thanks to the absence of legal and institutional frameworks for treating Syrians as individuals who decide for themselves in the fields of religious education and civil status.

During the Baathist period, the new and barely-legitimate elite lacked sufficient courage to resolve the tensions caused by positioning Sunni Islam as the dominant 'public religion'. It did, however, remedy problems related to the dominance of traditional notables within the governance of an emerging national state. Agrarian reform, nationalization of large corporations and private banks, and the expansion of education all provided a broader social foundation for national life, through which rural farmers were assimilated into modern state institutions of the educational, military, bureaucratic, and partisan (Baathist) sort. Before long, however, the policies of this new elite generated another tension, this time between the expanding base and the quite restricted political framework that had been forcibly imposed upon the country: one-party rule or, practically speaking, the rule of one person.

During the rule of Hafez al-Assad (1970–2000), the expansion of a national social base came to a halt, due to the increasingly authoritarian character of the regime as well as to the emergence of a new bourgeoisie. This new bourgeois class was constituted by two main groups: one that mediated between centres of power and the general populace (which I will call the 'local bourgeoisie' or the 'new notables'); and another that owned the most important resources of the country and controlled lucrative sectors of the economy (which I will refer to as the 'central bourgeoisie'). Throughout the three decades of Hafez's rule, several new or renewed tensions emerged within the structures of the Syrian state.

First, there was an intensifying conflict between contracting political structures and an expanding population (from 6 million in 1970 to nearly 9 million in 1980, and about 18 million in 2000). Both politically and economically, a large percentage of the population found themselves effectively on the margins, with 42 per cent living within the informal economy at the turn of the last century.

Second, Assad's state did not interfere with the status of the 'public religion', i.e. Sunni dominance in the fields of education, civil status and public religious ceremonies. On the contrary, the regime chose to leave these spheres untouched in order to maintain its position as the sovereign; the exclusive owner of political power.

Third, Hafez al-Assad's regime reproduced the class contradictions of pre-Baathist rule through its own authoritarian structures, which gradually developed fascist and totalitarian characteristics. During the reign of Bashar, the disparities between the local and central wings of the bourgeoisie and the impoverished and marginalized Syrian classes intensified. This was due to the introduction of a neoliberal model of development and the disintegration of populist mechanisms inherited from the early days of Baathist-Assadist rule. The most conspicuous tensions, frequently the source of violence in Syria, are closely tied to a deepening conflict between a very narrow power elite that completely controls the state and the vast majority of the economically and politically impoverished population.

But let us return to our conventional starting point of 1970, the year Hafez seized power in a military coup.

Securing the regime

Early in Hafez al-Assad's rule, it was obvious that the career soldier was preparing for a prolonged stay in power. Born in 1930,

Hafez was nineteen at the time of the first military coup in 1949, three years after the country's declaration of independence. He was still maturing during the political turbulence of the 1950s, a time of successive military coups accompanied by political pluralism under more open conditions. He became an officer and a founding partner of the secret five-man Baathist Military Committee in Egypt during the Syrian-Egyptian Unity (1958–1961), a period soon followed by the participation of Baathist and Nasserist militants in the Baathist coup of 1963. Hafez was a key partner in the 1966 coup, the orchestrator of the 1970 coup, and then the jailor of his former comrades. He imprisoned Salah Jadid, the Secretary General of the Baath Party, for twenty-three years until his death; he also imprisoned ex-President Nureddin al-Atassi for twenty-two years, not releasing him until it was confirmed that he would die of cancer within a few months.

During the twenty years that followed the country's independence, the dominant idea in Syria was Arab nationalism, first in a 'liberal' and then a 'socialist' variant. Both had a negative view of sectarianism, despite their distinctly mixed records on that score. However, regional divisions remained most prominent among the upper elite during the pre-Baathist and pre-Assad periods. Most areas of the country suffered from neglect in favour of the two major cities, Damascus and Aleppo (as well as Homs and Hama, to a lesser extent). The countryside and smaller cities were neglected, despite the fact that these were the areas where the military cadre of the Baath Party had originated, which widened the party's popular base.

He had learned a valuable lesson from his experiences: in Syria, staying in power is more significant than reaching it. It is quite evident that Hafez was doing everything he could to retain governance 'forever', an idea expressed every morning for the last two decades of his rule in the daily chants imposed on students in schools and soldiers in the armed forces.

Indeed, everything was his: from the songs that glorified his name to the massacres, from the countless statues to the 'spontaneous popular marches' and the prisons. All were his, and his possession always relied heavily on sectarianism.

First, Hafez established a brutal and feared security apparatus, which was led by family members and confidants. Top priority was given to his own clan, followed by his wife's, according to Hanna Batatu's book, *Syria's Peasantry*. Within his clan, however, priority was given to his immediate family. Throughout the years, Hafez followed the principle of clientelism as a rule of thumb. The regime's security and its 'pillars of sustainability' were handed over to his inner circle of relatives and confidants. Naturally, this practice lead to favouritism in military colleges and volunteer service in the army, and to the holding of high posts or key positions in state forces. Understandably, Alawites, who had been impoverished and despised for centuries under traditional Sultanic rule, took the initiative to volunteer for the army and in the security services whenever possible, even when there was no outright discrimination in their favour. Alawites turned to the military in substantial numbers during the days of the French mandate, something which can be partly explained by their need for work and income, along with particular encouragement from the French. Sunnis living in cities, however, had steered away from the army, driven instead by a preference for work in trade and scientific professions, as well as an aversion to serving in a foreign army. The Assad state's discrimination in favour of Alawites within security and military organizations was present from the first moment.

Hafez also built up military formations with security functions that were also headed by his relatives, such as the Defence

Brigades, the Republican Guard, and the Special Units. His brother, Rifaat, was the leader of the Brigades; his brother-in-law Adnan Makhlouf led the Republican Guard; and Ali Haydar was the commander of the Special Forces. At the same time, Hafez controlled the official army by heading each military unit with a commander, an official of the Baath party, and a security official. Promotion was often based on sectarian allocation, so that these three-headed formations wouldn't act uniformly. Additionally, overriding priority was given to the security official, who monopolized access to excessively sectarianized security centres. Hafez al-Assad was the military governor of Syria, and he weakened the army's capacity for taking an independent role in politics to the fullest extent, transforming it into a tool of internal and regional repression, in every sense of the word. It is worth mentioning that stripping the Syrian army of its active political character and turning it into a tool of oppression went hand in hand with turning the page on the war between Syria and Israel (1973–1974). Almost immediately—in 1976—a new chapter began with war waged against the Palestinians and Lebanese in Lebanon, and then against Syrians in Syria. The army changed from a highly politicized national army into a de-politicized military instrument or passive political tool, essentially serving as a guardian of tyranny. For this reason, it is not accurate to describe either Hafez's rule or that of his son Bashar as a military regime. The correct description is an intelligence system, or a system revolving around its own survival and security function, which is based on intelligence services in times of peace and on military units with a security function in wartime.

Security apparatuses are directly and exclusively linked to the President, and not to any civil authority. Independent connections among the various competing agencies were not tolerated. The

President is the Supreme Commander of all the competing security apparatuses: he stands at the juncture of information flows from these agencies, and possesses the most complete picture of any given situation. The chiefs of these agencies themselves have access to far less comprehensive information, whereas the Syrian populace is itself the subject of investigations.

The political system is based on loyalty to the president, whose position combines the presidency, leadership of the Army and Armed Forces, and the General Secretary of the ruling Baath party. In addition to this the figure of the president is the national symbol of Syria and the centre of public life in the country. He is immeasurably more significant than the Baath Party, the government, the army, the intellectuals, the people, the cities, or anything else. Hafez came to be described as a genius, as great and wise, the 'Master of the Homeland', 'Hero of War and Peace', 'Iconic Commander', the 'Greatest Man of the Nation'. He was the first teacher, the first physician, the first engineer and lawyer, and so forth. Images and statues of him were ubiquitous. Perhaps there was an additional and relentless purpose behind all this veneration that served all the institutions of power, something beyond convincing people of his genius, wisdom, and eternal survival; perhaps it functioned to intimidate them, and to paralyze any impulse to protest or object. It seems that the Syrian public realized that a regime capable of such a degree of self-exaltation might be willing to do anything to stay in power.

Tangible private gains were to be had from loyalty, endlessly exaggerated praise of the president, and the raising of banners that glorified him—all of which were used by individuals, families, and groups to intimidate others and to gain preferences at others' expense, as well as to achieve private interests within local or central public bodies.

But the true significance of all this bravado was to emphasize that only one person is free in the country (something in accordance with Hegel's racist idea of the 'orient'). This means there is only one politician and a single architect of policies: Hafez al-Assad. No political parties, no public political discussions, no political debates in the parliament or newspapers or universities, no free opinions, no independent and voluntary meetings, no public protests or collective embodiments of the word 'no'. All Syrians, save only their free master, are slaves, or politically dead.

However, they were in fact resisting all the time, and in different ways.

Assadism: a private state and a public sect

But what is the significance of a policy that favours Alawites, one that places them in high military and security posts? What does it mean when certain people, by virtue of their religious denomination, occupy crucial positions in the state, which is an institution of public government? It points to the transformation of a pre-existing social category into a public political caste that occupies a key position within the state. It goes without saying that not all Alawites—not even most of them—were appointed to such posts; only that posts of that sort were mostly held by Alawites. I refer to a 'public political caste' for the purpose of conceptually representing the discriminatory situation benefitting Alawites, without implying that the Alawites are politically free or that they are rulers—they are not. This point should be understood in the same light as the aforementioned situation regarding the public religious caste, Sunnis, whose doctrines were generalized socially through educational, symbolic and civil status laws. Such a system does not bring tangible benefits to all or most

Sunnis, but nevertheless counts as a structural advantage for Sunnis in these areas.

Aside from the attainment of a public caste status—and as a price for it—such discrimination in favour of Alawites within the state's main apparatus was also equivalent to privatizing the 'republic', or robbing it of the status of a public state and producing instead a private state. 'Assad's Syria' is the abridged name for this private state, with its implication that Syria is the property of its leader—a notion that eased the inheritance of rule following Hafez's death at the beginning of the current century.

The cornerstone of this project of privatizing the state is the process of sectarianizing the security apparatus, which is the covert dimension of the private state (or the 'inner state') that is the wellspring of actual power in the country.

The sectarian security apparatus and the extraordinarily brutal attitude of its components are most evident in the *shabiha* (Assadist thugs) phenomenon: these are private, unorganized groups surrounding leaders from the Assad family or other influential Alawite families, which practice *tashbih* (bullying and intimidation) against the 'public state' (which I will address later) and the general population. This is an old phenomenon dating back to the Syrian occupation of Lebanon in 1976; it flourished in the 1980s and reached a zenith during the revolution. Since the beginning of the revolution, the *shabiha* enthusiastically played an official security role despite having no official status—something clearly indicative of the public caste/private state situation, and of their close connection with what I call the 'inner state' (which I will also address). It is clear that the *shabiha* were institutionalized in late 2012 under Iranian supervision, within the so-called 'National Defence Forces' that are fighting alongside the regime against the Syrian revolution. In this way, the *shabiha* turned into an organized repressive force practicing indiscriminate violence, while the official security agencies were emerging as unrestricted forces of *tashbih* and criminality from the first days of the revolution—even before it was revealed in January of 2014 that those 'public' security agencies had, in fact, killed 11,000 Syrians under torture within the twenty-nine months since the beginning of the revolution through August 2013, enough to qualify them as instruments of mass murder.

What could have led the regime to rely on 'innate' or instinctive trust among relatives, instead of developing an inclusively national trust, despite the regime's own Arab Nationalism doctrine? The answer is twofold.

The first element can be traced to the debased development of the neo-sultanate's elite and the mixture of brutality, cynicism and malevolence within the personality of Hafez al-Assad. The regime took it for granted that the people were only concerned with making a living and that very few of them were truly oppositional in any case—prisons could take care of those. The regime also sanctioned generalized corruption, opening the way for later blackmail and extortion and making it impossible for the people to play an independent political role. For that reason, incorruptible individuals warranted the regime's resentment and wrath.

Second, there is the 'economic' principle. National trust is a political construct requiring considerable strategic investments in citizenship and ensuring political and legal equality, as well as the abandonment of the desire for perpetual reign. By contrast, 'natural' trust (what Ibn Khaldun called *asabiyyah*) of the sort related to tribes and sects is a cost-effective goldmine, capable of generating enough 'revenue' to secure the regime. Sectarianism functions like an alternative to oil, a form of compensation for the lack of oil resources such as those at the disposal of royal families of the Arab Gulf. The goldmine of 'natural' (sectarian) loyalty, however, has the same effect as oil wells and revenues: it provides the ruling elite with exclusivity and an independence from the governed. The royal families of the Arab Gulf are well-off without imposing taxes on their people, which puts them in a protected position when it comes to addressing any possible objections to their rule. The considerable revenues of sectarianism, in the form of straightforward identification with the regime and profuse loyalty, all place the Assad regime in a stronger position to confront the public. By contrast, the creation of a national trust is an undertaking requiring farsighted 'investors' to implement large-scale investments in education, the legal system, economy, and culture to secure long-term revenues.

The Assad regime could rely on Alawite kinship relations because Alawites had indeed suffered from extended marginalization, something that persisted until the French mandate, when the colonial principle of 'Divide and Rule' was applied to their apparent advantage. These circumstances later served as the basis for an active victimhood narrative that embraced nationalist discourses (Arab nationalism, Syrian nationalism) up through the 1970s, before lending its voice to the Assad 'state'.

The marriage between one-man rule and the sectarianized security and military pillars of the regime has always been accompanied by a process of differential identification with the state among Syrians: comfort for some while others are left alienated and frustrated. A generally divisive atmosphere is maintained—but the language of nationalism and national unity, propagated all the time by the state media outlets, conceals and suppresses such divisions. The regime monopolizes the definition of nationalism in order to prevent these relative identifications from surfacing in public life and to prohibit any public discussions of their possible social and political origins. In Syria, national unity is equivalent to the regime's absolute discretion on sectarianism and all related practices and the criminalization of those who break this taboo, under the pretext of 'inciting sectarian strife.' Not only does this tactic protect the regime's own sectarianism, it also inverts reality so that drawing attention to existing sectarianism becomes a discriminatory offense.

Before the Syrian revolution, it was striking that many intellectuals took it upon themselves to safeguard both the taboo against any attempt to address the issue of sectarianism critically as well as the nationalism built on that taboo by pointing the finger at scholars and intellectuals who worked to break it. By colluding with an inherently discriminatory concept of nationalism that was fashioned to mask sectarianism, in practical terms these intellectuals supplemented the role of the regime's ideological apparatuses by accusing those who violated the taboo of being sectarian. Such accusations effectively supported the actions of oppressive sectarian security apparatuses that suppressed debate on the issue and punished those who challenged the taboo. This kind of multidimensional effort to maintain this unspokenness shows that sectarianism is a dynamic process capable of continuously generating concepts, discourses, and practices in order to safeguard a discriminatory social and political system.

Since its inception, the regime's self-reproduction has been linked to the reproduction of sectarian divisions, accompanied by a decline in the strength of more encompassing national bonds. Throughout the years, Syrians became less Syrian, identifying more and more with their various denominational groups. This was not an accident, but rather the by-product of a systematically discriminatory policy that was enforced by means of the most sectarian state apparatuses, the security agencies. These are also savage and omnipresent. Sectarianism is an effective governing tool: not only has it proven reliable for ensuring the regime's security and continuity, but it has also promoted discord among the people, leading them to become estranged from and mistrustful of one another. Its importance is evident in the physical violence and humiliation practiced by the security apparatus against the people, similar to the relationship between the Israeli army and the Palestinians, for example, or to colonial relationships in general. The personal, intimate nature of this violence and humiliation produces and is produced by 'organic' bonds—the abused and humiliated rush to embrace kinship ties in an effort to obtain protection. This is an instinctive response, what someone attacked by powerful bullies would do: curling in on oneself to protect one's body from harm. It is difficult for those who have been abused to develop more open ways of thinking and values with a wider horizon than their organic communities (family, tribe, sect...). At the same time, revenge is as likely a response to humiliation and is also intrinsically linked to these same organic bonds. Violence visited upon an individual on the basis of his or her clan is humiliating and insulting, and the restoration of dignity in such cases is an issue for the blood community as a whole, not the individual. Sectarian strife is of a similar nature. The status, dignity, and honour of one's sect cannot be maintained without striking back against the offending community, in a way that would engrave that response in their memories for generations to come. Women have an important status with respect to this type of violence because it is often committed against them in the name of the honour of a clan. There are many recorded instances of such violence among patriarchal formations such as tribes and sects.

The concept of justice related to law and to the modern state separates punishment from humiliation (although not in relation to other countries, and especially other 'civilizations'). Punishment in a nation-state is individual and based upon abstract criteria. It does not explicitly attack the physical or moral integrity of the person punished. In contemporary Syria, however, justice has not developed in a manner anywhere close to this model. Instead, degradation has reached a record level during the Assad era, embracing humiliation, torture, collective punishment, massacres, and siege. This development is closely linked to the ways the state and legal principles of justice have been undermined, a process in which sectarianism has played an essential role. The regime's establishments generally hold that dissenters oppose it solely for sectarian reasons, to such a degree that one can find oneself obliged to prove one's patriotism in front of the most sectarian institutions in the country!

An identical dynamic appears among the intellectual guardians of the sectarian taboo: they tend to ascribe every radical opposition to the regime exclusively to sectarianism—which, by the way, is very comfortable for Islamists, and particularly for Salafists.

These observations are necessary in order to illustrate that sectarianism is largely a power relation. It is not a political expression of a community, religion, or culture, nor is it merely a framework for favouritism and addressing needs, as will be shown later. When we speak of sectarianism, we speak of hatred, coercion, discrimination, and mistrust; we speak of social and political privilege, of war, camouflage, and deception. Such demonstrable associations explain how, over time, sectarianism came to constitute a reservoir of pretexts for murder, crime, massacres, and endless wars.

In conclusion, the rise and spread of sectarianism has been associated with the unwarranted elevation of a particular societal group to essentially 'public' status, coupled with the rise of violence, torture, and hatred as the imperative laws ruling public life. Until the early stages of Assadist rule, Syria had never experienced this kind of massive, extreme violence streaked with hatred. The elevation of Alawites was part of a political strategy by Hafez al-Assad and his men for achieving permanent control and possession first of the public state, and then of the entire country. Public caste and private state are two sides of the regime, which was founded and shaped by one man, Hafez, before he bequeathed it to his son, Bashar. Inherited succession was not compelled from outside, but is rather foundational to the regime's neo-Sultanic form of governance. Sectarianism itself and sectarian identification of individuals are governing tools for the regime, which persists on reproducing its suitable *asabiyyah* (intra-tribal or intra-sectarian solidarity) so that it may be sustained 'forever'. Neo-Sultanic rule is eternal and hereditary by definition. Sectarianism is a prerequisite for eternity and inheritance.

Assadism: Outer State vs. Inner State

At an early stage in the reign of our story's protagonist, Hafez al-Assad, two distinct states began to take shape within Syria: a non-sectarian yet powerless visible state that I call the 'outer state', and an invisible one that I call the 'inner state'. The latter is private and sectarian, and enjoys sovereignty over people's fates, internal domestic affairs, public resources, and regional and international relations. The outer state is comprised of a government, administration, official army, educational and public institutions, the 'parliament', legislation, and the courts: it is the domain of executive officers who have neither power nor freedom. The inner state, on the other hand, is comprised of the president (and the entire Assad family, nowadays), security agencies, and military formations with security functions. Today, it also includes tycoons, principally Assad's cousin, Rami Makhlouf. Guarded by fear, the inner state is invisible to the public, who have no access to any of the mechanisms of decision-making within it. The security staff of the inner state describe themselves as 'regime men' or as the regime itself, whereas the workforce of the outer state are merely employees. The difference between senior and junior officials within the outer state is smaller than the gap between senior officials of the outer state and their counterparts within the inner state. In other words, the outer state really only has junior employees, since those who are truly senior work for the inner state.

To illustrate the duality of these two states, we should point out that Riyad Hijab, who had served as prime minister for a time in 2012 before his defection from the regime in August of that year, theoretically held the second-highest position in the 'state' after Bashar al-Assad. However, a high-ranking intelligence officer like Jamil Hassan, who serves as Head of the Syrian Air Force Intelligence Directorate (the most brutal division during the revolution in Syria), occupies a much more significant position within the state. Hassan is a 'regime man', and he gives orders more than he negotiates. By contrast, the prime minister can barely broker even trivial matters, such as the appointment of a new employee, and lists of dismissed staff are sent to him directly from intelligence. To understand this reality, we need to look beyond 'the state' and toward this dual reality of outer state and inner state.

Because of the inconsequential role played by public officials of the outer state (i.e., those working outside the elite military groups with security functions), we have seen many defections from across their ranks during the revolution, but none from among the men of the inner state, or from the political-security-financial complex that owns and rules Syria.

The inner state's character influenced the Alawites, who occupy the position of a public political caste, a process that can be observed in the strengthening of their ties with Assad's state. Originally, Alawites did not have a strong religious organization; their loose network of sheikhs (religious leaders) was loosened even further under the rule of Hafez al-Assad. Their communal consciousness came to be tied up with the 'state', which, gradually but steadily, became the focus of their collective identity. Among Alawites themselves, meanwhile, any independent political expression was suppressed. The Shubatis (Februarists, a Baathist group with a significant number of Alawites that seized power in February 1966) were detained and otherwise undermined, despite being Baathists with a more resolute ideology than the Baathists of Hafez al-Assad. Their leader, Salah Jadid (1926–1993) spent the last twenty-three years of his life in jail without any legal process. The 'Communist Labour Party', which had a high percentage of Alawites among its members, met with a similar fate in the 1980s and 1990s. It is highly likely that the September 2012 kidnapping and disappearance of a known member of that party, Abdul Aziz al-Khair, falls within the same logic: defeating the possibility that any Alawite expression independent from the regime would emerge.

However, that possibility was mainly bypassed by means of the de facto discrimination in favour of Alawites in the vital state agencies, particularly the security agencies, followed by media and the diplomatic service.

In this context, it is important to note that sectarianism is not a practice or circumstance that occurs at the level of the outer state. At that level, there is a type of pan-Syrian discourse that goes by the ideological name of 'national unity', something that is often implemented practically through an approximate sectarian balance in the distribution of positions. When Syrian intellectuals or activists reject descriptions of the regime as sectarian, they have allowed the outer state to deceive them (at least when they are not consciously guarding the sectarian taboo). However, this reduces their talk to apologetic ideology, one that fails to disclose the true sources of authoritarianism and subordination within Syrian society. Sectarianism is the principle of the inner state's coherence, and its implicit approach in dealing with the population. It is unfathomable that such a reality is not being addressed explicitly, since it is the source of falsification, prevarication, and denial in Syrian public life, besides being a powerful wellspring of hatred, violence, and massacres.

For a symbolic representation of the real relationship between the outer state and the inner state, it is worth paying attention to the national calendar and to the prominence of days glorifying Hafez al-Assad, in comparison with the holidays of the outer state. Since 1970, the most celebrated anniversary has been the day of the 'Blessed Corrective Movement, led by Mr. President Hafez al-Assad', 16 November. On this day, all media outlets are dedicated entirely to glorifying the occasion and its creator. He is praised by school teachers in their classrooms. Banners with pictures of the 'iconic commander' are seen everywhere in the streets and squares, as well as in front of the headquarters of official institutions and on their doors. The second most significant day is 8 March, the anniversary of the coup by which the militarists of the Baath Party seized power in 1963. What is supposed to be an inclusive national holiday, the 17 April Independence Day celebration marking the evacuation of French troops from Syria, has been demoted to a secondary position on the national calendar.

In this way, the national memory has been reconstructed so that Hafez al-Assad occupies the position of an irreplaceable foundation.

The pre-Assad era, on the other hand, has been fully concealed and is only mentioned as a matter of ritual, during which it is described as an obscure time of 'feudalism and the bourgeoisie.'

'Assad's Syria'

During the seven years of Baathist rule that preceded Hafez al-Assad's military coup, Syrians witnessed industrial and commercial nationalizations, agrarian reforms, and an expansion of social services. As he rose to power, these processes came to a stop, although none of the gains made during that short period were given up. The regime also began to loosen political and administrative restrictions on the economic activities of the traditional Syrian bourgeoisie.

In the early years of his reign (especially after the war against Israel in 1973, which was followed by a flow of funds from the Arab Gulf into the young Assadist state), a new class started to form within the Baathist realm. It relied on income generated from two sources: the monopolization of the business of public coercion; and the formation of compulsory partnerships with the remnants of the traditional bourgeoisie. This traditional bourgeoisie had been dealt major blows during the Syrian-Egyptian unity as well as during the pre-Assadist Baath era (1963–1970), when it was consigned to a secondary position and robbed of its independent political aspirations.

Gradually, the level of social justice began to decline. Occupying a position of public authority started to become a way of ensuring socio-economic advantage. Rifaat al-Assad, Hafez's brother and commander until 1984 of the strongest security formation protecting the regime, embodied both the marriage of power and wealth and the principle of compulsory partnerships with senior Damascene bourgeoisie. He reaped a fortune from these partnerships, as well as from deploying ruthless commercial tactics, the antiquities trade, and the acquisition of his own port (which was only closed in 1999, fifteen years after his expulsion from the country in 1984, because of his aspirations to replace his then sick brother). Furthermore, according to Mustafa Tlass (Defence Minister from 1972 to 2004, and a man worthy of the title 'happy idiot'), his brother compensated Rifaat handsomely in return for relinquishing his positions of power.

Security forces and military formations that had just emerged victorious from confronting both active social and political protests and armed conflicts against Islamists (1979–1982) were given the green light to commit atrocities to their heart's content against the defeated, robbing them of their lives, property, and social connections. Leaders of these divisions and squads were rewarded with privileges, directly or indirectly, including mandatory partnerships with local notables: landlords in the Jazira area; industrialists and traders in Aleppo, Damascus and other cities; and agents of foreign companies. Each one received a reward proportional to his status: seniors collaborated with seniors; juniors got involved with other juniors, or gained access to power by navigating between the regime (particularly its sectarian component) and the general population so as to practice extortion and bribery. The logic of security control, which practically put the country under occupation, placed security capabilities at the centre of social interactions (including economic exchanges), turning its agents into lords and masters who enjoyed great wealth through their ownership of public authority. Rifaat synonymous with schemes for gaining wealth through political power. After his struggle for power with his brother, the man moved to Europe (the Mecca for the 'central bourgeoisie') with his billions. But his name remained behind to signal a general tactic.

It is said that the military budget takes up a high percentage of the Syrian national budget. Most of it likely goes to groups and divisions with security functions. Aside from what has been described above, most of the income of senior, middle, and junior members within these arrangements comes from extorting large segments of the population, or from the direct transfer of income to the benefit of this feared security janissary. Such circumstances justify talking about an internal colonialism, or a colonial relationship, that provides a framework that allows armed Assadist squads, which are distributed all over the country, to seize private and public resources through *tashbih* and robbery. Eventually, a new class formed around senior officials of the inner state that included associates of the Assad family, their confidants and partners. The regime's idea of 'security' was to strip society of weapons and the ability to defend itself, moves that merge the Weberian idea of the state's monopolization of legitimate violence with the rule of a military junta that governs in a colonial style. It also provides the rationale for accusing every armed resistance of terrorism, in keeping with a tried and tested colonial approach, of which Israel's occupation is the most apposite example.

The above is sufficient to give a sense of the extent of our non-existent social justice. The legal system also fell to pieces. Security services handled judicial functions, conducted arrests, tortured, and imprisoned, all without any interference. Not once in the decades of Assad's rule was a security official held accountable for his crimes against the public, including cases of torture, murder, and confiscation of properties on a large scale.

There was a military judiciary and a Supreme State Security Court established by emergency law that also prosecuted civilians. On the other hand, civil courts deteriorated steadily, plagued by Baathist partisan and security-interest corruption and sabotage.

The status of political justice was far worse. Prisons were filled with tens of thousands of political opponents, from Communists to Islamists, as well as non-Assadist Baathists, Nasserites, and individual citizens who fell victim to state encouraged and sponsored slander. All of them were tortured and humiliated, except those whose release was ordered immediately by influential mediators. Some of them died under torture, and many of them spent long years in prison. Thousands of Islamists were executed in Tadmur Prison, where inmates were daily subjected to arbitrary torture until its closure in 2001 (only to be reopened in 2011). Victims were buried in mass graves, the whereabouts of which are still unknown today. The Hama massacre in 1982 was the endpoint—not to the conflict with Islamists, but to any political rights for all Syrians.

In short, there is no longer any justice in Syria. There is no authority of any kind to shelter the vulnerable and the powerless, or to receive their complaints about the aggressions of the Sultan's family and associates.

As the regime became increasingly and excessively centred around wielding power and controlling the people, everything else began to decline: education, the economy, the administration, culture, the army, and so on. To the extent that power was centred on the person of the president, loyalty to him became the greatest of values, and so producing loyalty became a new function across public, bureaucratic institutions; schools, universities, trade unions, government agencies (along with the army, of course), popular organizations and the Baath Party. Within these institutions, loyalty was closely linked to job security. Loyalty entailed the controlling of staff, writing security reports on those with questionable loyalties, and, when necessary, directly participating in repression. 'Reports'—secret written materials, sent to the security services by informants, professionals or volunteers—include information on certain people, in the presence of so and so, for saying something or doing something or refraining from doing something when they should have done it. An epidemic of report writing started in the 1970s under the influence of both fear and greed: fear of being reported for witnessing an incident and not reporting it, which could lead to severe punishment; greed for advancement opportunities and rewards for the sincerity of one's loyalty. Loyalty was always mixed with fear, and with personal gain at others' expense.

These practices were in effect a national training in treachery. Through slander, betrayal, and throwing false accusations against others, the security agencies were in fact schools for malice, treachery, and cynicism. But above all, they were factories of terror and murder. Getting rid of this system and putting its leaders on trial one day is a national duty, second to none.

It should be clear that such a comprehensive security function extends to far more than the dreaded security services alone. Obviously, the Assad state aspired to turn all Syrians into informers—into traitors. Moreover, it should be recognized that the success of this scheme for planting mines of hatred, bitterness, and vindictiveness in society was not negligible. I believe that the current series of social explosions within Syria is a testament to how thoroughly society and its path to the future have been planted with these mines.

Tests for gauging the success of these institutions in producing a mixture of loyalty and fear were provided by the so-called 'spontaneous popular marches' on 'patriotic and national events', such as the anniversary of the 'Corrective Movement' (Hafez al-Assad's coup in 1970) and the anniversary of the 'Glorious Revolution of 8 March' (the first Baathist coup in 1963). Government employees, state workers, and school students were forced to participate in them. They cheered for the life of the leader. Not only was there nothing spontaneous in these marches, they were rituals of submission to the ruler, public acts of rape paraded before the community. Marches were broadcast repeatedly on television, and described as 'Million Man Marches'. Over the years, these humiliating parades served to affirm Sultanic ownership, and resulted in the complete estrangement of the general population from public space.

A second test of loyalty was the referendum on President Hafez al-Assad that took place every seven years. Three years after the Hama massacre of 1982, at a time when tens of thousands of secularists and Islamists were detained in the regime's prisons, from 1985 onward this ritual became known as the 'Renewal of *al-Bay'aa*' (an Islamic oath of allegiance). *Bay'aa* is an old Islamic expression for the people's declaration of loyalty to the *khalifah* (Caliph, the leader of the Muslims), a practice that took place only once during the life of the Caliph, at the time of his inauguration. *Bay'aa* carries a substantial element of coercion, and also implies that anyone who does not pledge allegiance is outside the 'consensus of the nation'. It is an avowal of the public's subordination to the *khalifah*. Historically, the extent of this dependency was limited by the restricted presence of Sultanic power and by allowing communities a relatively extensive independence with respect to their customs and general affairs, or, as Abdullah Laroui put it, by a relationship of 'mutual exclusion' between the Sultanic State and the public. What is new within the Assad regime, in comparison to that of the *khalifah*, is that *al-Bay'aa* is renewed every seven years. And instead of sending delegations of *Ahl-ul Hal wal-Aqd* (notables who decide on local or regional levels) to support the new Sultan as a sign of allegiance and loyalty, under Assad the Syrian people were obliged to place their votes of approval in ballot boxes in a manner that was both ostentatious and carnivalesque, with security monitoring to inhibit those who might dare to vote no. It is likely that Hafez wanted to circulate the concept of *al-Bay'aa* to gain Islamic legitimacy, to guarantee the subordination of the population, and to ensure 'consensus' against 'divisiveness' and *fitna* (strife or sedition)—all of which configured objection to his regime as treason or *kufr* (blasphemy) and confirmed his *khalifah*, or sultan status, over Syrians forever.

After the massacre of Hama in 1982, pledges of allegiance started to be made in blood: loyal enthusiasts pricked their thumbs with a pin, and stamped 'yes' on the referendum paper. Others were then forced to imitate them out of fear of doubts about their loyalty. In those years, Hafez al-Assad received telegrams signed with blood, announcing senders' willingness to sacrifice their lives and their blood for 'the greatest man of the nation', the 'beloved leader', and declaring their 'absolute' loyalty to him. In those same years, after he had killed about 30,000 in 1982, he became known as *al-abb al-qa'id* (the Commander Father): in the years after the 1970 coup, his title had been 'the Good Son of the People'. The new title referred to the expectation that a father must have the obedience of all his children, and also signalled an expansion of patriarchy in culture and social relations.

Through *al-Bay'aa* and 'fatherhood', the Assad State became an unrivalled source of subordination and social regression. Ungrateful 'children' were punished with horrible cruelty, killed or imprisoned for years, their very existence denied. During the five referendums of his rule, the 'Commander Father' won over 99 per cent of votes in the 'renewal of the pledge'. His son-successor, the 'Leader of the March of the Party and the People' (this was his formal designation) and *habib al-malayin* (Beloved by Millions) received over

97 per cent on two occasions. The third time, in June 2014 (after he had killed over 150,000 Syrians) he won 88 per cent of their votes in the first 'multi-party elections' against two 'extras' from the regime. This farce showed the world that the regime was engaged in political reforms!

The founding father and his successor occupied the top positions in both the outer state and the inner state.

Meeting needs and the system of values

In the eighties, the Sultan—as a person and as a regime—became the most important thing in the country. Hafez al-Assad is the capital of Syria, its glory and pride—a phrase heard frequently. Rather than citizenship or abstract legal relations, submission to this great feudal lord was the type of a relationship with the general population that was produced, circulated, and guarded by the 'State'. Loyalty to Hafez was the key to every locked door. The highest value became power, with money and kinship competing for second place. The significance of values such as work, knowledge, competence, and culture was in steep decline.

How do people take care of their growing needs under such circumstances? All needs are political in every modern society, passing through the state: its devices, laws, and international relations. How are needs met in 'Assad's Syria'?

First, by being someone with power or close to someone with power. This is very effective, but not available to many. Not everyone can be an influential intelligence officer, army officer, minister, or senior Baathist official. These positions are conditioned by a principle of scarcity operating within the hierarchical, closed nature of the regime. While the regime is quite broad with respect to its control and supervision of all that is going on in society and invests precious resources for this purpose, it is very restricted with respect to serving people's needs and providing possibilities for *wasta* (mediation).

Second, by money. One may bribe influential people in order to: secure a job; obtain a passport; facilitate the processing of a transaction by a government agency; get a license to build an extra room on the roof of a building for a son who is getting married; dig an artesian well; get a permit to sing in Armenian at an Armenian wedding where only five songs are allowed in the newlyweds' native language; get a permit to sing in Kurdish (strictly forbidden); open a shop to sell falafel or a barber shop; get a landline phone, etc. These are real examples, without the slightest bit of exaggeration. The most ridiculous of these taboos are violated all the time, but the taboos are nevertheless maintained because they allow for the fining and looting of society. The ridiculous is very rewarding.

Nevertheless, in most cases applicants are people who already live in poverty; they find themselves in vulnerable positions without legal protection or social support. They express this state of affairs in simple language. This is *zulm* (injustice)! *Zulm* is a lack of money combined with a lack of an influential network. It is poverty and social vulnerability. For those capable of bribery, needs are met according to how much money they possess.

By addressing people's needs through money in this way, a system is built for transferring wealth to those with power and influence, at the expense of the public.

A third way of serving needs is kinship: your officer brother, your influential Baathist cousin or your mother's minister cousin; or a prominent cleric (Sunni, Christian, or Druze) whom the 'regime' wants to give 'privileges' in exchange for his loyalty; or an important Sheikh of a clan who repays the regime's services with his loyalty and the loyalty of his clan. The required rank of such mediators varies according to the needs and the personal influence of the applicant. An application for a landline phone may be secured by a special exception from the Minister of Communications, mediated by a member of the domesticated Communist Party to which the minister belonged (I personally got an exception for the transfer of a landline phone from Raqqa to Damascus in 2001, brokered by a friend in the aforementioned party). The release of political prisoners, however, requires 'very heavyweight *wasta*.' Our only Shiite comrade in prison was released in 1982, after a year and a half of detention, because his father secured a meeting with Hafez al-Assad; the father belonged to one of the National Progressive Front (NPF) parties (a coalition of pet communist and Nasserite parties under the leadership of the Baath Party—officially, the NPF is the highest political command in the country). Lifting a travel ban on a writer, a human rights activist, or a former detainee requires the influence of an important intelligence officer. Ministers do not dare to intervene in such 'political' or 'security' issues.

Undoubtedly, there are those who refuse to resort to *wasta*. These people simply do not get their needs served. I was without *wasta* when I applied for a passport in 2004 and 2007, and my applications were refused by the 'Officers Affairs [i.e., security] Branch' in Damascus, the institution to which I was referred when I was banned from travelling to Lebanon in 2004 (Syrians could visit Lebanon with their national IDs).

It is understood that power, money, and kinship are key to serving needs and interests. They occupy top positions in the hierarchy of values in a way that mirrors the social structure: the people of power at the top, followed by people with money and kinship. At the bottom are those with no money and no ties to power; these people are outside the system, and they remain invisible and unheard. Values such as work, knowledge, competence, and culture do not overcome obstacles or open closed doors. None of the influential third-party mediators is an intellectual, a scientist, or a leader in any independent or opposition party. To an extent proportional with their political and intellectual independence, such people are located outside the cronyism networks that connect applicants with mediators at local and central locations of power. In fact, they are marginalized or even expelled from the public patronage system; no one mediates or brokers for them. They generally live privately on the margins, having no impact on the conduct of the general situation in the country. This is how clientelism functions as a mechanism to stifle oppositionists and independents, in collaboration with mechanisms of direct repression and corruption.

In reality, there are hardly any independent positions. There are loyalists (or rather, followers) and there are opponents subjected to repression, but there are no real independents, not even among the well-known intellectuals. Independence is structurally impossible, even as it remains ideologically possible. During the years of Hafez's reign, not a single scholar was able to express their independence openly in the public sphere. It should be kept in mind that the expression of independence and then bearing the consequences is precisely what independence is.

Some intellectuals have never faced problems 'getting by', especially with regard to overcoming travel bans through the use of intelligence networks. But this comes at the cost of sacrificing their independence. Those individuals do not fall outside the mechanisms of submission or corruption. Some intelligence officers 'befriend' intellectuals, exchanging ideas and enjoying lavish meals with them. There is also a class of tame 'oppositionists'. They keep the telephone numbers of key intelligence officers (these are given to activists, dissidents, and writers when they are summoned to intelligence headquarters for some reason): this allows them to masquerade as mediators between their partisan 'sects' and the intelligence services (the only channels through which the regime will deal with them).

In contrast with their public rhetoric, these 'oppositionists' are practically part of the regime through the role they play as intermediaries, their participation in clientelism and their patronage of intelligence officers. Here, too, we find the dual outer/inner structure: just as the sectarian inner state hides behind the pan-Syrian outer state, the submissive position of this dominated section of the dominant 'new notables' hides behind a (falsely) oppositionist discourse. This fact sheds some light on the divisions among the Syrian opposition, both old and new.

In other words, submissive relationships prior to the revolution included sectors of the opposition, but only the least rebellious ones. As Lenin differentiated between 'His Majesty's Opposition' and 'Opposition to His Majesty' before the Bolshevik Revolution, one should distinguish between 'His Excellency's Opposition' and 'Opposition to His Excellency' in Syria. The presence of the former is contingent upon the existence of His Excellency, and would disappear with him.

Kinship circles are wider than circles of money, and both are more extensive than the circle of power. But kinship circles are not equivalently wide, nor are they distributed equally in the community. There are, for example, greater numbers of intelligence officers, army men, and other influential, powerful men in the Alawite milieu (10–12 per cent of the population) than there are in other confessional communities. This is indisputable, and certainly has a dangerous social impact. The density of the Alawite networks of favouritism and the consequential availability of *wasta* among them is a dynamic source for sectarian feelings. Even when financial conditions are equal, some facilities and services remain unavailable to other groups, particularly within the Sunni archipelago. As mentioned earlier, a sense of 'injustice' stems from the need for income and 'vitamin W' (as Syrians call *wasta*) in a political environment where legal justice is absent. The availability of clientelism to Alawites partially makes up for a lack of money and, consequently, modifies the severity of injustice.

It is not known exactly what the ratio of Alawite military intelligence officers to the total number of officers is, but it is many times higher than their proportion within the whole population. Their influence is stronger than that of others holding equal rank. This is also a known fact in Syria, one that points to an invisible inner system of positions and orderings that conflicts with, and is destructive to, the publicly apparent outer state.

There are also bishops and businessmen in the Christian milieu (about 5 per cent of the population, before the revolution) with whom the regime is keen to reconcile because they are mediators for the needs of people within their community. The regime gives special attention to Christians to expand its social base, and to enhance its 'international' legitimacy—posing, in fact, as the protector of minorities and of Christians in the eyes of the 'secular' West.

Moreover, there are Druze Sheikhs and political or security influencers in the Druze community (3 per cent of Syrians) who mediate for those within their group.

In the Sunni community (about 70 per cent of the population), there are also well-heeled, influential clerics and tribal leaders who mediate for their relatives. However, the percentage of influential figures here is not sufficient to provide for the needs of so many people. There are sub-communities within the Sunni community that operate within networks of relatively dense favouritism, including in particular the Damascene network, which consists mainly of wealthy men and clergymen around which the 'Damascene sect', so to speak, is constituted.[1] However, widespread discrimination and the lack of access to *wasta* in non-urban Sunni environments (which have a high percentage of the poor, and therefore more experience of *zulm*) help to explain why political mobilization in the Arab Sunni community takes an Islamic form.

Among Kurds (8–10 per cent) there are influential figures as well, although this small network consisting of a few individuals is likewise unable to mediate for the whole Kurdish community. This deficit is reason for the high level of political mobilization within the Kurdish community, and helps explain why it takes a nationalist form.

These realities help explain the fact that the strongest victimhood (*mazloomiyya*, a word etymologically related to *zulm*) narratives in Syria today are Kurdish and Sunni. In the Alawite community, by comparison, a narrative of superiority (self-attributed to 'modernity' in general and 'secularism' in particular) is more prevalent today than the narrative of victimhood that had been very powerful until the 1970s.

To summarize, religious and sectarian groups possess varying amounts of social capital: that is, access to 'vitamin W' and various advantages. Substantially independent from material capital, social capital is peculiar to the Sultanic system and makes it easier for individuals to take care of their business. Sectarianism is a matter of inequality in social capital, and is linked to the discriminatory structure of the political system. In obtaining *wasta*, admission into military and security formations, and overseas employment, in managing to avoid the worst humiliations and punishments including murder—in all these matters, your chances of success are simply greater if you are descended from a certain group of people than with respect to equivalent material capital. This is sectarianism, which is enveloped in a great deal of discretion, and it must be kept in mind when talking about class inequalities and social disparities in Syria. Furthermore, members of minorities usually have higher social capital; a fact not disconnected from essentialist international (Western in particular) prejudices against Arabs and Muslims, and from 'minority rights' dogma.

The kinship industry

It is useful here to recall three important points.

First, a routine, publicly available means for meeting people's needs barely exists. The competency of an already corrupt bureaucracy has declined steadily, with loyalty being the top priority in the appointment of staff. People do not only require a broker for exemption from general obligations or to attain unlawful privileges; brokers are also necessary for taking care of their legitimate needs without disruption or infinite delays. The court system, like the bureaucracy, is dysfunctional, corrupt, and slow. Routine meeting of needs is ultimately an exception to the rule. This has been the reality since the 1970s, and is another facet of the centralization of public life around the Sultan.[2]

The second point is that money performs all the functions of favouritism, but is also governed by a principle of scarcity. Economic sufficiency is the prerogative of very few people. Material adequacy is conditioned by continuous growth, which requires the extortion of others and the protection of this extortion. This path is not available to many.

The third point is that one is required to look for *wasta* among relatives, but not among strangers. The latter wouldn't respond to requests in any case, because there would always be awkwardness and an implicit estimation of costs and benefits. Why should one mediate for benefits for a stranger when there is always a risk of being 'dismissed' and turned down? On top of that, the 'favour' will have to be returned one day and success is not guaranteed. So what is one to do? Seeking help in brokerage should be kept among relatives, and relatives alone. Apart from strengthening internal bonds of the confessional groups through this system of *wasta*, and thereby strengthening those of influence within those groups, the system itself is designed to condemn the intervention of strangers for the benefit of strangers: this is none of your business, why interfere? An Armenian arrested or summoned to the security apparatus would probably hear the following: 'You are Armenian, why bother with the affairs of others?' A Christian would be told: 'Why work in politics? We protect you from "fanatics", (meaning Sunnis) and if it weren't for us, they'd kill you!' A Druze would hear: 'The people of the city of Hama hate your people and would love to eliminate you!' These examples provide just a glimpse of what I have heard from those involved, or learned from their writings. People are pushed ever more deeply into their narrow communities and away from the general Syrian public, which is no longer perceived as a unifying framework for trust. Of course, this process weakens the voluntary and artificial bonds of 'civil society' while encouraging the cohesion based on kinship and hereditary communities (i.e. 'organic' society).[3] First comes blood kinship (one's family and clan), then moral kinship (one's religious, ethnic, or provincial group). The chances for forming an efficient clientelism network increase when the community is small, and decrease when it is big.

A *mujtama' ahli* (a society of hereditary bonds) is the only form of society that can be formed under the Sultanic state; it is by no means a 'state society comprised of individuals' (as it was characterized by a Syrian state worshipper, Aziz al-Azmeh), nor is it a civil society composed of independent, voluntary ties.[4] In truth, the society of the Sultanic State amounts to an annulment of individuals, who never surface in Syria except in the context of objection and resistance to Sultanism and its state—a resistance that the state worshippers are always in position to oppose.

The modern society of the neo-Sultanic state is not a 'traditional society' in any way: one comprised of families, neighbourhoods, and confessional communities, in a relationship of 'mutual exclusion' with the Sultanic State. Rather, it is an artificial modern society that functions as a framework for relations of subordination. Its relationship with the neo-Sultanic State is one of overlap, interdependence, and ontological coexistence. In such a situation, relations of mutual exclusion pertain among 'organic' communities, but not between these groups and Sultanic rule. Only those who challenge Sultanic rule transgress the boundaries separating these communities that all have their backs turned to each other—but such challengers are always besieged by the Sultanic state, its apparatus, and its ideologues (both paid and voluntary).

The world of *wasta* is a fragmented world that is comprised of regressive and isolated groups. For example, it is unlikely that an Armenian would mediate for an Arab Sunni, an Arab for a Kurd, a Shiite for a Druze, or a Circassian for a Palestinian. The world of *wasta* is a world of kinships and mutual exclusions; the borders that separate these communities are policed by the mechanisms of the Sultanic apparatus.

This state of affairs is reinforced by the very structure of clientelism or favouritism, since it is built on resorting to relatives in a way that maximizes the value of blood and moral kinships and puts them in high demand. Kinship becomes the necessary framework for pursuing and meeting one's needs. The family, clan, and caste consequently acquire public functions, essentially playing the role of political organizations in serving the needs of the population. Over time, it is likely that the rising value of kinship will transform casual, weak confessional links into much more coherent ethnicities that then will constitute the frameworks for connections to power and determine the acquisition of private and public benefits. This process already permeates victimhood and superiority narratives, conflicts and risks, violence and victims—all things that the neo-Sultanic regime has engendered in abundance over the past two generations.

The Assadist state's reinforcement of relations of subordination and 'organic' ties explains the ways that the impact of kinship has been strengthened. Through these means it has engineered a profound social decline in relation to the general direction of Syrian history since it took its modern form at the end of World War I.

The sectarian relationship

Whether figured as real or artificial kinship frameworks, sects are closed networks of favouritism, condensed around people of influence who mediate with local or central authorities on behalf of people in need who belong to the mediator's sectarian group. This situation is reminiscent of the role of notables during the Ottoman Empire, when influential elders within their communities or local religious or kinship groups mediated between these groups and the local centre of power, or with the Ottoman centre in Istanbul. This system has been well studied by historians, including Albert Hourani and Philip Khoury.

Sects are intermediary bodies formed around mediators or notables, who connect segments of the population with the centres of power. Collectively, these constructs constitute an 'organic society' (*mujtama' Ahli*) as opposed to a 'civil society' (*mujtama' Madani*), and their respective components are mutually exclusive.

The importance of the mediatory role of sects is part of what justifies describing Assad's state as Neo-Sultanic, or one that is always busy in 'organizing' society, de-civilizing it, and transforming it into a composite of 'organic' communities subordinated to a unified centre of power. Additionally, the Neo-Sultanic State is premised on the following components: *al-Bay'aa* as a method of ensuring the collective obedience of the 'organized' society to the Sultan and his apparatus; the inheritance of power in perpetuity, which is contrary to the logic of a contractual and constitutional national state; a monopoly on politics; the persistent exclusion of any independent voices; the use of violence to crush social protests; a generally instituted state violence that deploys humiliation and revenge; the spread of an ideology that denies the right to social protest and any similar public claims under pretext of fear of *fitna*; and an emphasis on *Ata'* (superior power giving to the needy) and *makruma* (generous donations from the rich and powerful to the poor and weak). When Hafez issued a decree increasing the salaries of state employees, these were *ata*'s and *makruma*s from him, as opposed to rights. This of course implies the ruler's appropriation of the country, and the treatment of public resources as the ruler's personal property. The inheritance principle within the Assad dynasty is the most perilous institution to have plagued the Syrian Republic since independence, especially since it could not have occurred had the Father not murdered tens of thousands in the 1980s, arrested, tortured, and imprisoned tens of thousands more, and succeeded in building a 'state' based on submission.

To conclude these remarks about sects, let us observe how they are structured around relationships of subordination that combine three elements within a hierarchical social pyramid.

At the base stands a large crowd, comprised of the entire needy population; of those who cannot create a way of life that is independent of or removed from the state. The state does not provide general mechanisms for meeting their legitimate needs.

Below the summit is a small crowd of new notables: officers, clergymen, businessmen, tribal leaders, senior Baathists and government agents. They have enough influence and authority either to serve the needs of their inferiors or to mediate for them with those of higher standing. They also have access to various facilities and privileges in exchange for their loyalty to the Sultan: financial services; special conveniences for themselves and their families in housing and business; greater opportunities for assignments overseas in diplomatic missions or education (overseas deployment is the second most sectarianized sector in Syria, after the intelligence and the military); and access to foreign agencies, companies, and banks.

At the peak stands a much narrower group, one that used to include only Hafez al-Assad himself in his day, along with leaders of his agencies and military and security units. Today, it includes the entire Assad family, senior security officials, and businessmen. This elite can hold anyone accountable but it cannot itself be held accountable.

One should also visualize sub-pyramids within this general pyramidal structure to grasp the social structure of the neo-Sultanic state more fully. In each region of the country and within every social group, the same structure is found. At the base are many people in need, above them is a smaller number of intermediaries and liaisons to address people's needs within specific regions or classes. Higher classes have greater needs, which means their intermediaries need to be more influential. However, the lower classes are mostly left out of the world of favouritism—without any connections or Vitamin W, their needs are never met. This is a fundamental point: a regime based on clientelism deprives large segments of the population from having any useful intermediaries.

The regime requires that mingling among groups stay limited, with a low level of mutual trust. Mutual exclusion characterized the relationship between the traditional Sultanic state and its governed communities. Within this neo-Sultanic state, mutual exclusion is transformed into heightened exclusion among the *ahli* ('organic') components, with some of these components overlapping with structures of governance. We are not looking at the structural independence of the state from society, as the state-worshipping dogma of Aziz al-Azmeh would have it. Rather, we are looking at overlapping, unequal relationships, which I described above in terms of uneven identification with the state, and at the emergence of a general, political sect.

The new notables are divided into two categories: a local group made up of clerics, tribal leaders, and wealthy people; and an official one made up of officers, government officials, and senior Baathists. As mentioned earlier, clientelism is exclusively internal with regards to the local component: a mediator mediates for those from his group (regional and/or tribal and/or sectarian). However, the Baath Party also formed a framework for mediation (*wasta*) in the years of Hafez al-Assad, and offered some opportunities for socializing among people of different origins—something that has almost completely faded away upon the arrival of Bashar to office. Officers and ministers provide mediation in exchange for money; this fills their pockets and impoverishes the governed, and also has the effect of providing an alternative to kinship and its sectarian complements when it comes to serving people's needs.

Bashar's era: Neoliberalism and the collapse of Baathist Populism

Sectarian practices became more prominent than ever during the years of Bashar's rule, even more than they had been in his father's era. This was due to the accelerated deterioration of Baathist methods of social mobilization such as the Baath Party itself, along with the decline of its 'popular organizations' such as the Revolutionary Youth Union of the Baath Party (which accommodated theoretically all young Syrians), the National Union of Syrian Students (the only organization available for college students), the Labour Union, and the Farmers Union. The same applies to the syndicates of scientific professions that were restructured in 1981, after their boards took positions opposed to the regime and introduced democratic demands in public statements the previous year (1980). These organizations were weak, but their membership extended throughout the country, and they served as social mediators between large segments of the population and the centres of power. All these institutions have deteriorated during the years of the 'modernizing' Bashar, who relied on the bourgeoisie (I will explore their structure later) which had evolved under the auspices of his father. Bashar also adopted a neoliberal vision for 'reforming' the economy, so that wealth was accorded a more important status within the hierarchy of public values than it had enjoyed under his father.

It should be noted that the deterioration of the Baath Party and its organizations under Bashar's rule was the second wave of its decline. The first began under his father at the beginning of his rule: Hafez favoured intelligence agencies and the inner state, but maintained Baathist organizations as tools of censorship, social control, and mediation. In the era of the Son, Baathist outlets were once again dispensed with to the benefit of the new bourgeoisie and their organizations, such as The Syria Trust for Development, headed by Bashar's wife, Asma' al-Assad. But the Baath Party was dead before that, and showed no signs of objecting to the constitutional article in 2012 that dismissed it from 'the leadership of the state and society'. The party was never in charge, not even for one day—it was merely bearing false witness to itself and to Syrians.

One of the factors that promoted the rise of sectarianism during the Son's reign was the very act of succession from his father, which established a ruling dynasty and introduced a de facto inner constitution decreeing hereditary rule within the Assad family. Just as he was heir to his father, Bashar's basic duty will be to pass power to his son, whose name is also Hafez.

There were other favourable factors, including the proliferation of a global culturalist and 'civilizationalist' intellectual climate that is sectarian to its core. These developments were connected to the defeat of communism and ideologies of practice (as opposed to ideologies of identity) like third world nationalism, with its values of equality, freedom, and social and national liberation, as well as to the rise of neoliberalism and multiculturalism, postmodernism, and ideologies of identity. Starting in the 1990s, this climate became the habitat for most Syrian intellectuals, as much for those who held on to a nominally leftist rhetoric, as for those who abandoned it. We now live in a post-September 11 world, however, one that has placed 'Islam'—Sunni Islam in particular—in the position of a global villain. We are also living at the time of the American occupation of Iraq, the rise of Iranian Shiite political hegemony, and the emergence of al-Qaeda and Sunni jihadists in Iraq—along with the Assad regime's devices for manipulating them.

This climate has revived old colonial discourses centred on Islam and fundamentalism. These discourses advocate a coercive secularism and systematically denigrates the 'unenlightened' and the 'irrational'. Any cruelties visited upon such people are greeted with tolerance and leniency by both the Western and domestic 'first world'. It is appropriate to categorize the works published during the 1990s and 2000s of Syrian writers such as Adonis, George Tarabichi and the like as examples of internal orientalism and renewed colonial discourse. They also cannot be separated from the birth of Sultanism and the emergence of a privileged internal 'first world' that safeguards itself with both extreme brutality and the discourse of reason, enlightenment, and modernity—all of which signals the rise of a genuine internal colonialism.

With the decline in the social functions of the state (though by no means its repressive authority) and the rise of the role of wealth that accompanied the liberalization of the economy, the importance of kinship and sectarianism increased. New forms of severe deprivation emerged—37 per cent of Syrians were living below the upper poverty threshold ($2/day in 2007) while 11 per cent were below the lower poverty threshold (near $1/day in 2004)—simultaneously with the decline of agencies of populist mobilization that we discussed earlier. Meanwhile, Syrian society continued to be excessively impoverished politically because it was prevented both from expressing itself and its needs within public space, and from independent gathering and organizations. Sects, besides being patronage networks geared towards serving people's needs, also came to define the boundaries of political poverty.

Sects functioned as social solidarities, ensuring trust and safety for segments of the population. They possessed collective discourses. Sects are most efficient when they are small in size: the system seems designed in a way that divides larger groups to the benefit of the smaller, most cohesive groups.

For many in Sunni Syrian environments, practiced religion (i.e., gatherings of worshipers in mosques, religious holy texts, and religious adages) marked the boundaries of political poverty. Intuitively, such a confluence of religion and politics is destined to have a sectarianizing effect, albeit partial (not encompassing all Sunnis) and incomplete (without open political expression). The diversity of Sunni (to which around 70 per cent of the population belong) environments along with the heavy censorship imposed on Sunni political activity both worked against the achievement of an all-encompassing Sunni sectarian identification.

In truth, the efficacy of religious sects, whatever the extent of their respective patronage networks, is even less guaranteed than was the case for the Baathist 'popular organizations.' The sectarian machine is not designed to serve the needs of the general public—it subordinates the populace at large first to the pinnacle of power, and then to the influence of the new notables. Sometimes clientelism fails. Not all notables have the same influence, nor do they have equal access to centres of influential power. *Wasta* is also less available to people who have no money. The poorest have no mediators or support networks. This is one of the system's sources of tensions. Most people of the lower class never have their needs served, and have no access to the 'keys' through which their needs can be met. This is a spring of resentment and anger.

What I have described above was also a driving factor behind the revolution. The Syrian revolution broke out due to a confluence of two things: a chronic failure of the regime, the consequences of which were suppressed by the so-called 'wall of fear' in Syria; and positive, successful examples in Tunisia and Egypt that gave the impression that it was possible to topple Sultanic fortifications.

Initially, the main participants in the revolution came from two sectors: the 'working society', who wanted legal justice, relations of citizenship, and 'freedom'; and the impoverished sectors of the population, who had no 'backing' or 'vitamin W' and were deprived of social and legal justice.[5] Later, these were joined by some secondary, less influential members of the new notables, such as ministers, members of parliament, and ambassadors—those whose power did not go beyond that of the outer state, or who had limited influence within it.

During Bashar's era, before the revolution, the neo-Sultanic state modernized its symbolism by reducing its emphasis on the military. For example, spontaneous popular marches were no longer done in uniform, but in civilian clothing or fashionable shirts; the podium that used to be put in place two days prior to the delivery of a senior state official's speech in front of huge crowds was replaced by gatherings in squares or major streets. Before, we would see grim images of Hafez printed on sheets of cloth with the same image visible twenty times in a setting, and dull 'nationalist' and 'socialist' slogans saluting the commander written on cloth banners were made especially for the occasion—using a special budget allocated by each institution that also provided opportunities for theft and self-enrichment. Today there are images of a smiling Bashar printed with expensive materials and made into strips of cloth that can be extended over an entire side of a multi-floor building, with phrases written in colloquial Syrian such as *Menhebbak*! ('We love you!' in colloquial Damascene dialect), or flirtatious expressions such as 'Syrians know their Bashar best!' In line with the regime's policies of 'modernization', even love for the leader was privatized, where it had previously been the affair of the Baath Party, trade unions, the Revolutionary Youth Union, and schools. Public displays of love flowed light heartedly from economic institutions, private companies, and businesses. The Syria Trust for Development, headed by Asma' al-Assad, mother of Hafez Jr., then entered the market of symbolic goods, largely replacing popular Baath Party organizations.

We have not escaped Sultanism in any way. On the contrary, it has become engraved into our society and has acquired the new tastes of a nouveau-riche class, made up of the sons of officers, ministers, and senior Baathists. Most of the founding fathers came from rural families, or were minor notables descended from people of the countryside and medium-sized towns, according to Hanna Batatu. Now in their forties, their sons are wealthy, speak at least one foreign language, and are familiar with Western culture and the joys of life for the wealthy. They have no history of social conflict, political battles, or national struggles. They meet all their needs by money or by force.

One last point concerning the neoliberalization of the Syrian economy: why have we not seen privatization of the public resources and facilities in Syria, when we know that privatization is an essential item in the neoliberal prescription? The answer is simple: the Sultanic transformation. Through this transformation, the state and the country as a whole became the property of the Sultan and the ruling dynasty. Privatization is unnecessary because of the private condition of the state.

Units of Sultanic rule

From theoretical and practical points of view, one can't help but make an important observation about sectarian relationships and how they function within the social pyramid, whose base is too broadly comprised of the poor and in which, closer to the top, notables and new dignitaries mediate with those at the peak on behalf of some of those at the base. Sectarian relationships vertically link influential people and dignitaries with a public that resides at the bottom and with a centre of decision-making above. They do not take place in a separate world, or outside of horizontal class relations. The new notables and dignitaries occupy the position of a 'middle class' in the neo-Sultanic formation, and their relationships with each other are broader and more solid than the ones they have with people at the bottom, whom they ensure stay divided. By contrast, the majority of the 'needy' occupy a position that is divided against itself: interactions among them are limited. At the very peak was the neo-Sultan, Hafez—today, it is Bashar and the family. If the situation stabilizes for Bashar, there is no doubt that he will bequeath the throne to his son, Hafez. The inner 'constitution' of Sultanic rule is succession, a phenomenon that is not dissociable from the tripartite sectarian relationship of Sultan to notables to general public—they are two sides of the same coin in the reign of a neo-Sultan.

In summary, sects are political components of neo-Sultanic rule because they are obligatory pathways for serving the needs of the general population. The Sultanic regime can only be sustained if the population is subordinated and stripped of political capacities. Sects are excellent frameworks for this subordination because they deprive residents of political agency and turn them into subjects and accomplices.

The revolution against Sultanic rule will not be complete until the political role of sects is crushed—only then will the population be emancipated from the status of subjects and from the chains of dependency.

Sultanic rule transforms social conflicts into religious *fitna* or sectarian conflicts, a tactic second to none for intimidating the population with the prospect of prolonged unrest and chaos.

Originally, *fitna* was the other face of *Bay'aa* and Sultanic governance—Bashar al-Assad used the word sixteen times in his first speech after the revolution broke out. In essence, a Sultanic state is a management of *fitna*: it subdues or summons it according to its survival needs. It holds the monopoly over *fitna*, which it nationalizes when necessary. This is what happened during the Syrian revolution.

Sectarianism and classes

The world of sects is not located in a distant galaxy, separate from the world of classes, nor is it far away from the world of unjust social and political privileges: it is part of this world, as I illustrated above with my example of the social pyramid. As the representative of the ruling family, Bashar orders and is obeyed. He does not need mediation because he is above the law. He only need follow one rule: ensure that his family stays in power. Absolute authority is condensed and concentrated at the top of the pyramid. At the top, there is also enormous wealth (Rami Makhlouf is the treasurer of the Assads' money), and full unity. In an interview conducted by the late Anthony Shadid on 10 May 2011, Makhlouf said, 'We believe there is no continuity without unity. As a person, each one of us knows we cannot continue without staying united together.'[6] At the bottom of the pyramid there is political and economic destitution, disintegration, fragmentation, conflict, distrust, and a lack of confidence. In the middle, there is comparatively greater wealth and power, and also a degree of consolidation. The new notables exchange benefits among themselves, and are closer to one another than they are to the divided social base—and they are closer than those at bottom are to each other. In turn, they are kept under supervision and control from the summit, which does not allow them to act independently. The new notables are a sector unified by dependence on what is above; through them—and also by other means—the division of those below is ensured. By virtue of their position, they are Janus-faced: a public face looks up to the Sultanic peak; a private face looks down at the *ahli* (organic) communities. The most proximate forum for alliances within this sector is the 'Parliament'. But the sector itself is certainly much more extensive than that institution, and includes all ministers, governors, and senior people of influence, both civilian and military.

In order for the Sultanic summit to remain united, the bottom needs to remain divided and fractious and the new notables must remain in their role as obedient aides in return for the privileges and amenities they receive. The policies of neo-Sultanic rule are based on spreading *fitna* among the governed, so that it may remain above all the rest, lofty and condescending.

The world of sects is close to the world of classes, but distant from that of religions and beliefs. When we examine sectarianism, we are in the heart of a world of politics and power, wealth and influence, social privileges and social deprivations, sovereignty, and subordination: we are not in the world of faith, piety, beliefs, fanaticism, and rituals. Sectarianism is not an ideology of identity. As Benedict Anderson has argued, sectarianism—like racism—is an ideology of class. Which is to say, it rebuilds and redirects identities to support and disguise current relations of power and privilege. Sectarianism (like racism) is not only an ideology: rather, it is a system of conditions and practices based on discrimination among the population according to their religious or confessional backgrounds. It is the designation and description of groups of the population in ways that warrant discrimination for or against some of them. However, the peculiarity of sectarianism is how it hides the reality of social privilege and discrimination behind a cultural heritage of differentiation. What is hidden behind sectarianism is not sect but class. Social and political privileges are concealed within it, not cultural distinctions.

Sectarianism is a specific form of racism in that it is a discriminatory system of labels, descriptions, and classifications. It does not owe privileges or their lack to race but rather to faith or culture, which makes it seem as if the general circumstances of certain groups are principally the product of their beliefs and culture—in other words, something independent from issues of power, politics, access to decision-making, and to public resources. The type of sectarianism that Antonio Negri and Michael Hardt identify as 'differential racism' in their book *Empire* is a cultural or civilizational racism. The doctrine of a 'clash of civilizations'—which is nothing but sectarian struggle at the global level—is an example of such 'differential racism'. Like local sectarianism, global sectarianism is more closely related to class than to identity. It is more related to First World privileges than to Western culture or Christianity.

An ideology of culturalism and 'civilizationism' is suitable for obscuring racism while depicting the fortunes of certain groups as a true reflection of their cultural identities, so that neither social nor political privilege has an influence at the local level and nor do the current conditions of global control. There is only a transparent, competitive marketplace of identities in which some of us are destined to be affluent while others are destined to be losers. The marketplace merely enables the measure of the entitlements attached to identities.

Civilizationism, which I use here as a synonym for culturalism, flourished in Syria in the two decades prior to the revolution, and in the second decade more than the first. It told a Manichean tale of struggle between fundamentalism, obscurantism, and irrationality, on the one hand, and modernity, enlightenment, and rationality, on the other. Because social and political conditions were interpreted in terms of culture, the facts of privilege, power, repression, and looting were practically obscured.

In many well-known examples across our region, sectarianism is preferentially coupled with power, prestige, and influence, and with the social privileges that ensue from enjoying an excellent position of power—more than would be the case on the basis of one's economic class alone, strictly speaking. This is related to the fact that the possession and exercise of power, rather than material production, is the basis of class and privilege. He who has power gets a class promotion, and loyalists get better opportunities to climb the class ladder. Sectarianism is an instrument of power, and power is an elevator of class.

The reality of the regime is power and social privilege: not the faith of the ruler and not the society's cultural character. Sectarianism itself is not the regime's reality: it is a strategy of political control, a tool for governing, subordination, and the protection of privileges and privileged segments of society. Sectarianism is a socially divisive power that obscures the fact of political and social disparities behind the diversity of identities and religious beliefs.

This, in fact, is where the paradox of the sectarian regime lies: it is only sustainable to the extent it provides discriminatory identifications for a certain sect or sectarian alliance, but its ultimate goal is to create personal profits and privileges for first the Sultan and then for the new notables. The regime acts as patron for those who identify with it, and distinguishes them from others so they can better serve the regime. It sustains itself by feeding differences of identification, and by generating disparities among different sectors of the lower class as well. The regime succeeds so long as the barriers that divide the poor at the bottom are greater than the ones that separate the lower class from the middle. Barriers between Sunnis and Alawites, for example, should remain higher than the barriers that separate a lower-class Alawite from an Alawite notable (an Alawite officer, for example, or an Alawite Director-General) and also higher than the barriers between a lower-class Sunni and a Sunni dignitary (a minister, for example, a wealthy man, or an influential cleric). What is important for the elite of the sectarian regime is the power and wealth in its possession. The rights or dignity of the people are secondary, mere rhetorical tools of governance.

The two faces of the sectarian regime

As noted above, mediation is not available to many, and may not work even when it is available. The regime is not designed to meet all the needs of people, but only the needs of the powerful in proportion to their influence. What, then, keeps the pyramid together? What prevents the revolt of those who are frustrated by being deprived of access to *wasta*? What holds the hierarchical structure together, keeping the lower class in its place while ensuring that those above remain on top? The answer is 'security', or the general function of the security system, whose central role and prevalently sectarian character I discussed earlier. Security has a fundamental role, one that is institutionalized and cultivated and on which the regime relies to reproduce itself. The Assad regime presents an example of the forceful takeover of a community and its resources by overgrown, omnipresent intelligence agencies that are designed so that the regime 'lasts forever', just as it exemplifies a comprehensive system of patronage in which sects are the Sultanic form of 'civil society'.

It has also been noted that the regime's security system's area of operation is very wide, allowing oversight of the entire society. However, the areas of it that allow access to 'vitamin W' are limited: they are not necessarily available to cronies and influential dignitaries when needed. Security control from above is stronger and more pervasive within society than patronage influence from below. All people are under security control and only a few of them have access to *wasta*. On the one hand, sectarianism is embodied in the protective armour that surrounds Assad's Sultanate, consisting of 'a class of guards' that penetrates society with a far-reaching network capable of scrutinizing the slightest of activities. On the other, sectarianism ensures that patronage networks split the population vertically, which allows for the surveillance of the lower class via the new notables, for the benefit of the centres for power. The relationship between the guards and the patronage networks is interlocking. It is common for an effective mediator to be an officer or his equivalent—but networks are generally intra-sectarian, while guarding is a more public function. Simply put, guards are a state device, while networks are social fields in which civil and governmental parties are interwoven. The upper hand is always given to the guarding shield and not to the narrow, sectarian networks of intermediates. The regime is keener to keep people in check than it is to serve their needs.

The vertical subordination of the governed and the horizontal mutual exclusion of groups guaranteed by clientelist networks isolate non-sectarian and non-subservient people, turning them into vulnerable, worthless souls within the system.

The ubiquitous security shield is what protects the regime as a whole, and it has a particularly strong presence at times of subaltern rebellion against Sultanic rule. Yet both the shield and the network systems failed to prevent the rebellion of the 'oppressed', and this despite the emergence of strong reserves within the Sultanic forces, exemplified by phenomena such as the *shabiha*, which began as salaried repressive power in the early stages of the revolution. Later, they were allocated some conquered neighbourhoods to loot, such as Baba Amr and Karm al-Zaytoun in the city of Homs during March of 2012. This development preceded their reorganization, at the end of that same year, into a private army with considerable salaries under Iranian command. The *shabiha* opened what they themselves called 'the Sunni Market' with goods looted from neighbourhoods in and around Homs, about a year after the outbreak of the revolution. With its combination of the words 'market' and 'Sunni', this phrase affords a deep glimpse into sectarian phenomena as relationships of power and coercion—here, as a direct tool for looting and transfer of wealth. Such things are not, under any circumstances, a matter of beliefs and identities, nor of their detached or distorted expressions.

Sectarianism operates within a political framework that facilitates access to wealth for those in power. One outcome of nearly two generations of Assad control is a subordinate new bourgeoisie, consisting of 'new notable' intermediaries and the upper bourgeoisie who are also partners to Sultanic rule.

Through its relation to power and privilege, and in the context of ongoing struggles for power and privilege, sectarianism is a polarizing phenomenon that tends to institute a bipolar society, and not a multipolar society of multiple belief groups. Regardless of any debate about the policy of an alliance of minorities at the local and regional levels that is attributed to Hafez al-Assad, this situation is evident in Syria mainly with respect to the Sunni Muslim majority.

A sectarian regime is not a decentralized cultural pluralism, as it is with the 'multiculturalism' of Anglophone countries and, to a lesser extent, in Lebanon as well. It is a hierarchical system based on privilege that is centred on a general power. In the Syrian version, this system is directed towards ensuring the eternal power of the Assad Dynasty.

In sum, I want to say that sectarianism is not just a social mechanism for serving the needs of people from certain sects. Perhaps this was the case earlier in Lebanon—and I have borrowed the depiction of sects as networks of patronage from the prominent Lebanese researcher, Ahmed Beydoun. In Syria, the matter extends to the sectarianization of the political centre and the security function, or the 'inner state'. Lebanon is a neo-Sultanic state without a Sultan, and should either fill the gap and assign a Sultan with a well-developed general security shield, or turn the page on the sectarian patronage system and evolve toward a state of citizenship and equality. In the context of present interconnections between the two Sultanates, Lebanon is the incomplete one with a large 'security branch' (i.e. Hezbollah) that is leaning more towards Sultanism, and the complete model is currently beset by a revolution. However, the situation in Lebanon follows the situation in Syria, and the very Syrian Sultan today follows the Iranian imperial centre, as does the Lebanese 'Intelligence Branch'.

The comments above touch on the regional face of sectarianism, which I will not discuss here except to say that the key to approaching it is the Sultan and territorial control. The key is not, under any circumstances, religious and sectarian groups, Shiites, Sunnis, and so on. Sectarianization is a tool for political control and a result of it. Power comes first, and sects are creatures of power.

'New notables' and the 'central bourgeoisie'

in keeping with the duplicity of the state, outer and inner, and the duplicities of sectarianism, a security shield and a favouritism network, there are also two related origins for the development of the regime's bourgeoisie. First, there are the 'new notables', who are distinguished by their mediating functions. The origin of the second group, the upper or central bourgeoisie, is the seizure of public resources, land confiscations, and the annexation of the most profitable sectors of the economy. The first group can also be called 'the outer bourgeoisie', and is composed of members of the government, its departments and Baathist organizations, and the parliament, as well as those who work through sects in networks of favouritism. Generally, this is a local bourgeoisie, whose members reside in environments close to their religious, tribal, and regional backgrounds. But there is another component of this outer bourgeoisie: a governmental and Baathist one whose personnel are not necessarily local: those subjected to its looting are not their *ahli* followers. This component is made up of local functionaries like governors, secretaries of Baath Party branches, regional administrators, heads of military recruitment divisions, etc.

The second group merits the title of the 'inner bourgeoisie' as well. It is generally a central bourgeoisie—not because of residency (though it is almost exclusively in Damascus and Aleppo), but because of their proximity to the centre of power, i.e. the Assad family and the security services. It is through the latter that they earn their wealth, in partnership with those at the pinnacle of the neo-Sultanic state, through the acquisition of national public resources, especially land. This bourgeoisie was organized in the form of two superpowers: Cham Holding and Souria (Syria) Holding, which were founded around the same time

(Cham Holding in December 2006; Souria Holding in January 2007). Rami Makhlouf, a cousin of Bashar, was a key partner in the first. Rami's name was not listed among the founders of the second, although his brother Ihab's was. Together, the two companies formed a semi-exclusive central bourgeois club in which Rami occupied a key position. A few years before the revolution, the expression *ramrameh* (Ramization) became popular, referring to how the most lucrative sectors of the Syrian economy were handed over to Rami and the Assad family, effectively making him the 'economic sultan' of Syria. In that period, there was a common joke that reflected the close links between the pinnacle of power and the central bourgeoisie: the Syrian economy is either *Mukhalef* (unlawful) or Makhlouf.

Undoubtedly, we need well-documented studies about the formation of the central bourgeoisie and its relationship with both the class of new notables and the centre of power. It seems to me that the central bourgeoisie is multi-sectarian, with a large share of Damascenes and Christians. But its head is undoubtedly Rami Makhlouf by virtue of his kinship. The questionable character of his dealings, including his mobile phone business as well as the acquisition of property in Damascus, would not have been possible for the likes Nabil al-Kuzbari, Muhammad Hamsho, Saeb al-Nahas, or Naji Shawi. These people might be very wealthy, but Rami is rich in money and power. He is sovereign, they are not.

The 'outer', local bourgeoisie is highly sectarian and generally plunders its own sects. But it is possible that its governmental component could manage to loot a wider segment of the public, either by belonging to the public sect, or by having greater weight within official or governmental circles. For its part, the central bourgeoisie plunders public resources and wider society. The central bourgeoisie also distinguishes itself from the outer bourgeoisie through its monopoly of revenues from economic exchanges with the outside world and with agencies of foreign companies, along with projects and assets outside Syria (whether in Abu Dhabi, Swiss banks, or the Virgin Islands). By contrast, the outer bourgeoisie is exclusively domestic.

One could say that the new notables are the Sultanic middle class in the literal sense because they link the general public to the Sultanic centre and its sub-Sultanic centres across the thirteen Syrian governorates, according to their positions and the local communities. This class acquires its income without the use of direct force—or with very little of it—but that acquisition is always premised on the structural relationship of coercion instituted up by the Sultanic state with regard to the governed. But here again we can recall the distinction between non-coercive, *ahli* components and the governmental components, with the latter well positioned to use political or physical coercion in order to accumulate wealth. The inner or central bourgeoisie is an essential component of the Sultanic State: direct coercion and the confiscation and occupation of land all played large role in their accumulation of wealth, as did their monopoly on foreign economic exchanges (a practice that could justify describing it as an 'external' bourgeoisie as well).

Just as the official security component of sectarianism, the 'guard class', is superior to the social component of 'new dignitaries', so the central or inner bourgeoisie is superior to the outer and local one. The central bourgeoisie is not a mediating class, but one that simply appropriates—as is fitting for a partnership with the Sultanic summit.

As much as the outer or internal bourgeoisie enjoys ties with local groups, especially in their *ahli* component, their survival is not existentially linked to the regime. The central bourgeoisie owes everything to the regime, and its battle alongside the regime is a matter of life and death.

There is no doubt about the existence of partnerships and other interactions between these two bourgeoisies, but the aforementioned structural determinants allow meaningful distinctions between them to be made.

But is there any justification for using the concept of the bourgeoisie in naming these two groups? Is it sensible to talk about the bourgeoisie within a Sultanic framework based on personal dependency? Should we not rather talk about feudal lords, or a subsidiary aristocracy—a Sultanic aristocracy, for example? Especially when political coercion, both structural and capricious, plays a more significant role in the collection of wealth than does the role of economic coercion, which is distinctive of capitalism?

With regard to the central group, a preference for the term 'bourgeoisie' is somewhat justifiable, given its ties to international markets and capitalism, as well as the initially contractual nature of its projects, which are predominantly services (banks, communications, foreign agencies, real estate, and so forth). Despite the political restrictions against most Syrians, they are not serfs tied to their places of work. The notables group, especially its official part (governors, members of the parliament, local intelligence officers, and local partisan leaders), is closer to becoming a neo-feudal one, though without the traditional stability of land ownership. As for the *ahli* part (rich people, clerics, tribal leaders), who comprise a lower sector within the internal bourgeoisie, and within the new bourgeoisie as a whole, the coercion plays a lesser role in producing their income; consequently, there is less justification for labelling theirs a truly 'feudal' system.

Another thing that justifies my hesitation to describe these groups as feudal is that they are not stable hereditary classes. This in particular might explain the obscene looting practices for which they are known. At the same time, there is a definite development toward heritability, a hallmark of feudalism, ever since Bashar succeeded his father.

In any event, it is necessary to link the Syrian bourgeoisie under the Assad Sultanate with the factors that distinguish it from the classical bourgeoisie. I speak of a 'new' bourgeoisie not only to distinguish that class whose conditions for materializing were prepared in the Assad era after the old bourgeoisie was shattered by Baathist rule, but also to say that we are looking at a distinctive form, one that is a match in quality with the Assadist political formation of the neo-Sultanic State.

Collectively, the new bourgeoisie and the Sultanic centre form what might be called the society of white Syrians, superior in class and culture to a black, backward, intolerant, and obscurantist public. These racist ideas justify the whites' contempt and torture of blacks, killing them when they rebel. They are generally seen as a source of danger, terrorism, and incivility.

The society of white Syrians is not composed of a sect, nor is it an aggregate of 'minorities', although the latter enjoy special affection within the globally-dominant Western consensus among all its left-wing, right-wing, liberal, and fascist currents. It includes the 'enlightened' and 'civilized' Sunni Muslims who are loyal to the Sultanic centre, and who renounce all the democratic opponents of Sultanism, those who are actually preoccupied with issues of justice, equality, and human dignity, regardless of their religious and sectarian backgrounds.

Sultanic structure: dual or triple?

Is the society of 'Assad's Syria' composed of two components: a new bourgeoisie, both internal and external, and generally urban (on the one hand) and a 'working society' alongside other impoverished, marginalized classes within peripheral urban neighbourhoods and rural areas (on the other)?

The makeup of the al-Mezzeh and Kafr Sousa neighbourhoods in Damascus, for example, suggests rather a structure composed of three components: a security component, which includes fortified security agencies that give passers-by an impression that the builders of these fortresses are truly preparing themselves 'to burn the country' before the would give over power to 'nobodies'; gated residential towers, with organized, glittering malls; and a more popular quartier that is relegated to invisibility. This arrangement might give the impression of a tripartite division: the two wings of the bourgeoisie, the surveilled and marginalized general public, and the blatantly distinct force of guards. The latter, with its strong yet non-exclusive sectarian nature, protects the regime, which in return protects the bourgeoisie and keeps the public under its thumb. The supervisory function of the guard force and its function as a source of information about the society—including the new bourgeoisie—are no less important than its protective function. However, the guard forces, leaders aside, are not part of either of the two sectors of the bourgeoisie. In fact, the guards often complain about the bourgeoisie and openly resent them.

Despite the explicitly negative feelings, the guard forces do not rebel against the bourgeoisie. Instead, they hold to a fundamental loyalty to the regime and hostility toward its opponents as well as toward the general population. The regime has never had a problem using it as a cudgel against all opponents. Security and military forces with security functions, the upper ranks of the army, and the police have never, not even once, sided with the general population or expressed a sense of connection with them. After the revolution began, defections were very rare.

This third component within the Syrian social structure, the guard force, signals the independence of sectarian formations from class status; through its loyalty to the regime, it also illustrates the independent efficacy of sectarianism within the Sultanic confines of contemporary Syria.

The Sultanic pinnacle directs the attunement of this margin of independence. It enjoys the loyalty of the guards and makes use of them frequently, without having to grant them direct social privileges. However, the opportunity to benefit from favouritism is greater among the guards by virtue of their predominantly Alawite composition. After the revolution their 'social capital' has been coupled with growing opportunities for looting: trivial looting for juniors and major looting for seniors.

The guard force is the Sultanic centre's tool of social control, one that monitors even the new bourgeoisie, and, especially, the internal bourgeoisie.

The Sultanic centre

The Sultanic centre is what makes the system a living, coordinated organism: Hafez al-Assad himself during the thirty years of his reign; and the Assad family since his death. If the guards force was the regime's eyes, ears and muscles, or its nervous and motor systems, and the patronage system provided important nourishment for his clients, then Hafez was the head of the Sultanic organism and also its ego—he occupied the command centre for that oversaw the Sultanate itself as well as the effective coordination between inside and outside of the regime, which is the position of orientation and 'politics'.

The Sultanic centre monopolizes relations with the outside world, and controls the movement of the regime's external resources; it dominates the inside the way a man controls his own body. The inside is the body of the Sultan and that which sustains it.

His position as governor and founder of the state is indivisible from being a husband, a father, a brother, an uncle, etc. He is a public figure and a private figure, abstract and tangible at once. It is not possible to separate his use and exchange values. Like the commodity for Marx, he is 'abounding in metaphysical subtleties and theological niceties.'

I find the Sultan concept most appropriate for expressing such a supernatural merger, one necessitated by inheritance and the building of a dynasty. Sultan is an Arabic word that expresses power, authority, and dominance, and also refers to one who possesses these three attributes. Hafez is as exceptional father as he is an exceptional president, and as great a son as he is father and president. All of this so-called greatness produces reverberations. A mural in Masakin al-Haras (the region also called *Al-Areen* or the lion's lair, inhabited only by Alawite officers of *al-Haras al-Jumhoori*, the Republican Guard) depicts Hafez bowing to kiss the hand of his mother, her head surrounded by a halo.

This is a real Sultan, with real Sultanic blood. One can neither abstract from nor separate these two qualities, which, by way of contrast, are not found together in any other person. Whether as employees in public office or as individuals, all others are immeasurably inferior. The building of a dynasty is 'predestined' by this essential privilege.

The amount of supernatural glorification bestowed upon the man throughout the years of his rule and beyond is related to the principle of the regime's coherence, its sacred religion. A basic function of his state was the public glorification of the president to ensure people's submission. Assadism is a religion and a state, and its religion is its state. Speaking of 'a cult of personality' is probably insufficient for Assad. Hafez is a sacred founder in the eyes of his loyalists, particularly his sectarian followers. He is not merely a unique governor or a genius leader. He is unique and a genius because he is blessed, not vice versa. Here, one might also speak of the outer, rational face of Hafez—his genius and uniqueness—and an inner, metaphysical side—blessed and holy. This face is only visible to his Alawite followers. Hafez's mausoleum in Qardaha is visited as a sacred monument. A few years ago, a cardboard sheet came into my possession, showing pictures of Alawite religious chieftains over 1000 years (a sort of a family tree drawing), the last of which was Hafez al-Assad, who was described in religious terms.

For decades, the official media tried in earnest to enshrine the worship of Hafez al-Assad. It went so far that many Syrians were dumbfounded by this sort of disregard for their minds. But its meaning resides in its function: raising the Sultanic centre above politics and social debate, and the virtual consecration of the regime to ensure its eternal life. Holiness generates a lot of wealth, fame, influence, and Sultan (lordship and dominance).

Through sanctification and loyalty to the Holy Sultan, in his simultaneity as a president and a person, Hafez became a dynamic power for undermining citizenship and the concept of the nation-state, as well as a well spring of patriarchy and personal subordination.

The death of Hafez inaugurated the time of the dynasty. The Assad family has taken the place of the father—not only because Bashar is weaker than his father or less qualified, but because the logic of inheritance and building of dynasties leads to that result. Whoever succeeds Hafez is an heir, a son among others, he is not the founder nor is he the greatest. Bashar cannot neutralize the family unless he renounces the logic of inheritance to become another founding father who either ends dynastic rule altogether or establishes his own dynasty. Bashar is too small for both. The Sultanate belongs to his family and not to him. Sticking with him is required for the cohesion of the Sultanic family and the Sultanate as a whole, but this does not signal an appreciation of his personhood. Bashar has no personal use value, only an exchange or public value. When necessary, he can be replaced. That is possible, one day.

The ideologies of sectarianism

at this point, it should have become clear that the issue of sectarianism is a matter of political and social privilege, not a question of identity, culture, or religion. Consequently, sectarianism cannot be dealt with by holding religious conferences—those where Muslim and Christian clerics, or Alawites and Sunnis or Shiites, for example, sit together and call upon their followers to practice tolerance and love, while remaining silent on the sources of discrimination and privilege. Similarly, sectarianism cannot be addressed by a kind of state-worshipping authoritarian secularism that fails to take into account either the conditions of discrimination and social and political privilege or the rights and conditions of the most disadvantaged social segments, but instead blames the people for their circumstances, like many ideologues of the 'internal First World' in Syria and abroad do.

Moreover, sectarianism cannot be addressed by avoidance, as if it is some kind of shame (as some ideologues do under either nationalist or leftist pretexts); nor can it be addressed by silence about the origins of its political formation (as loyal intellectuals and politicians do), or by attributing progressive, values to certain sects and backward values of other sects (as do others). There are no good sects and bad sects except in sectarianized eyes. All sects are bad and backward (this statement is not in any way an attack on confessional groups, and is not meant as disrespectful to them), and all are politically constructed. The worst and most backward, however, is the political organization in which sects are formed as political units or political alliances: neo-Sultanism.

We ended up with barely any liberal, secular resistance to sectarianism in Syria, thanks to two things: first, the violent repression at the hand of the most sectarian apparatuses of any public debate about this vital issue; second (and of no less importance), the elusive nature of the discourse of its diverse ideologues (nationalist ideologues and 'anti-imperialists', or the ideologues of modernity and anti-fundamentalism), all of whom tried to monopolize the definition of nationalism in a way that blurred the fundamentally sectarian nature of Assad's rule. During the years before the revolution, to bring up the phenomenon of sectarianism was to find oneself accused of sectarianism from the guarding ideologues of the inner state and the Sultanate's organic intellectuals. During the reign of Bashar, these were not Baathists, but rather representatives of the system of privilege: ideologues of the 'internal First World', duality that replicates the duality of the outer state and inner state, the duality of sectarianism in its *wasta* and security faces, the duality of the bourgeoisie as internal and central. It is a duality of governmental intellectuals who play the card of 'national unity' while protecting the prohibitions that guard the sectarian taboo, and those 'modernist' and 'civilized' intellectuals (Huntingtonian intellectuals, in fact) who defend Sultanism as an enlightened oppression in the face of potential 'tyranny of the majority'—to borrow the formulation of Aziz al-Azmeh, George Tarabichi, and Kamal Dib. These are some of 'White Syria's' intellectuals from the era of Bashar, who can be distinguished from their predecessors, the 'leftist' intellectuals from Hafez's time.

It is interesting that, in his book *Crisis in Syria*, the Lebanese-Canadian Kamal Dib suggests that power be shared equally between 'minorities' and Sunni Muslims who (according to him) make up 75 per cent of the population—virtually giving a 'minoritarian' three times the political fortunes of a 'majoritarian'! This even surpasses the system of consociational democracy in Lebanon, to which this 'secular' author objects. According to Ahmed Beydoun, the Lebanese system is based on an equation that gives a Christian (only) twice as much weight as a Muslim!

Throughout the book, it is remarkable that the words 'Islam' and 'Muslims' are never mentioned in a positive or a compassionate context. Throughout Dib's book, these two words are used in an uninhibited, remarkably straightforward manner: they always and exclusively appear in a negative context, in connection with the dangers of terrorism, beheadings, and the persecution of women, intellectuals, Christians and 'minorities'.

While one would assume that a secularist would inevitably call for equal rights for all people, perhaps with special emphasis on 'the rights of minorities' as the most vulnerable groups, it should already be clear that the rights of minorities in the Syrian context are exclusively pitted against the rights of the religious majority, and by no means against the Sultanic regime. Are there any emancipatory implications in talking about 'the rights of minorities' in the calls for sharing power equally among three-quarters and one quarter? Are we seeking equality, or rather privilege? What is racism, other than insisting that 25 = 75, i.e. 1 = 3? This 'secular' discourse has strong links with colonialism, only this time the mediator is White Syrian society with its 'civilizational' beliefs.

The chances for the emergence of a reasonable secular resistance to sectarianism has been weakened by the following factors, which have, in combination, created the right conditions for confronting sectarianism with sectarianism: long-standing brazen racial injustice; the marginalization of cultural independence and critical thought; and the suppression of social opportunities for the emergence of a grassroots social opposition. This is what we see today embodied in Salafists who aspire to occupy the position of Assad's Sultanate on the basis of a different ideology. The sectarianism of Salafists is principled and combative, and seems to resonate among the impoverished and despised elements of the Sunni rural public.

Nevertheless, the Muslim Brotherhood's version of 'Islam' can also be a mask for sectarianism—more precisely, for a Sunni privilege to discriminate in favour of Sunnis. While a distinction should always be drawn between, on the one hand, sectarian and illiberal animosity against Islam (which is very common, with the above mentioned racist preacher calling for 'parity' serving merely as one blunt example) and efforts to expose advocates of racism and demonstrate their political and class bias, on the other, there are no excuses for exempting aspirations for Sunni dominance from criticism. The troubles of uniting all Sunnis within one group should not obscure the presence of many Sunni sectarians—active, aggressive, and not limited to Salafists.

The fate of the Assad Sultanate

Faced with popular protests in 2011, the Sultanate worked to disseminate *fitna*, or strife. Bouthaina Shaaban, the bigoted and deluded advisor to Bashar, brought up strife and Salafi emirates only about ten days into the revolution. Later, she became known for her statements about the victims of the chemical weapons attack in Ghouta, saying they were abducted children from 'the

Coast', (i.e. Alawites) and attributing her words to the people of the region. Following the 'Caesar' report early in 2014, which revealed that 11,000 people had died under torture between March 2011 and August 2013, her poor reputation was reinforced by the way she lashed out in response to a question from CNN about the victims of torture. Advisor Shaaban said: 'Isn't the West Christian? Do you not care about the fate of Christian nuns who were kidnapped by the terrorists of Ma'loula?'

Bashar himself talked extensively about *fitna* in his first speech after the revolution on 30 March 2011. Early on, the regime's journalists attributed a slogan to the protests that I personally believe was coined by Michel Samaha: 'Alawites to their coffins, Christians to Beirut!' This slogan was designed so efficiently that it could simultaneously taint the protests with Sunni extremism, justify sectarian alliance between Alawites and Christians, cajole the West and instigate the Western public against those violent backward Sunnis. It is unfathomable how such a slogan would reportedly arise only during demonstrations in Latakia!

In addition to its dissemination of strategies for arousing discord, the regime hired foreign forces to save the Sultanate, a method known to royal dynasties throughout history, including Arab ones both ancient and contemporary (most recently the Kuwaiti dynasty, merely a generation ago). What autocracies have in common is appropriation of the countries they govern. They are not national governments. It is not Assad who is Syrian: Syria is Assadic. According to this logic, it is not the Assads who need to prove their patriotism by serving the people of Syria. Rather, Syria is positioned in such a way that it is required to honour and show loyalty to the Assads. 'Assad or no one! Assad or we burn the Country! Assad or to hell with the country!' are all slogans issued with the assumption of ownership: I shall destroy what I might lose, so that no one may use it afterwards!

Practically speaking, what has happened since mid-2012 was a handover of leadership to the Iranians and their followers from Lebanon, Iraq, Afghanistan and elsewhere. The 18 July 2012 assassination of top Syrian military and intelligence officers in the bombing of the National Security Headquarters could have been an inside settling of accounts to the benefit of Sultanic hawks and their Iranian patron. We recall that, until this time, peaceful demonstrations were on the rise; the highest number recorded was in June 2012, when there were more than 700 demonstration locations. Warplanes began to be used against cities in July. Bombing of the bread lines in front of bakeries in Aleppo and neighbouring regions took place in August 2012. We also recall that before the end of 2012, chemical weapons and Scud missiles began to be used. The *shabiha* were institutionalized before the end of that year as well, becoming a supportive sectarian militia in the 'National Defence Forces', with many of its members receiving training in Iran. All this was preceded by well-known sectarian massacres in Houla, Al-Qubeir, Karm al-Zaytoun, and Banias, and by the emergence of the 'Sunni Market'.

Earlier, within its framework for disseminating *fitna*, the regime also released jailed Salafi jihadists whose 'programming' was known all too well to its intelligence agencies—between Iraq and Lebanon, it had engaged with them for years before the outbreak of the revolution. Meanwhile, the blogger Tal al-Mallouhi, the eighteen year-old girl who was framed as a spy for a foreign state and sentenced to five years, is still in Adra prison. Tal was arrested on 26 December 2009.

While Assad's Sultanate has furthered the growth of this jihadi presence, the latter has also helped spread discord and *fitna*. It has contributed to sectarian entrenchment, and destroyed the secular democratic opposition forces. Almost as if by design, combatant

Salafism did its best to crush non-sectarian opponents of the regime, disseminate sectarianism, and grant the regime the full right to represent Alawites and non-Sunni Arabs in general. So far, it has recorded a level of success for the Sultanate that even the Sultanate itself could not have anticipated.

In sum, the Sultanate has led Syria to destruction through co-optation of Alawites, open avenues for Iranian control, and the rise of the combatant Sunni sectarianism—although, apparently, it has managed to preserve some of its inherited property.

Resisting sectarianism

Because of this whole approach, I believe that a policy of emancipation from sectarianism starts with liberating the public state from private ownership, that of a family or of a sect. First and foremost, Syrians must regain their country from its current neo-Sultanic rule. 'Syria is ours, not Assad's!' said Syrian demonstrators in Daraa, 'the cradle of the revolution' since its early days. Syria belongs to Syrians, in other words, and not to an inherited dynasty. No particular group should have privileged access to the state.

Second, Syria needs an effective system of administrative and legal justice that ensures people's needs are routinely met regardless of their kinships and their wealth, as well as a system of social justice that provides resources and services to the poorest segments of society so they do not need to seek the help of notables or any new sorts of dignitaries. There should be apolitical system of political justice, based on the principle of common policies that no one is entitled to monopolize; this system should be specifically based on the understanding that the Syrian people are all partners in three important respects: in public speech; voluntary association; and peaceful protest.

Moreover, emancipating the state requires liberating Syria from the absolute rule of 'the internal first world' and the society of White Syrians, instead of blundering about with identity politics and regenerating political slavery on religious grounds. The experiences of nearly four years now have shown that resistance to 'the internal first world' does not succeed when it does not include opposition to the external first world and its regional supports.

All of this in turn requires facing an unaddressed and unresolved contradiction relating to the status of public religion and Sunni dominance in the fields of education, personal status, and public religious ceremonies. Sectarianism is not another name for Alawite dominance, which means that Sunni dominance is not the solution. Sectarianism is an essential element of Sultanic governance, one that Salafist groups are working today to renew and intensify. This promises to force all non-Salafists into slavery or genocide, including non-Sunni Muslims, non-Salafist Sunni Muslims, and Salafists with a different approach from the most powerful one. Contemporary Salafism is a schismatic phenomenon, hostile to the world; it generates hatreds within the community, within its groups, and even within the same individual. Its only destination is death. In my opinion, Daesh has stepped up because the revolution as an aspiration to own life and liberty has stumbled and fallen. Salafism emerged because there are no social revolutionaries in Syria. Salafists' social bases have overtaken those of the social revolutionary forces.

The fundamental positive principle involved in transcending the Sultanic system is equality among Syrian confessional groups as constituent groups of the national body. The first constitutional principle of the Republic should state that Syrians are not to be divided into vertical majorities and minorities; this would be a sounder and more sensible idea than a constitutional text on

'Protection of Minorities', or 'equal sharing and guarantees', as Kamal Dib put it. While this seems impossible in light of the Salafi ascendency and the erosion of the revolution, it is now apparent that the rise of Salafism is a source of major national and social problems—challenging it provides a chance to fix old problems in the structure of the Syrian body-politic. Whatever the political paths leading out of the current situation may be, it seems that opportunities for deliverance from jihadist Salafism (including Daesh, al-Nusra Front, and others) will be limited without deliverance from the Assads. Assad's Sultanate and jihadist Salafism are two sides of a single process of national destruction.

It may also be necessary to open a discussion addressing the perception of a homogeneous central state that shapes the population using a uniform template and which works to impose assimilation by forcing homogeneity on the people. This kind of orchestrated, homogenizing approach may appear to be anti-sectarian, but actually the opposite is true. Centralization strengthens the state at the expense of society, allowing influential individual and group aspirations to take over the state and creating opportunities for allegedly national doctrines and policies to be shaped in ways that are secretly hostile to *ahli* expressions from below, while succumbing to sectarian practices and sectarian discrimination from above. Homogenization then evolves into an ideological camouflage for Sultanic mechanisms of mutual exclusion. From there, it is but a short step to instrumentalizing sectarianism in order to rule this cherished central state, headed by a brutal tyrant and guarding its bigotry by criminalizing any debate on sectarianism.

In any case, homogenization is an agenda of repression and domination, not a liberal or a progressive plan, and is a supreme value only for modernist worshippers of the State.

In fact, the neo-Sultanic state is nothing but a specific, modernized form of the traditional Sultanic state, which had a unified, centralized state apparatus grafted onto it as well as a forced doctrine of social and cultural homogenization—but not legal equality, social justice, or public freedoms.

What we need in Syria is a combination of social and legal justice, and a mixture of republican political activity along with a greater degree of local democratic governance. This would address legitimate Kurdish demands, respond to vital development needs, and reduce sectarianism as well as the prospect of emergent state-dominating sects or denominations. It would also put an end to continued political, intellectual, and physical investment in a centre of power whose history over half a century has been one of social destruction, exhaustion of natural resources, massacres, and large-scale killings. The problem lies in the centralized homogenizing model, its culture and its identity, more than in a particular application of it. Hafez al-Assad himself was a by-product of this model, though his state was a draconian example of it.

At the same time, we should recognize the religious, confessional, and ethnic plurality of Syrian society, and encourage public social expressions of it. There has never been a problem with the variety of local socio-cultural self-expressions. The problem has been discrimination at the level of the state and in the institutions of governance. Sectarianism is the result of discrimination from above; it is never the product of a society's local variety of expressions from below. Such expressions must be supported, and the emergence of the specific character of local environments as well as the manifestation of diverse cultural and political practices must be made easier.

If we have no choice other than turning the page on the status quo of the public political sect, we must ensure equal rights for

Alawite Syrians as individuals and as a community. We need to think about liberation from sectarianism and the Sultanic state as liberation of Alawites, not from them. The Assad Sultanate is not the state of Alawites, although it has used their labour and blood in order to rise above all Syrians.

On the other hand, there is no escape from closing the book on the public religious sect. Alawites are not Sunni, and neither are Druze, Ismailis, or Shiites: they should not have to endure Sunni education in schools or refrain from public expression of their own identities. Similarly, the Kurds are not Arabs: they should not be stripped of their personality and language, and Arabic should not be imposed on them.

After all this, and if we are lucky enough to close the book on the Assad Sultanate, we will need to learn the virtues of tolerance and forgetfulness. We will need to be tolerant of each other. We will need to forget things about our contemporary history. These are possible after a basic level of justice has been achieved and the main architects of murder have been dealt with: the Assad family; senior guards; and the central bourgeoisie. A negative attitude towards tolerance is characteristic of the organic intellectuals of 'White Syrian' society, like Adonis and his ilk: on the surface, it seems like a liberal dismissal of tolerance on behalf of equality, while in reality it is a dishonest trumping of social demands for respect and the possibilities of living together. In other words, this contrast between tolerance and equality is a sort of ethical extortion, meant to divert pressure away from the regime and towards the population. The 'problem' lies in the 'head' (i.e. the heads of Syrians) and not in the 'chair' (Bashar and his regime), as the man said in early 2013. The outer/inner binary opposition is at work here as well.

It remains to say that the first step toward achieving a liberatory policy will be the development of effective thinking tools in order to understand the problems of sectarianism as well as its general social and political context. Here, I have tried to develop some conceptual categories that might be useful: public sect, private state/outer state/inner state, and the idea of the neo-Sultanic state, for example, along with the distinction between the two sides of sectarianism (guarding and clientelist), and the distinctions between segments of the new bourgeoisie. New tools are crucial for launching a public debate about sectarianism; also crucial is allowing a liberal public opinion to emerge regarding this sensitive issue. A collaborative society creates and builds by means of lively public debate.

It is always necessary to demystify sectarian fraud, whether in its traditional nationalist form, in today's secular modernist version, or in the contemporary political Islamic form (i.e. using 'Islam' to mask Sunni domination). Sectarianism rarely appears barefaced, but instead cloaks itself under a thick hijab of high values, whether modern or ancient: modernity, secularism, enlightenment, or civilization; 'authentic' values such as Islam (represented as singular); or novelty and 'uniqueness'. But behind the veil, there is nothing to be found but Sultanism and racial discrimination.

NOTES

FOREWORD

1. "Syria and the World: Reactionism is Back, and Progressing", Aljumhuriya.net,http://aljumhuriya.net/en/critical-thought/syria-and-the-world-reactionarism-is-back-and-progressing?print=pdf
2. 2008 interview with al-Hayat cited in Joshua Landis, 'The National Salvation Front Folds', 23 April 2009, http://www.joshualandis.com/blog/the-national-salvation-front-folds/
3. https://douma4.wordpress.com/2014/08/11/yassin-haj-saleh-on-samira-khalil-translation/
4. The English-language site can be accessed at http://aljumhuriya.net/en/
5. 'Interview with Yassin al-Haj Saleh: Syria and the Left', New Politics, Winter 2015, http://newpol.org/content/syria-and-left
6. From 'Syria, Iran, ISIS and the Future of Social Justice: In dialogue with Yassin al-Haj Saleh', Radio Zamaneh, 29 May 2015.

2. THE *SHABIHA* AND THEIR STATE

1. *Harper's Magazine*, June 2011, http://harpers.org/archive/2011/06/
2. Mamdouh Adwan, *The Animalization of Man*, 1st edition, Damascus: Mamdouh Adwan Publishing, 2007, p. 134.
3. See this Al-Jazeera report on the '*Shabiha* Phenomenon' (Arabic): http://bit.ly/2s6D98g. See also Ibid. Adwan describes the '*khaal*' (uncle) as the '*shabiha*'s umbrella,' adding he is 'above the law, mostly due to his blood ties to a state official', p. 138.
4. An altercation broke out in 1993 between the *shabiha* of Fawaz al-Assad (son of Jamil al-Assad) and the *shabiha* of the Deeb clan (led by Rabah

Deeb, whose mother was from the Assad family). In the end, Rabah Deeb was sent to Latakia Prison, until his *shabiha* men attacked the prison and set him free, killing a few police officers in the process. Note that due to the scarcity of written references, I often have to use information made available to me by friends, and I only quote confirmed and recurrent narratives.

5. In 1994, a young man, Safwan al-Aasar, was killed because he defended a young woman who sought his protection from *shabiha* on a public bus.
6. Compare to: 'The Militias of '*Shabiha*'... Special Forces Above the Law', *Asharq Al-Awsat*, http://bit.ly/2r6vxUk
7. See article by Rosa Yassin Hassan, 'On the *Shabiha* and their Masters, a Fear-Colored Memory,' http://www.aleftoday.info/article.php?id=7701; the writer says she alluded to Abu Rammah in an article she wrote before the uprising, but did not dare to mention his name at the time.
8. Mamdouh Adwan, who was perhaps the only writer who talked about *shabiha* and *tashbih* prior to the revolution: '*tashbih* is a loaded word, a blend of *za'arana* (gang bullying), *salbata* (seizing possessions by force), and *taballi* (falsely accusing someone of an offense); it is everything that breaks the law flagrantly.' Adwan, *The Animalization of Man*, p. 135.
9. During the summer of 1997, while I was at a college military summer camp, a Baathist student accused our coach of sectarianism after telling a funny joke about the people of Homs. The student collared him and yelled in his face, 'I'm from the National Leadership (of the Baath Party) security!' The topic of sectarianism is one of the worst political taboos in Assad's Syria. Not only is it a source of intellectual and political paralysis, but also a mask that hides the regime's sectarian practices and its manipulation of Syrian society.
10. The video is available at http://www.youtube.com/watch?v=kVZk_VMWJsg
11. The video is available at https://www.youtube.com/watch?v=lk8EUrC4KV4
12. The video is available at https://www.youtube.com/watch?v=a0Ctla7Rs0Y
13. There is, however, a difference between a smuggler and a *shabih*: while

the former is 'a brave, adventurous, risk-taking night creature of the night who might very well clash with the state,' the latter 'uses a state car and smuggles at the height of the day in a busy street, even obstructing traffic': Adwan, op. cit., p. 136. This distinction reveals the *shabiha*'s legal immunity within the regime.

14. [Note added in 2014]—See this article by Dima Wannous describing the typical appearance of *shabiha* and their leaders (Arabic): http://www.almodon.com/Culture/Articles/9237
15. Under his leadership, they attacked Al-Haram Exchange Company in broad daylight in Damascus in 2005, and seized all the money they found there. They also made false accusations against political prisoners in Adra Prison in 2006.
16. [Note added in 2014]—The *shabiha* phenomenon was institutionalized in what is known as the National Defence Army, established in late 2012. It was led by Hilal al-Assad, Bashar's cousin, who was killed in Latakia on 24 March 2014. On the murder of Hilal, and for information on his son Suleiman, see (Arabic): http://ara.tv/g39uu
17. In many of his works, Ahmad Baydoun tackled the connection between patronage and sectarianism in the Lebanese regime. See, for instance, *Adventures of Diversity: The Lebanese as Sects, Arabs and Phoenicians*, 1st edition, Beirut: An-Nahar Publishing, 2005, p. 20.
18. According to information obtained by *The Telegraph*, the founders of the *shabiha* were Maher al-Assad (Bashar's brother, also the commander of the Republican Guard and the Army's elite Fourth Armored Division) and Rami Makhlouf, his cousin and the family's treasurer. See: http://www.telegraph.co.uk/news/worldnews/middleeast/syria/10716289/How-Bashar-al-Assad-created-the-feared-shabiha-militia-an-insider-speaks.html
19. See this report (Arabic): http://cnn.it/2qpLbIV
20. [Note added in 2014]—The militarization of the revolution has inevitably changed the situation, whether by marginalizing outgunned *shabiha*, or, more dangerously, through arming them. I remind readers that this essay was written during the autumn of 2011. By the end of 2012, the *shabiha* phenomenon was institutionalized by the Iranians in what became known as the 'National Defence Forces'.

21. [Note added in 2014]—For more on alleged *shabiha* financiers see Sam Dagher, 'Assad's Not-So-Secret Weapon: Loyal Syrian Businessmen,' *Wall Street Journal*, 24 May 2013, https://www.wsj.com/articles/SB10001424127887323528404578453043883699474
22. Reported here (Arabic): http://www.all4syria.info/Archive/19669
23. Report can be found here: http://www.lccsyria.org/wp-content/uploads/2011/11/11.pdf
24. Ibid., p. 17. It is worth mentioning that seizing the possessions of citizens has more than one historical precedent, most notably the plunder of Hama in February 1982.
25. This information was taken from the personal profile of Ismaeel Alhamed, a respected doctor from Mount Zawiya, Idlib (https://www.facebook.com/Ismaeel.alhamed?ref=ts) on 25 August 2011. Sums ranged from 25,000—1,000,000 Syrian liras. It is likely that there is a commission paid to those involved. Those who do not pay remain under arrest until further notice. [Dr. Alhamed was kidnapped by Daesh on 2 November 2013 while walking the streets of Raqqa city, where he worked and lived with his family. Since then, no information has been received about him.]
26. During the first Assadist war in 1980 and since, members of Saraya ad-Difaa under the leadership of Rifaat al-Assad; the Special Forces units of Ali Haydar; and the 4th Armored Division of Shafiq Fayyad, placed their guns in front of them on their desks while taking their final exams in Junior High (Ninth Grade) and their High School diploma exams. They cheated overtly, and no one dared to stop them. That same year, members of the armed units who were formed to fight along with the regime were given extra school credits to facilitate their admission into the college of their choice. Needless to say, they were the worst morally and academically. Today, many of them work as professors at Syrian universities. The well-known caricaturist Ali Farzat got into hot water with Saraya ad-Difaa after he drew a student paratrooper landing with his parachute on top of the faculty of medicine.
27. [Note added in 2014]—This was the situation during the autumn of 2011. Many traditional oppositionists have been arrested since then, and no information is available on many of them, including Abdul Aziz

Al-Khair, Fa'iq Al-Meer, Jihad As'ad Mohammad, and others. Some suspect they have been murdered. In general, it is still accurate that the ratio of the traditional opposition's detainees is low in comparison to the overall number of detained revolutionaries.

28. [Note added in 2014]—This is according to numbers provided by the Local Coordination Committees, which serve as the framework through which protest activities are organized, media coverage is provided, and casualties documented. Their statistics, in my opinion, are more accurate than those of the UN and the international human rights organizations. Three years into the revolution, the number of casualties of the revolution today has surpassed 150,000.
29. There are reports about the regime having resorted to Assad the elder's security men, such as Ali Douba and his ilk. However, it is difficult to ascertain the validity of this information.

5. THE ROOTS OF SYRIAN FASCISM

1. Hamza Al-Khatib was a thirteen year-old boy from Daraa in southwestern Syria. He participated in protests during the early stage of the revolution, and was detained by the notoriously brutal Air Force Intelligence. His mutilated body was delivered to his parents in May 2011, showing a broken neck, severed genitals, and gunshot wounds in his chest and arms.
2. The constitution of the Arab Socialist Baath Party is available here: https://web.archive.org/web/20050203235613/http://baath-party.org/eng/constitution.htm
3. Ibid.
4. Ibid.
5. Photos of individuals worshipping the military boot (commentary in Arabic): http://bit.ly/2qmlRI1; http://bit.ly/2qtJJol; http://bit.ly/2rIEt52; http://bit.ly/2rrNBv9; http://bit.ly/2qmqzFM. Here is another monument of the military boot, also built in Latakia on the anniversary of Al-Baath Party in April 2014: http://bit.ly/2pvw5ov
6. See article by Saado Rafi, 'The reality of the Druze in the Syrian Revolution: Between fear and the historical role' (Arabic): http://arab-worlds.blogspot.co.uk/2012/01/blog-post_6826.html. The author

writes, 'After the bloody events in the province of As-Suwayda in 2000 [between the Druze inhabitants of As-Suwayda and their Sunni Bedouin neighbours], where dozens were killed and injured, the regime propagated a rumour that an officer from Hama had issued the orders to shoot the As-Suwayda protestors in retaliation for the murder of Adib Al-Shishakli.' Adib Al-Shishakli of Hama was a prominent figure in the Syrian regime between 1949 and 1952, becoming the outright dictator between 1952 and 1954. He suppressed Druze protests in 1954. Years after he had been ousted from power, he was assassinated by the Syrian Druze Nawwaf Abu Ghazalah while in exile in Brazil. Rafi adds, 'Even during the Hama events in 1982, the regime and associates spared no effort in spreading rumours across the mountain that the events were an effort to deter the 'strict Sunnis of Hama' from returning to power, in which case the residents of the Druze Mountain would incur severe losses, according to the theory of vengeance between 'Al-Shishakli's Hama' and the Druze.'

7. The Syrian Armenian Aram Karbit, who was detained in 1987 for his membership of a communist party, said he was told by an officer during his interrogation that the regime was protecting them from strict Muslims, in his book: *Moving to the Unknown*, Alexandria: Dar Jidar, 2009.s. Many oral narratives give the same indication.
8. See Baraa Al-Sarraj: *From Tadmur to Harvard: The Journey of an Opinionless Prisoner*. Al-Sarraj spent twelve years in Tadmur Prison, then moved to the USA after his release to specialize in immunology, having previously taught electric engineering at Damascus University. See also: *The Shell*, a novel by Mustafa Khalifa, available here (Arabic): www.achr.eu/القوقعة.pdf
9. A Human Rights Watch report, 'By Any Means: Responsibility of individuals and leaders for crimes against humanity in Syria,' issued in December 2011, is available here (Arabic): http://www.hrw.org/ar/reports/2011/12/15–0
10. See Chapter 2, 'The *Shabiha* and Their State'.
11. See the author's *Walking on One Foot*, Beirut: Dar Al-Adab, 2012. Chapter 4: 'Political Economy...', pp. 147–200.
12. Rami Makhlouf was and is Syria's best-known business figure, but his

statements in the *New York Times* following the protests (in an interview with the late Anthony Shadid) reveal a very politicized character, explicitly advocating on the regime's behalf. His comments from the article: 'The decision of the government now is that they decided to fight... We believe there is no continuity without unity... As a person, each one of us knows we cannot continue without staying united together... We will not go out, leave on our boat, go gambling, you know... We will sit here. We call it a fight until the end... They should know when we suffer, we will not suffer alone.' He warned that the alternative—led by what he described as Salafists, the government's term for all Islamists—would mean war at home and perhaps abroad. 'We won't accept it,' he said. 'People will fight against them. Do you know what this means? It means catastrophe. And we have a lot of fighters.' Makhlouf's full interview is available here: http://www.nytimes.com/2011/05/11/world/middleeast/11makhlouf.html

13. In the absence of serious economic and social studies, herein is some useful material that calls a spade a spade: 'Who are the new bourgeoisie (the characters, size, and economic impact)?' Available at: http://5oole.mam9.com/t81-topic
14. The process is nevertheless not always guaranteed for the regime. It is noteworthy that markets affiliated with the old bourgeoisie, such as Al-Harikah, Al-Hamedya, Medhat Pasha, and Al-Buzuriyah Souq were those which went on strike on 28 May 2012, and during the days that followed, in protest at the Houla massacre. They were partially, and reluctantly, joined by Al-Shaalan, Al-Salehia, and the Jisr Alabyad markets, each closer to the new bourgeoisie.
15. Names (including Tlass, Shalish, Al-Akhras, Makhlouf, and Suleiman) of powerful families who have long occupied high positions in the Assad dynasty rule, also occupy vital positions in the new bourgeoisie. The sons of Abdul Halim Khaddam were cut from the same cloth, before being expelled from the upper class by their father's political ambitions. On the general staff of the new bourgeoisie, see the article 'The Assads: A Predatory Clan,' published in *Le Monde*, available here (French): http://www.lemonde.fr/a-la-une/article/2012/04/17/les-al-assad-un-clan-predateur_1686641_3208.html

16. *Al-Watan* is owned by Rami Makhlouf, while Addounia TV is financed by Mohamed Hamsho (a favourite of Maher al-Assad's), Suleiman Maarouf, and Omar Karkour, all of whom are members of the new bourgeoisie, i.e. they made their fortunes under the auspices of the two Assads, or joined its social, security, and political networks.
17. In the interview mentioned above Makhlouf claims, 'This is a priority for Syrians. We have to ask for economic reform before speaking about political reform.' Taking leave entirely from all sense, he adds, 'but if there is some delay, it's not the end of the world.' Mr. Makhlouf, of course, is not in a hurry, for he has never experienced hunger, detention, or humiliation.
18. This facilitation was useful for the 'opposition' politicians who were able to turn to one of the regime's officials and have them mediate with the authorities, or could personally turn to the very authorities that issued their travel bans and provided their reasons for travel. Most of them needed official approval each time they intended to travel abroad, which put them at the mercy of the intelligence services. Those who had no mediators had little hope of coming to any such arrangement.
19. See Chapter 2, 'The *Shabiha* and Their State'.
20. Modernist ideology cannot be reduced to solely internal social conditions, as we can see its varieties in most Arab countries with no remarkable differences. In fact, this ideology is linked to international developments represented by the collapse of the Eastern bloc and of communism, globalization and neo-liberalism, and the rise of 'clash of civilizations' theories and the international culturalist tendencies in general, in addition to the rise of Islamic currents and the emergence of the post-9/11 world order centred on the 'War on Terror'. In all its variations across the globe, modernist ideology is always seen near the centres of power and wealth. There is no progressive or humanitarian modernist ideology, let alone a democratic one.
21. Amjad Jadallah, 'What Will You Do to Reduce the Population Growth to 2.1%?' This article addressed Abdullah Al-Dardari, Syria's former Deputy Prime Minister for Economic Affairs. The article is available here (Arabic): http://www.thefreesyria.org/f-s-1/parid-121210.htm
22. Nabil Fayad, 'The Disturbing Silence of the Intellectuals: In Defence

of Truth and Syrian Security!' The article is available here (Arabic): http://www.aramaic-dem.org/Arabic/Archev/N_Fayyad/41.htm

23. George Tarabishi, *The Culture of Democracy*, Beirut: Dar Al-Talia, 1998, p. 21. The author did not change his stance when he republished the same text in 2006, under the title *Hartaqat* [Heresies] Beirut: Dar Al-Saqi, 2006.
24. Referring to Adnan Al-Aroor, a populist Sunni cleric who regularly appears on a salafi TV channel based in Saudi Arabia. Since the revolution, he switched from attacking Shiites in the context of the Sunni/Shiite sectarian conflict between Saudi Arabia and Iran, to public incitement against the Syrian regime. Until then only known within religious circles, after the revolution erupted he became widely known in Syria for his incendiary TV appearances, and through the hostile propaganda deployed against him on behalf of the regime.
25. According to Bassam Abu Abdullah, supposedly a professor of international relations in Damascus University. He repeatedly made these statements on Addounia TV and during his public appearances. On 12 May 2012, the 'professor' appeared on the same TV channel and called upon the Syrian government to expel every non-Syrian from public functions, which in reality could only be applied to Palestinian refugees. Condescension over the lower classes and 'foreigners' is characteristic of extremist right-wing currents, especially the fascist variety. One day prior to his TV appearance he called for 'chopping' the tongues of Burhan Ghalioun and Hassan Abdul Azim to prevent them from speaking on behalf of the Syrian people.

6. THE RISE OF MILITANT NIHILISM

1. I placed the word 'Islam' between quotation marks precisely for this reason: Islam forms in a way that meets the social, political, and psychological demands directed at it by Muslim masses who feel isolated, and by Muslim ideologues who prefer extremist versions of Islam that let them instrumentalize religion with absolute power.
2. Kamran Bokhari, 'Jihadist Opportunities in Syria': http://www.stratfor.com/weekly/jihadist-opportunities-syria

3. For more than a year, demonstration Fridays were titled through a poll on a popular Facebook page at that time: الثورة السورية ضد بشار الأسد, 'The Syrian Revolution against Bashar Al-Assad'.
4. See my *Myths of Successors: A Critique of Contemporary Islam and a Critique of its Critiques*, Beirut: Dar Al-Saqi, 2011, particularly the chapter, 'The Nihilism of the Overabundance of Meaning,' pp. 143–151.
5. Though one could argue this tendency is more strongly present in Christianity under the influence of the doctrine of original sin, and in Buddhism, which regards the world as an illusion. Sufism is yet another form of Islamic nihilism in that it shares the withdrawal of trust from the world, and its despair of life, but unlike militant nihilism, it recedes from the untrustworthy worldly life. Jihadist nihilism does not recede from the world; it withdraws meaning from it and works to destroy it. Moreover, unlike Salafism, Sufism has many intermediaries and mediators. Saleh, *Myths of Successors*, pp. 122–143.
6. It is not impossible to conceive of an atheist, anti-religious Arab nihilism, but living under 'secular' dictatorial regimes over two generations has bestowed upon Islam the power of revolt and protest, eliminating all the conditions for the creation of an atheistic nihilism. It is true that there exists today a nihilistic, anti-religious Arab inclination against Islam, but it lacks intellectual seriousness and has produced no new ideas. Its representatives are often found within the existing regimes, or as individuals living in the West who enjoy good relations with the most racist right-wing tendencies there. Perhaps a post-Arab Spring, atheistic, nihilist inclination will emerge because of the Islamists' domination of a broader public space in their countries.
7. One can refer to al-Qaeda strategist Abu Bakr Naji's book, *Managing Savagery: The Most Crucial Stage in the Life of the Nation*, where the author charges the Muslim Brotherhood with pursuing a secular project.
8. In his article 'Islamism and the Syrian Uprising,' Nir Rosen says one of the reasons behind the absence of sectarian massacres of the Bosnian kind in Homs is the strong influence of opposition sheikhs. The article isavailablehere:http://foreignpolicy.com/2012/03/08/islamism-and-the-syrian-uprising/

9. In Rosen's article above, he says Abu Sleiman, a drug-dealer-turned-Salafist in Sednaya prison—a story reminiscent of Abu Mus'ab al-Zarqawi—tried to establish his own emirate in Mount Zawiya, but the population united against him. One of the leading local fighters said, 'When people learned he wanted to establish a private emirate, the entire mountain turned against him.' 'We are all brothers, from here all the way to Daraa,' he added. 'We are revolutionaries first and foremost.'
10. In my *Myths of Successors*, I differentiated between 'hard' and 'soft' secularism. The first is based on considerations related to science, rationalism, modernity and universalism. The latter is more related to the social and political needs of the population, and is open to values like justice, freedom, and respect. Hard secularism is centred around religion, while soft secularism is society-oriented.
11. For a definition of absolute Arabism, see my 'Political Reform and the Reconfiguration of National Identity in Syria', 2008, available in English here:http://www.yassinhs.com/2007/06/14/political-reform-and-the-reconfiguration-of-national-identity-in-syria/
12. Freedom is the second of the Baath Party's three goals. However, its predication on a presumed Arab 'essence', not on the existing Syrian population, caused its regression into autarchy and isolation from the world under the banner of national independence, accompanied by authoritarianism and deprivation of freedom and rights from the Syrian masses.
13. See Naji's *Managing Savagery*, previously cited. For Naji savagery is a desired condition after the collapse of a state, preparing the ground for the work of jihadists, though it is also 'the most dangerous stage facing the [Muslim] nation'.
14. 'Desperation' is addressed in Chapter 3, 'The Danger of a "State of Nature"'.
15. Daesh did not appear until one year after I finished writing this text, but it is the embodiment of excess nihilism and scant revolution. It is indeed absolute nihilism without any revolutionism; a fascist death machine, explicit in its fundamental anti-revolution tendencies, and its existence is a boon for the regime.
16. Amnesty International, '"I wanted to die": Syria's Torture Survivors

Speak Out', available here: https://doc.es.amnesty.org/cgi-bin/ai/BRSCGI/MDE2401612?CMD=VEROBJ&MLKOB=30437270000; 'Report of the Independent International Commission of Inquiry on the Syrian Arab Republic,' 22 February 2012: http://www.ohchr.org/Documents/HRBodies/HRCouncil/RegularSession/Session19/A-HRC-19–69.pdf

17. Sarah Leah Whitson of Human Rights Watch has reported on this: https://www.hrw.org/news/2012/03/20/open-letter-leaders-syrian-opposition. On all of these issues, see the author, 'Justice of the Revolution does not Guarantee the Justice of the Revolutionaries' *Al-Hayat*, 8 April 2012.
18. I remind readers that the text was written in May 2012, when it was still unconfirmed that the al-Nusra Front was an actual organization and not a mere invention of Syrian Intelligence. Also, Daesh had not yet formed. It was to break from Al-Nusra Front in April 2013.

9. THE DESTINY OF THE SYRIAN REVOLUTION

1. See Chapter 5.
2. The first generation were the founders, most of them born during the second decade of the twentieth century (Michel Aflaq, Salah al-Din al-Bitar, Akram al-Hawrani etc). The second generation were the power holders, most of whom were born in the 1930s (Hafez al-Assad, Abdul Halim Khaddam, Mustafa Tlass, Rifaat al-Assad, Ali Duba, Mohamed Makhlouf). The third generation are mostly their descendants, born during the 1960s and 1970s (Bashar al-Assad, Rami Makhlouf, the sons of Khaddam and Tlass before their 'dissent' from the regime). See the chapter 'Economic Liberalization: An Approach of Third-Generation Baathists,' from my *Walking on One Leg*, Beirut: Dar al-Adab, 2012.
3. Human Rights Watch counted ten attacks, claiming more than 100 casualties. HRW, 'Attacks on Bread Lines': http://www.hrw.org/ar/news/2012/08/30; According to the East Ghouta Unified Revolutionary Medical Bureau, the total number of casualties approached 10,000, of whom 67 per cent were women and children. See a video report issued by the Bureau here: https://www.youtube.com/watch?v=faxCgsiPHmc

4. A direct testimony of a young man friend who shall remain anonymous, who spent months in the airport bunkers in 2012. See also an investigation on the airport prison here: http://archive.aawsat.com/details.asp?section=4&article=703673&issueno=12401#.UiCRxdIwprc
5. See a report by the Violations Documentation Centre in Syria: 'The Hell of the Fourth Brigade Detention in Damascus,' available here: http://www.vdc-sy.info/index.php/ar/reports/4thdivision#.VYW6s_lViko
6. According to Human Rights Watch's report, titled, 'By All Means Necessary: Individual and Command Responsibility for Crimes against Humanity in Syria,' issued in December 2012, available here: http://www.hrw.org/ar/reports/2011/12/15–0 (The report speaks of 2500 detainees in prison.)
7. See Human Rights Watch's report 'Cells of Torture,' available here: http://www.hrw.org/ar/reports/2012/07/03–1. 'Syria: Detention and Violation of Female Activists,' available here: http://www.hrw.org/ar/news/2013/06/24. See also Dara Abdullah, 'I'm Alive in Prison,' available here: http://www.almustaqbal.com/v4/Article.aspx?Type=np&Articleid=576241. A report by the Violations Documentation Centre in Syria, including testimony by Ahmed Abu Ali, known also as Abu Tammam, on Air Force Intelligence—Daraa Province, available here: http://www.vdc-sy.info/index.php/ar/reports/daraaairforce. A report on al-Khatib Branch—State Security, testimony of detainee Yasser Abdul Samad Hussein Karmi, available here: http://www.vdc-sy.info/index.php/ar/reports/khatibbranch#.VYW_ZflViko. A report on the horrors of al-Mantiqa Branch No. 227, available here: http://www.vdc-sy.info/index.php/ar/reports/militarybranch227#.VYXAEflViko
8. Many prisoners who died under torture are documented by name. See detailedlistshere:http://www.vdc-sy.info/index.php/ar/martyrs/1/c29ydGJ5PWEua2lsbGVkX2RhdGV8c29ydGRpcj1ERVND fGFwcHJvdmVkPXZpc2libGV8ZXh0cmFkaXNwbGF5PTB8Y29kTXVsdGk9Niw3LDksMTB8. Later, it would be proved that the estimations above were very modest. Early in 2014, it turned out that in Damascus alone, 11,000 victims died under torture by the end of August 2013, nearly four times more than the number mentioned in the report of the Violations

Documentation Centre. See: http://www.theguardian.com/world/2014/jan/20/evidence-industrial-scale-killing-syria-war-crimes

9. See Lauren Wolfe, 'Syria Has a Massive Rape Crisis,' available here: http://www.womenundersiegeproject.org/blog/entry/syria-has-a-massive-rape-crisis. Also, Human Rights Watch, 'Sexual Assault in Detention,' available here: http://www.hrw.org/ar/news/2012/06/15–1
10. Reports issued in May of this year spoke of more than 270,000 people handicapped.See:http://www.aljazeera.net/news/pages/75a1131d-03414c6d-b1d7-aff2c9dd424d
11. Paul Wood, 'Face-to-face with Abu Sakkar, Syria's "heart-eating cannibal"', BBC News, 5 July 2013, http://www.bbc.co.uk/news/magazine-23190533
12. See Chapter 8, 'An Image, Two Flags, and a Banner'.
13. Jack Moore, 'Lebanon Sentence Ex-Minister Michel Samaha to Hard Labor for Plotting Assassinations with Syria Regime', *Newsweek*, 8 April 2016, http://www.newsweek.com/lebanon-sentences-ex-minister-michel-samaha-hard-labor-plotting-assassinations-445566
14. Naela Mansour, 'My Name is Kafra-Nbel, I Need No Courses in "Estimation of Needs,"' The Republic Group (Arabic): http://aljumhuriya.net/6504
15. Régis Debray, *Critique de la Raison politique* (Paris: Gallimard, 1987).
16. See Chapter 8, 'An Image, Two Flags and a Banner.'
17. '*Al-Arabiya* monitors manual oil refining in Syria,' *Al-Arabiya* (Arabic): http://bit.ly/2s0LfQJ
18. 'Syria's al-Nusra Front—ruthless, organised and taking control,' *The Guardian*, 10 July 2013: https://www.theguardian.com/world/2013/jul/10/syria-al-nusra-front-jihadi
19. Gilbert Achcar, *The People Want: A Radical Exploration of the Arab Uprising*, translated by Omar El Shafei, Beirut: Dar al-Saqi, 2013, p. 233.
20. For example: Noam Chomsky, 'Sykes-Picot Is Failing,' *Al-Akhbar*: http://www.al-akhbar.com/node/185107. For example: Alaa Al-Mawla, 'Cooperation Council of the Levant: Necessary and Possible,' *Al-Akhbar*: https://al-akhbar.com/node/186210. Also, Nahedh Hattar, 'Cooperation Council of the Levant': http://www.rasseen.com/art.php?id=36504b73135ab0b8070bb2e3f50be050a36f0bf1

21. See my 'The Syrian Revolution and the Condition of an Absolute Revolution,' available here (Arabic): http://alhayat.com/Details/460137
22. Edward Luttwak, 'In Syria, America loses if either side wins,' *The New York Times*, 25 August 2013: http://www.nytimes.com/2013/08/25/opinion/sunday/in-syria-america-loses-if-either-side-wins.html
23. One of the most active networks associated with the revolution, formed with the Local Coordination Committees, which conduct protest and political activities as well as relief and documentation. There are many independent activists, men and women, who work under harsh conditions within the country. For militants, I refer to a series of portraits of fighters, which I carried out in the months of May and June 2013 in Eastern Ghouta, particularly of Abu Khaled Ghazlani: http://www.nytimes.com/2013/08/25/opinion/sunday/in-syria-america-loses-if-either-side-wins.html. Abu Qusai: http://aljumhuriya.net/7017 and Abu Najm al-Qadmousi: http://aljumhuriya.net/8814

10. THE NEO-SULTANIC STATE

1. Yassin al-Haj Saleh, 'The Remaining Group: Sunni Syrians and Politics,' Aljumhuriya.net, 2012: http://aljumhuriya.net/237
2. 'Sultan' in Arabic is sovereign power, and the person who is the supreme position in the any power hierarchy.
3. In Arabic, we differentiate between *mujtama' madani*, i.e. civil society (voluntary gatherings that one chooses to join, such as parties, youth and women's organizations, leagues of intellectuals or sports people etc), and *mujtama' ahli*, i.e., social formations based on kinship, religion, locality etc, of which one finds oneself a member.
4. Aziz al-Azmeh, *Dunia ad-Din fi Hader al Arab* ('The World of Religion in the Arabs' Present Times'), Beirut: Dar at-Talia'a, 2002, p. 54.
5. For the concept of the working society, see my 'The Common Syrian: The uprising of the working society!' Souria Houria, 2011: http://bit.ly/2s73Wl5
6. Anthony Shadid, 'Syrian Elite to Fight Protests to 'the End',' *New York Times*, 10 May 2011: http://www.nytimes.com/2011/05/11/world/middleeast/11makhlouf.html?pagewanted=all&_r=3&

INDEX

INDEX

INDEX

INDEX

INDEX